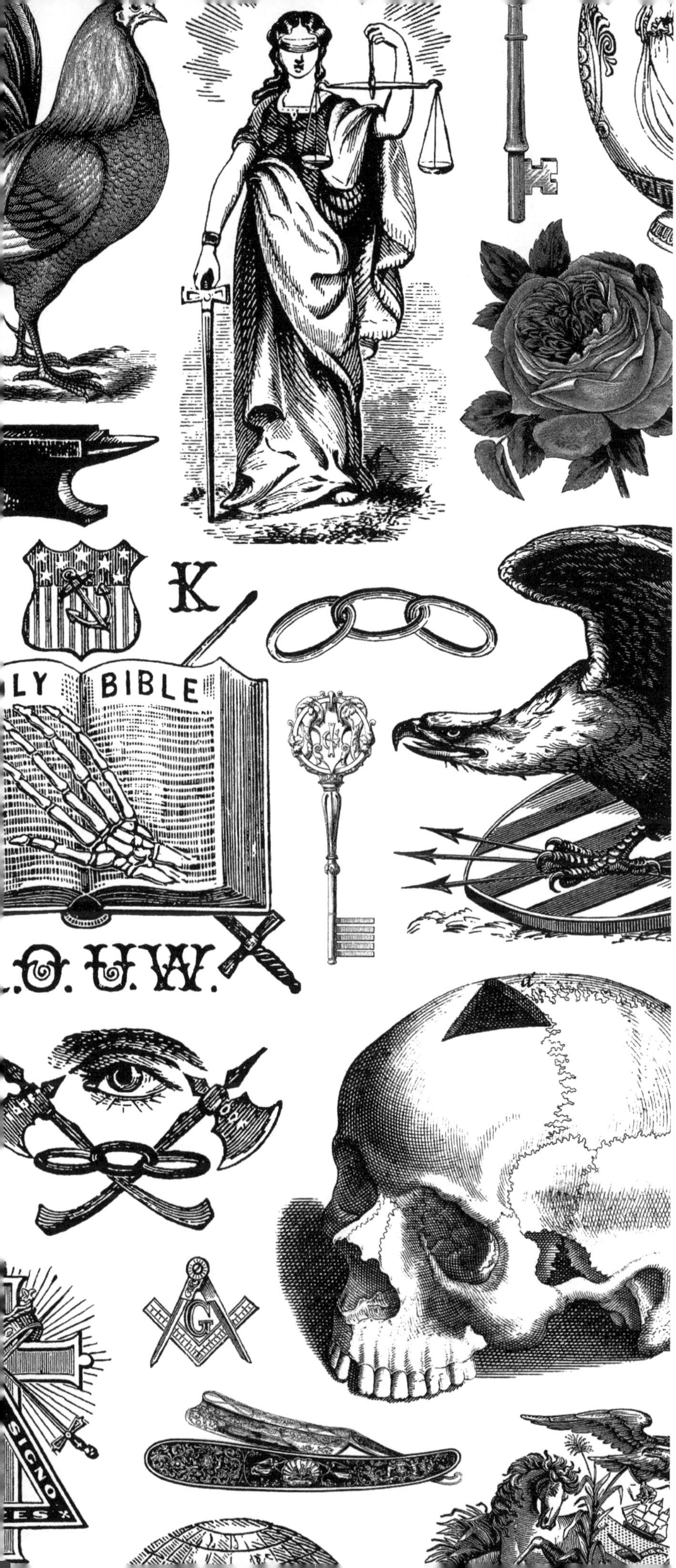

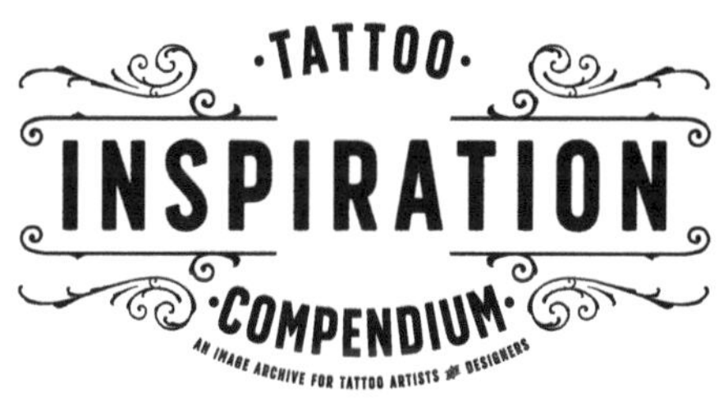

EDITIONS Vault

INTRODUCTION

This pictorial archive is a unique collection of rare 18th and 19th-century imagery that inspired the rich aesthetic and symbolic imagery we see in neo-traditional tattoo culture today. Featured within these pages are over 500 beautifully restored high-resolution images of skulls, masonic emblems, snakes, spiders, toads, eagles, owls, vintage Americana, sea monsters, tall ships, filigree, ornamental designs, religious iconography, death, hands, roses, heraldry and much more.

Image Download Included:
Each book comes with a unique download link providing instant access to high-resolution files of the hundreds of images featured. These images can be used for tattoo designs, art and design projects, or printed and framed to make beautiful decorative artworks for your home or studio.When downloading your assets, you will also get access to the Vault Editions Skulls and Anatomy sample pack completely free.

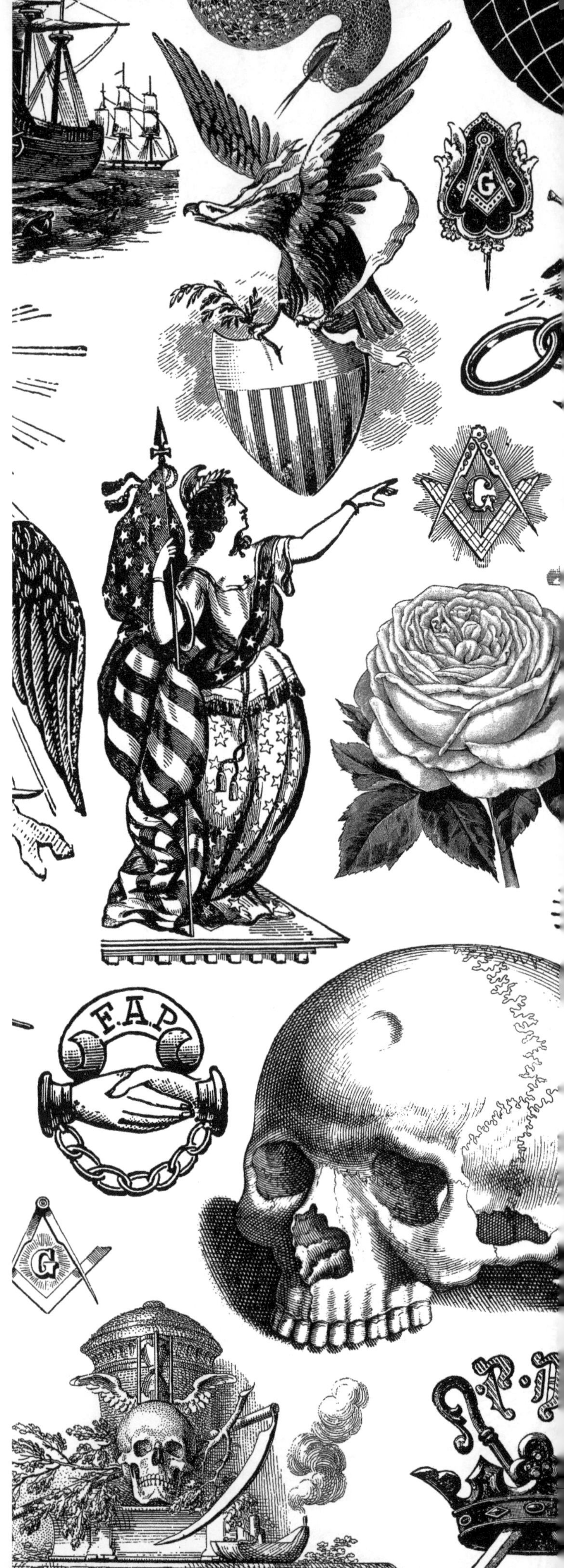

TABLE OF CONTENTS

Society Emblems 01-06
Eagles 07-10
Religious Iconography 11-15
Vases 16
Keys and Locks 17-18
Snakes 25-29
Americana 69-70
Clocks and Watches 30
Military Medals 31-32
Insects 33-38
Women 39-42
Men 43-44
Rings and Jewellery 45-48
Hands 49-52
Skulls and Skeletons 53-58
Crowns 59-60
Roses 61-62
Tall Ships 63-64
Sea Monsters 65-70
Barbering 71
Roosters 72
Various Animals 73-74
Toads and Frogs 75-76
Owls 77-78
Death and Mortality 79-82
Ornaments 83-92
Heraldry 93-94
Rocaille Ornaments 95-100
Miscellaneous 101-102
Download Your Files 103

DOWNLOAD YOUR FILES

Downloading your files is simple. To access your digital files, please go to the last page of this book and follow the instructions.

For technical assistance, please email:
info@vaulteditions.com

Copyright

Bibliographical Note

This book is a new work created by Vault Editions Ltd.

ISBN: 978-1-925968-60-6

SOCIETY EMBLEMS

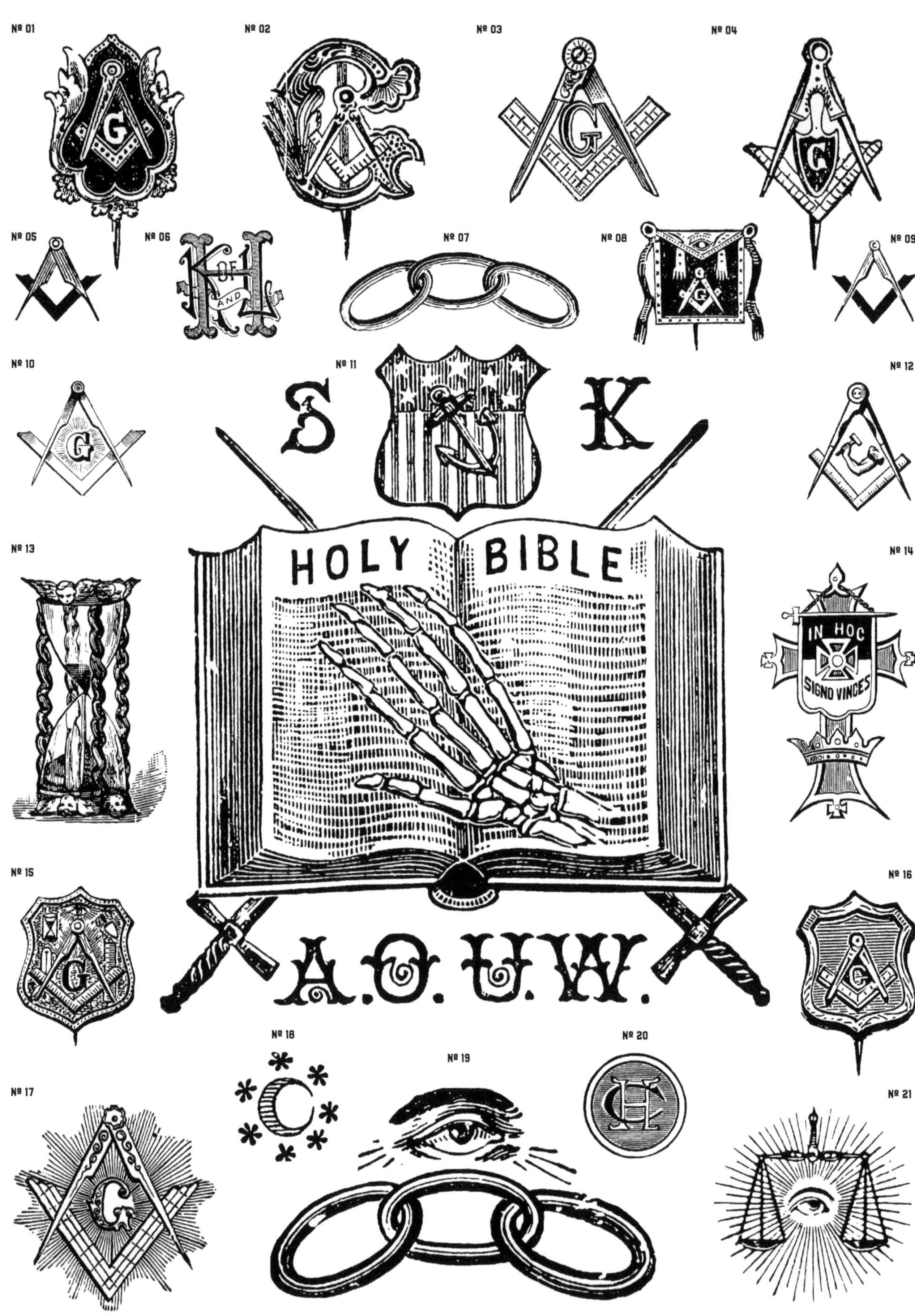

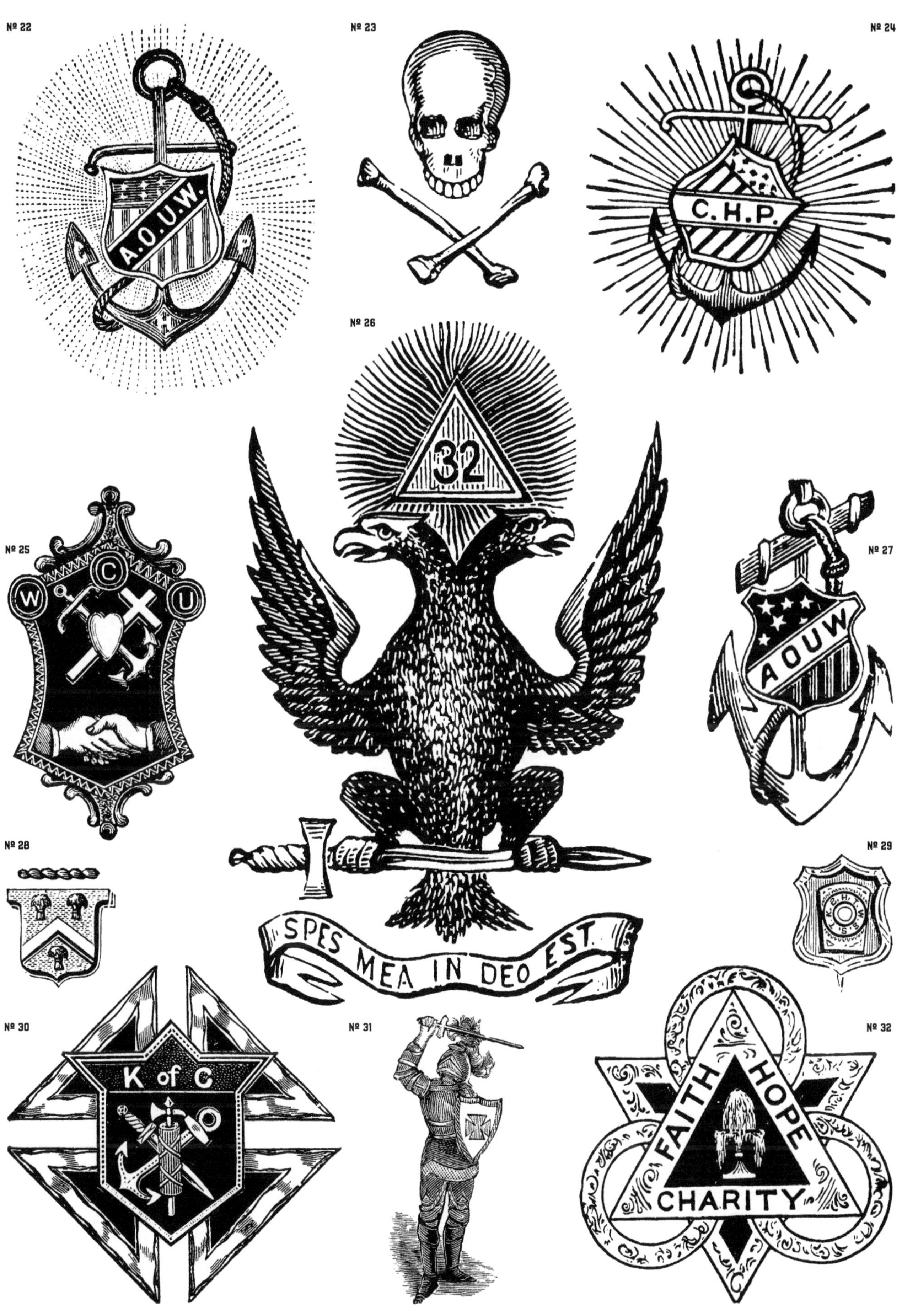
№ 22
A.O.U.W.
№ 23
№ 24
C.H.P.
№ 26
32
SPES MEA IN DEO EST
№ 25
W
C
U
№ 27
AOUW
№ 28
№ 29
№ 30
K of C
№ 31
№ 32
FAITH
HOPE
CHARITY

SOCIETY EMBLEMS

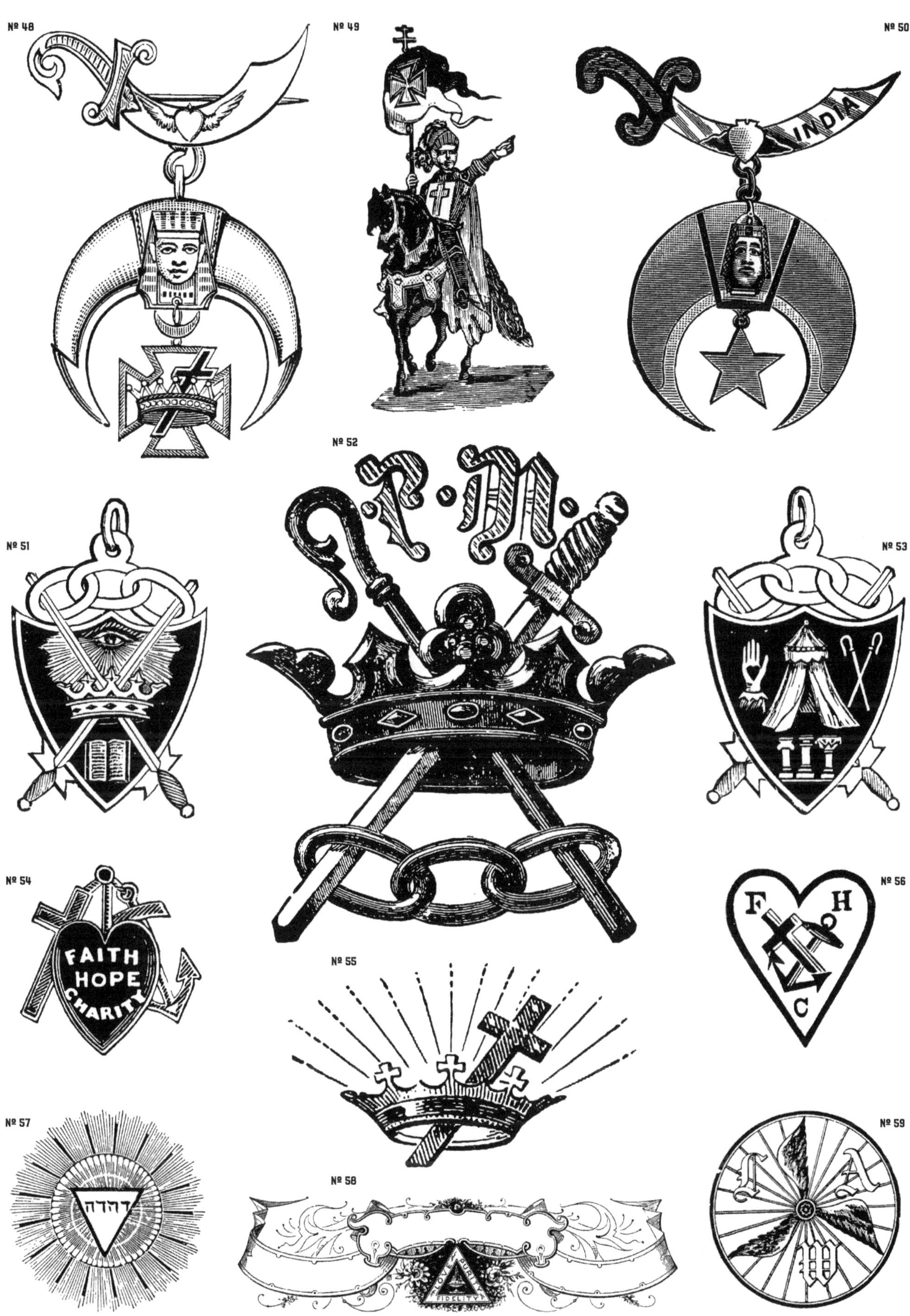

SOCIETY EMBLEMS

SOCIETY EMBLEMS

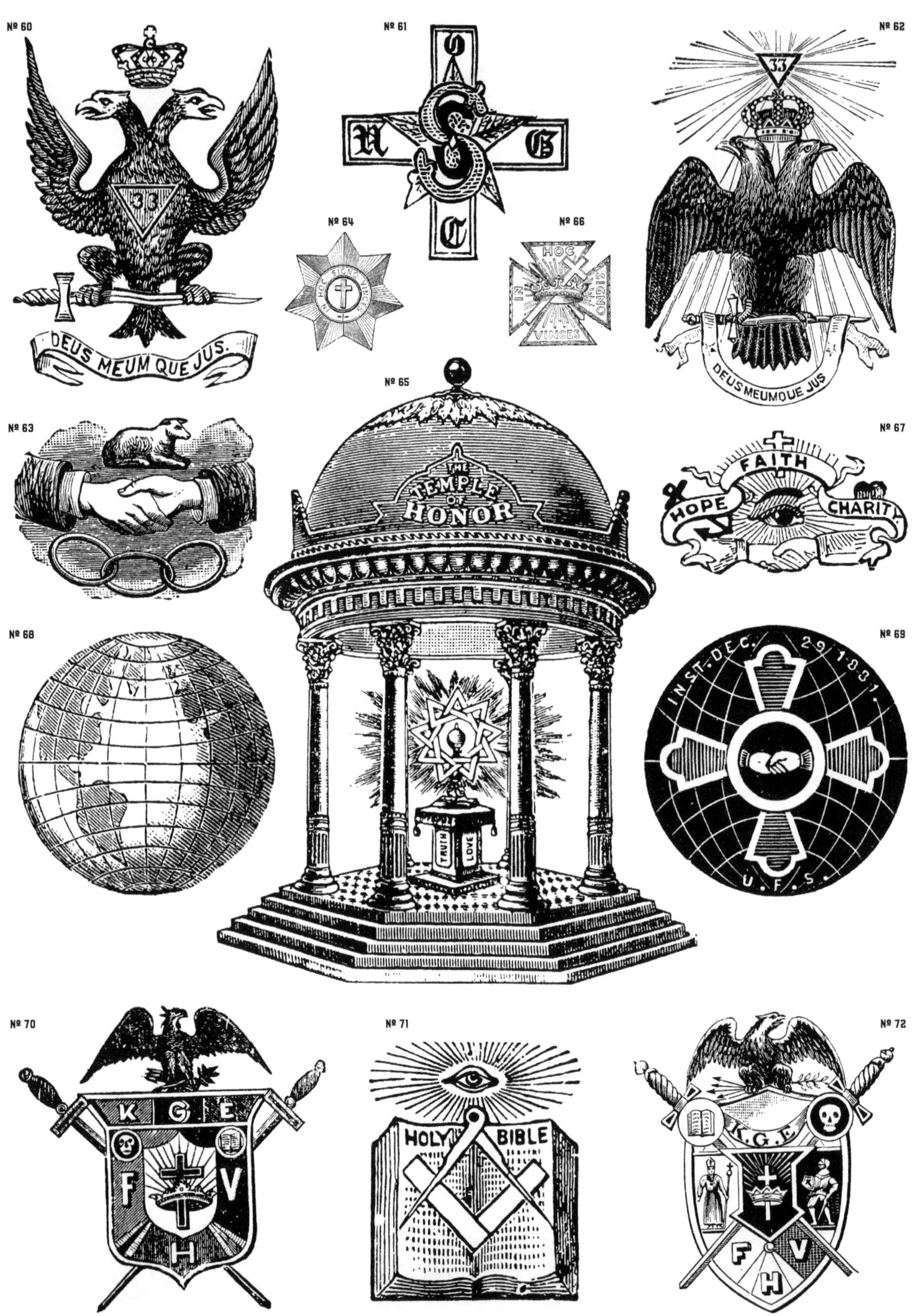

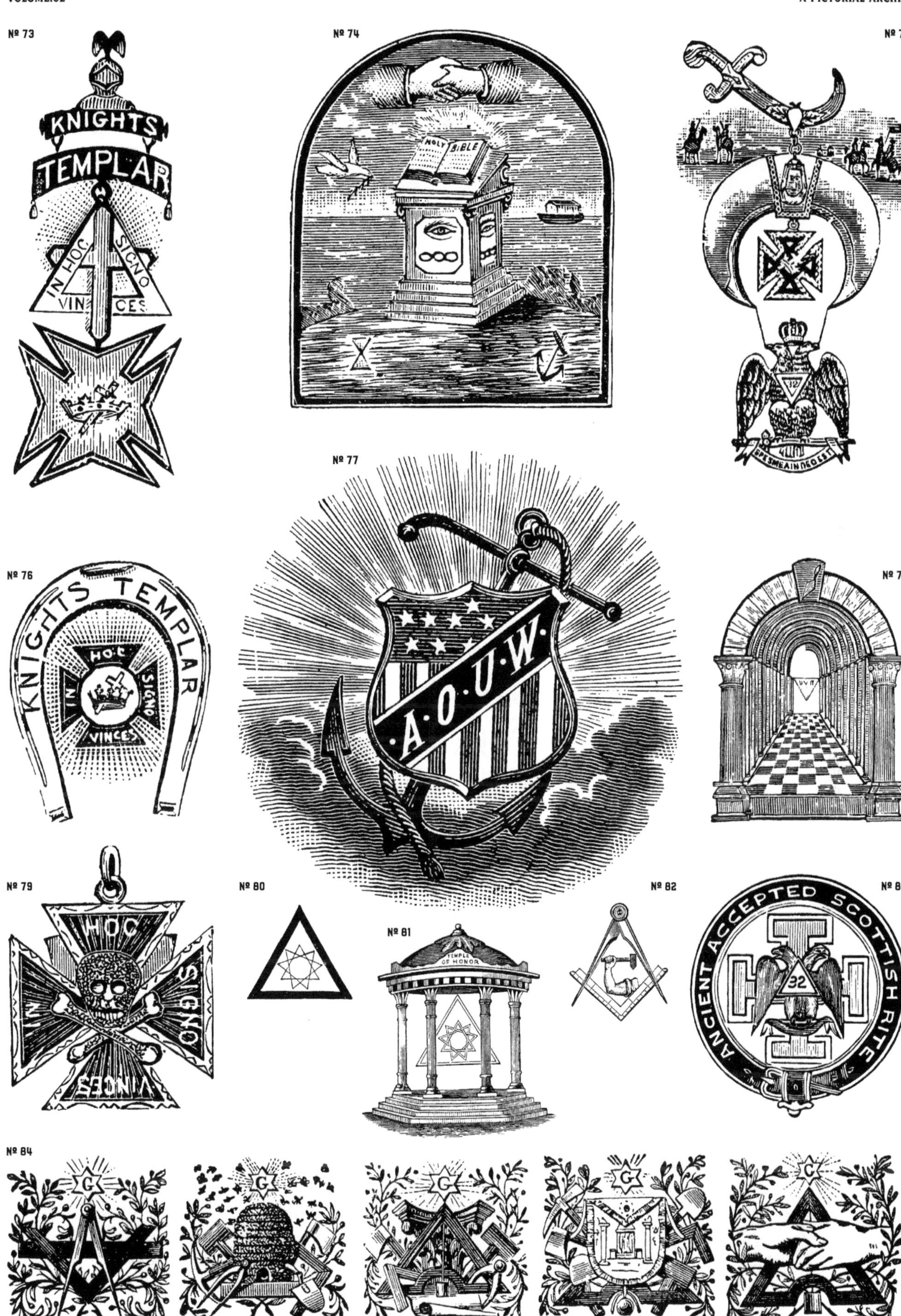
№ 73
KNIGHTS
TEMPLAR
IN HOC SIGNO VINCES
№ 74
HOLY BIBLE
№ 75
№ 76
KNIGHTS TEMPLAR
IN HOC SIGNO VINCES
№ 77
A·O·U·W
№ 78
№ 79
IN HOC SIGNO VINCES
№ 80
№ 81
TEMPLE OF HONOR
№ 82
№ 83
ANCIENT ACCEPTED SCOTTISH RITE
32
№ 84
G

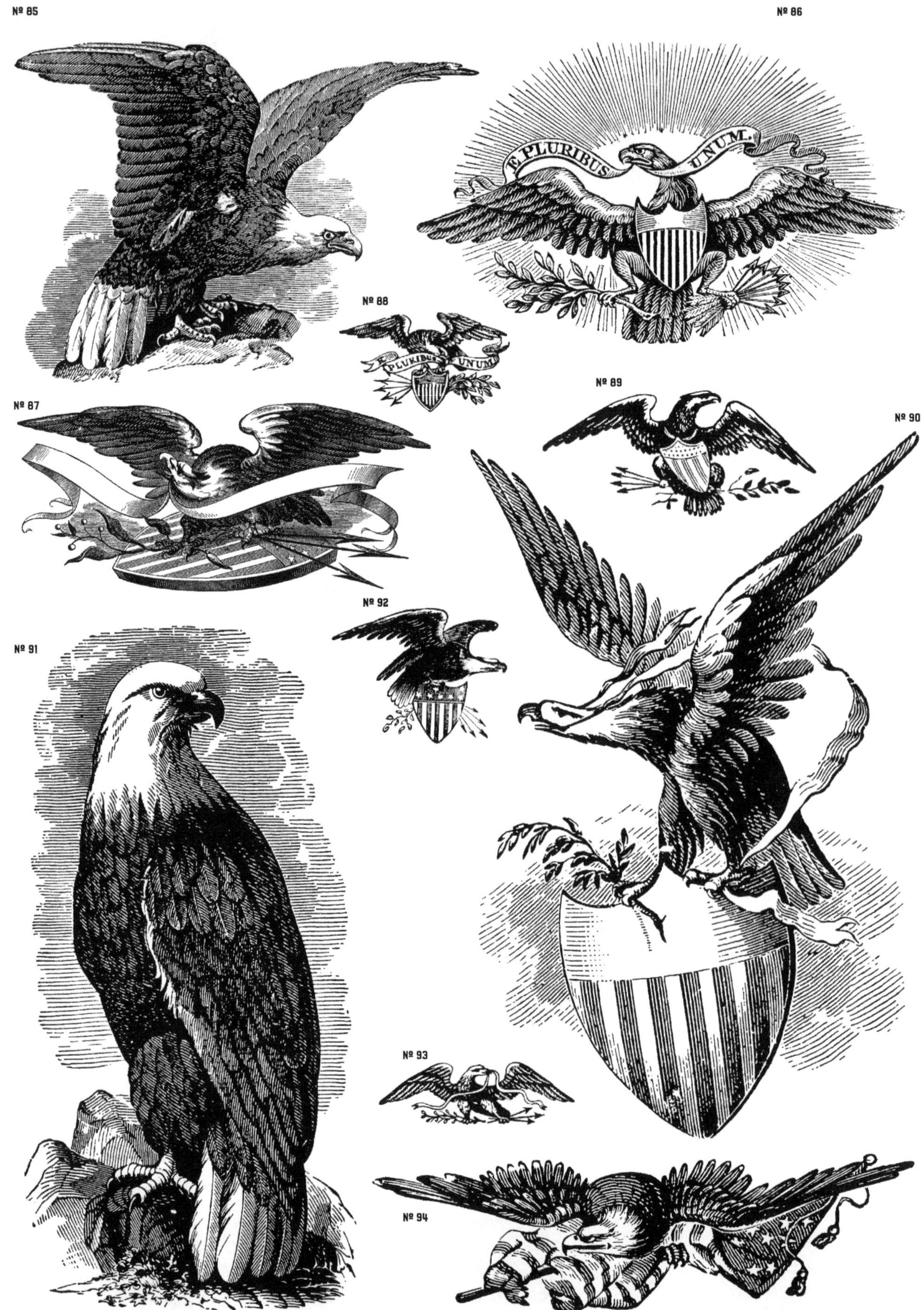

Nº 85

Nº 86

Nº 87

Nº 88

Nº 89

Nº 90

Nº 91

Nº 92

Nº 93

Nº 94

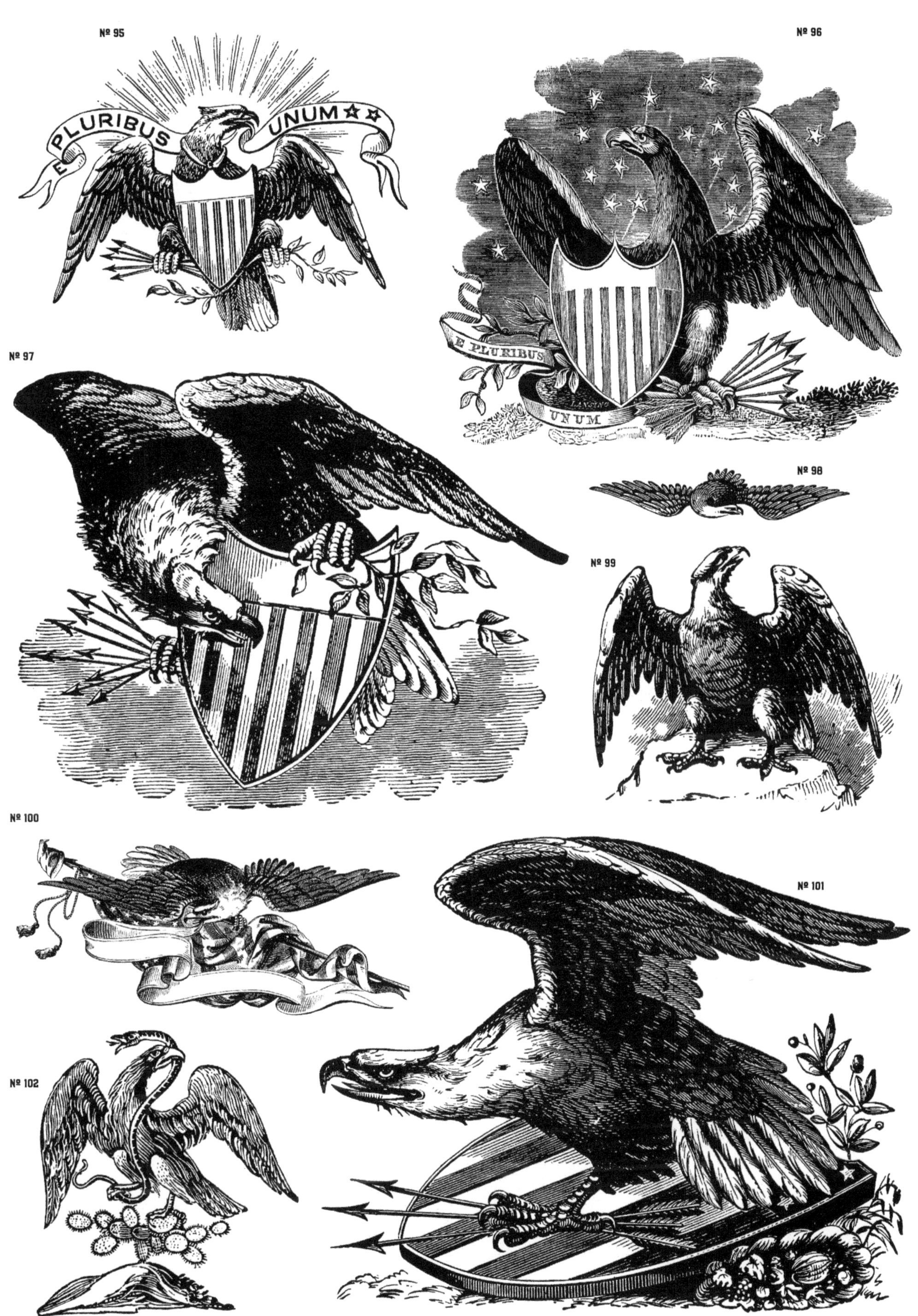
Nº 95
E PLURIBUS UNUM
Nº 96
E PLURIBUS
UNUM
Nº 97
Nº 98
Nº 99
Nº 100
Nº 101
Nº 102

№ 103
№ 104
№ 105
E PLURIBUS UNUM.
№ 106
№ 107
№ 108
E PLURIBUS UNUM
№ 109
№ 110

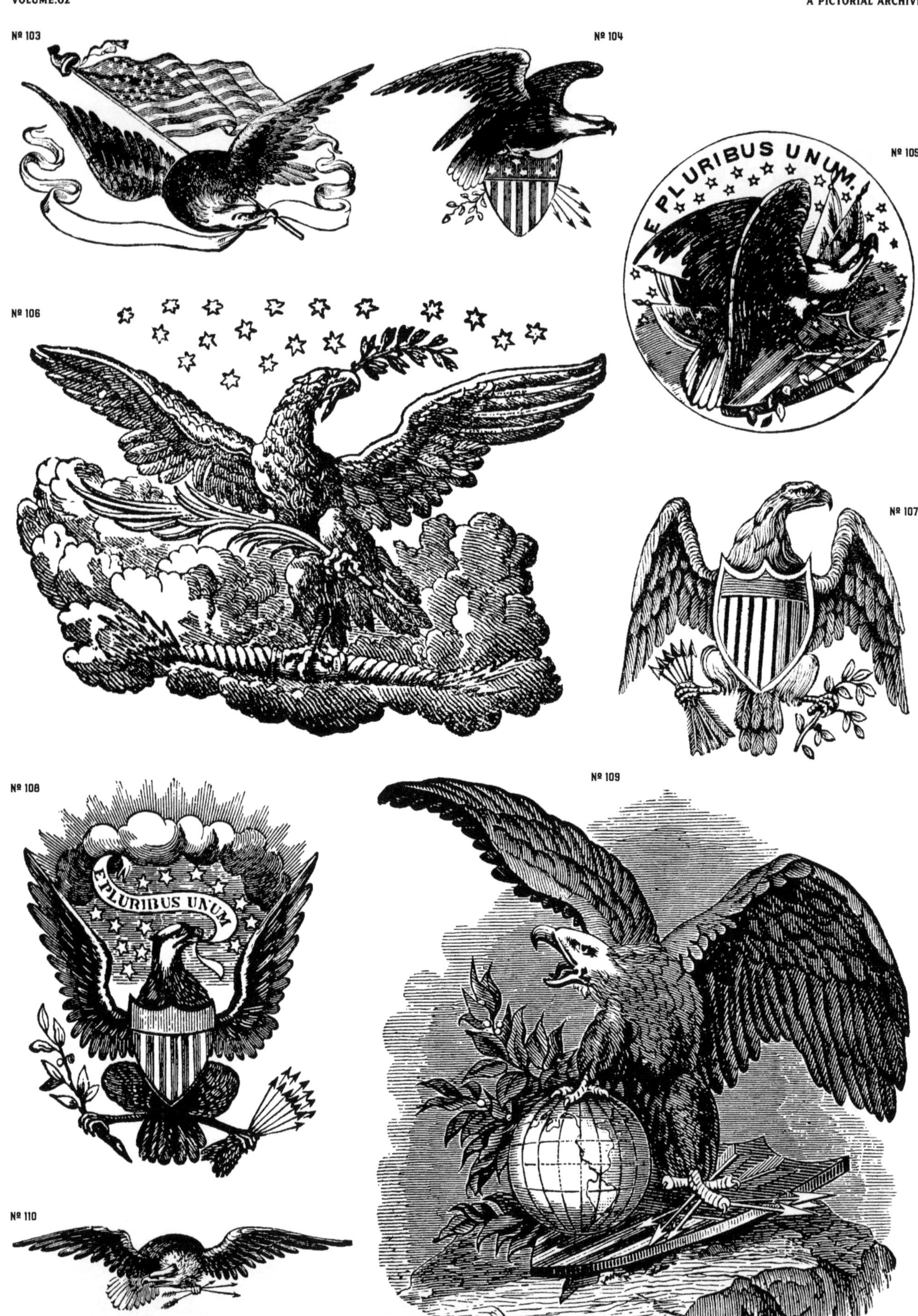

EAGLES

№ 111
STATE
SOVEREIGNTY.
NATIONAL UNION
№ 112
E PLURIBUS UNUM.
№ 113
№ 114
E PLURIBUS
UNUM
№ 115
E PLURIBUS UNUM
№ 116
STATE
SOVEREIGNTY
NATIONAL UNION
U S
№ 117
E PLURIBUS
UNUM
№ 118
№ 119

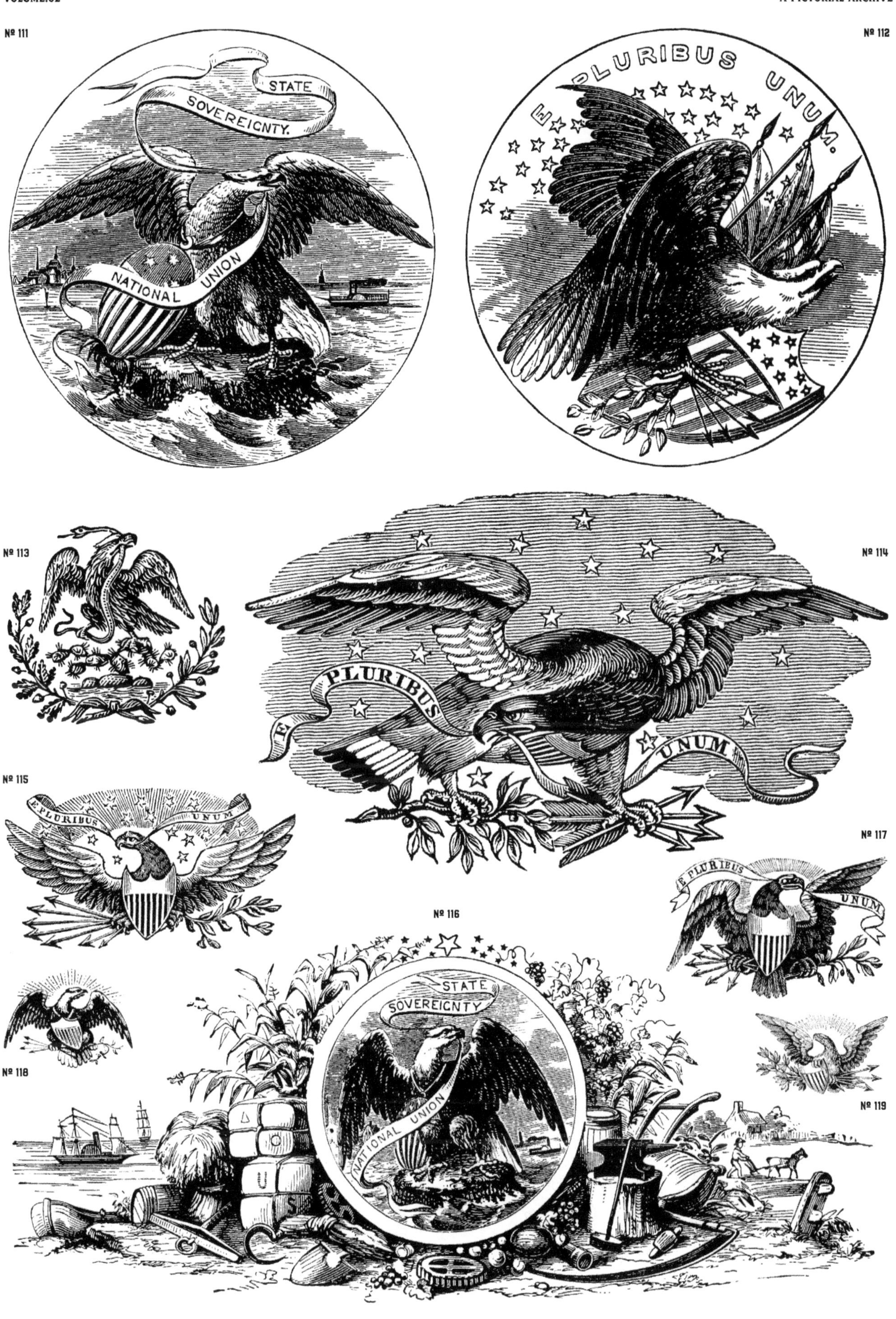

EAGLES

RELIGIOUS ICONOGRAPHY

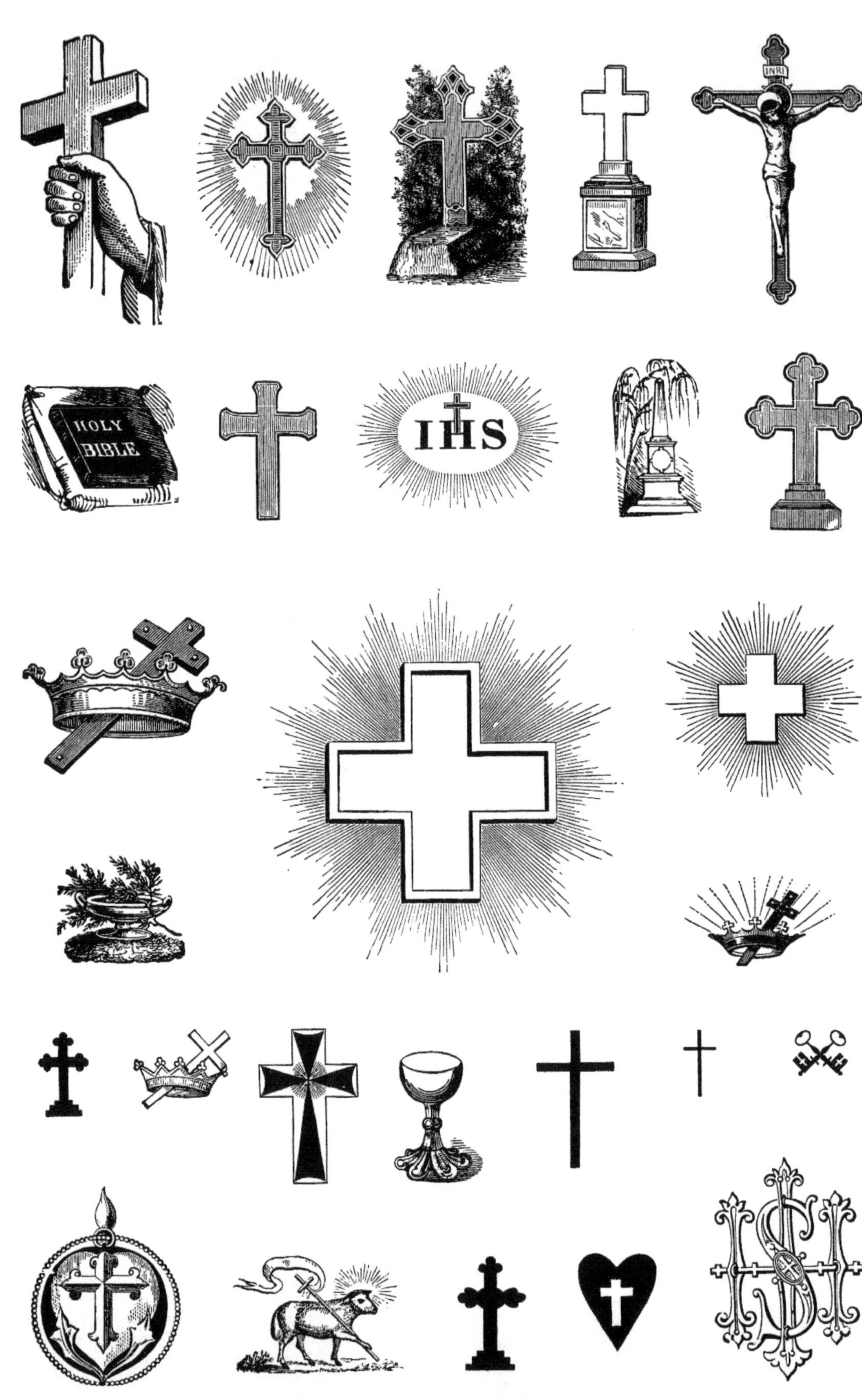

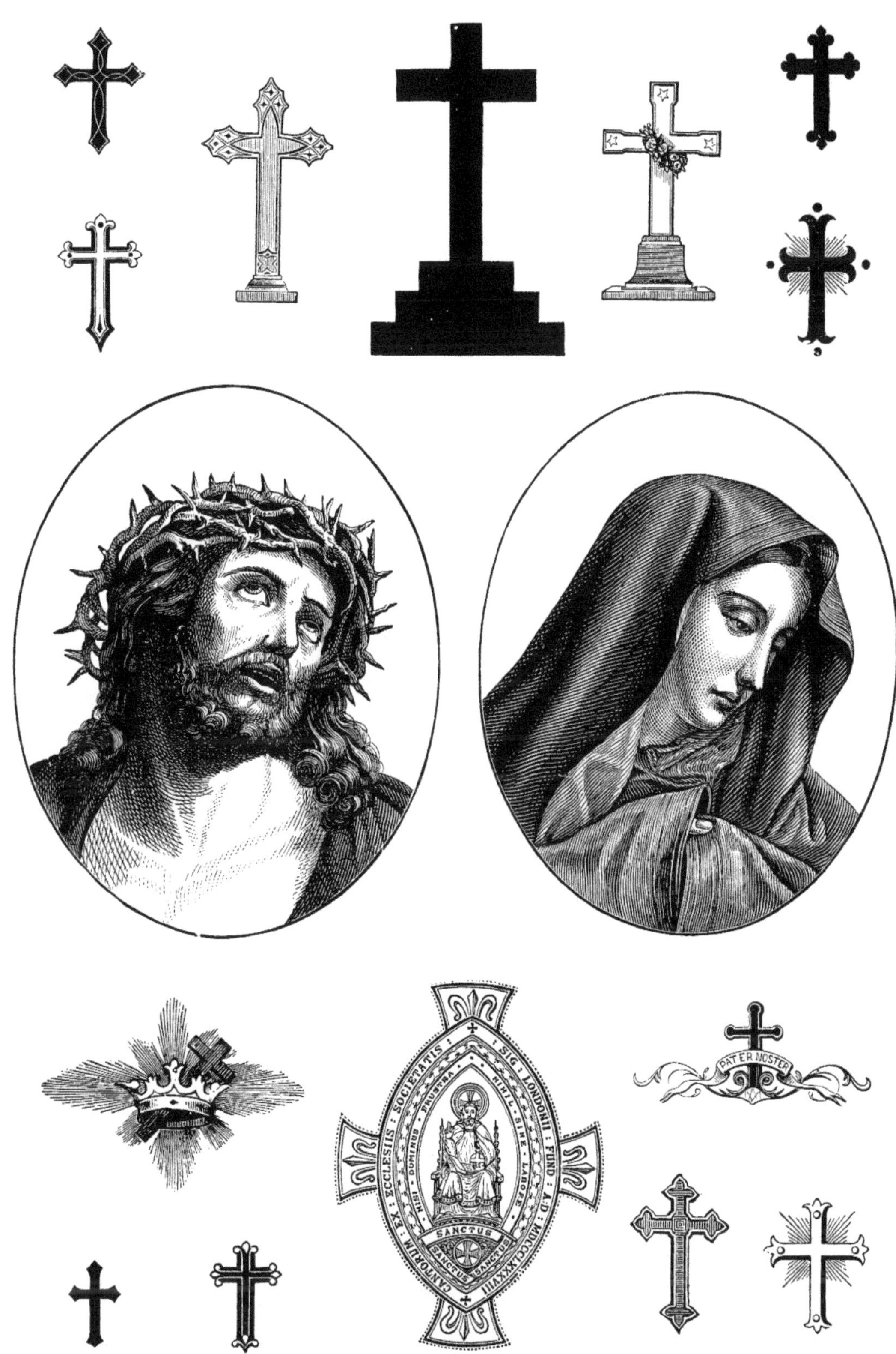
PATER NOSTER
SANCTUS

№ 122

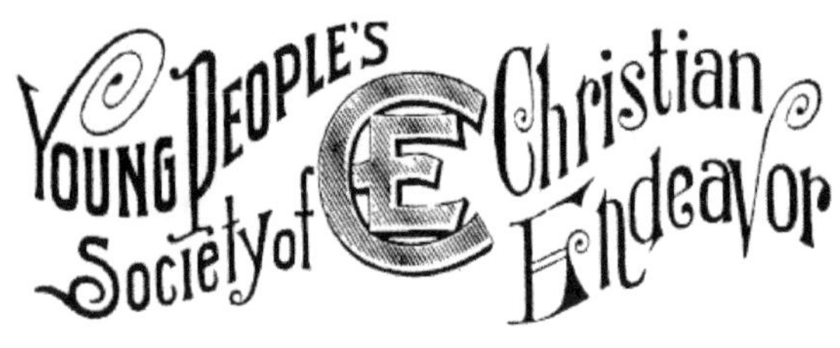

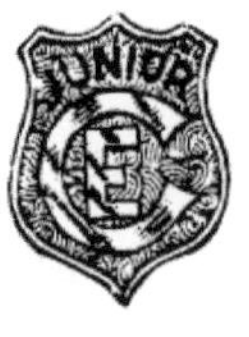

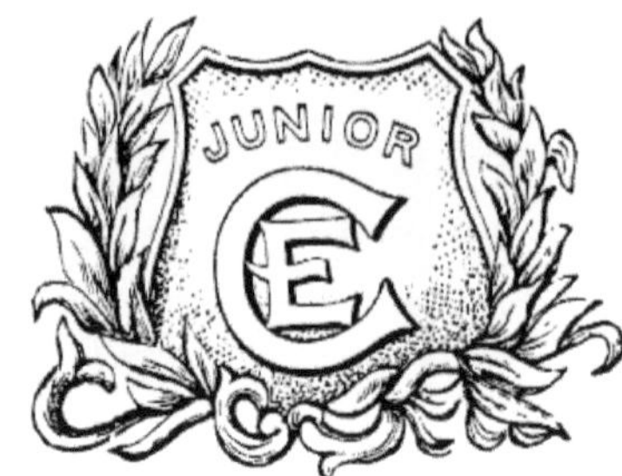

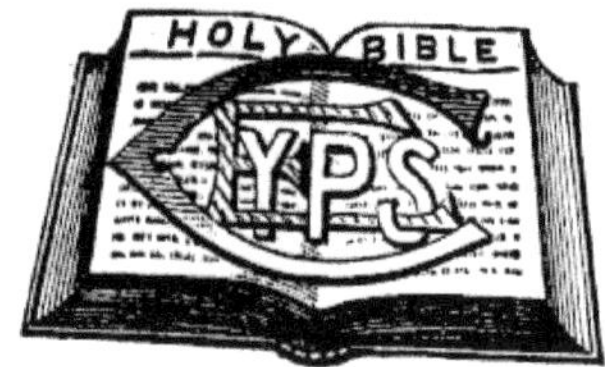

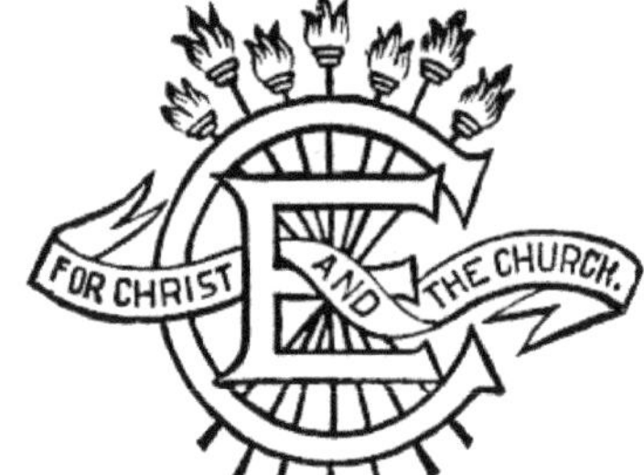

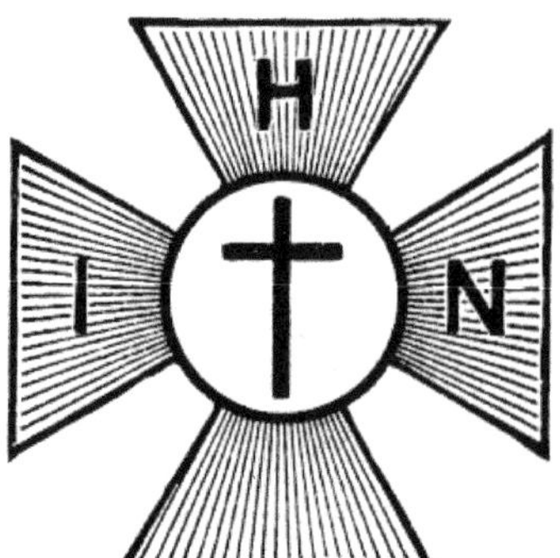

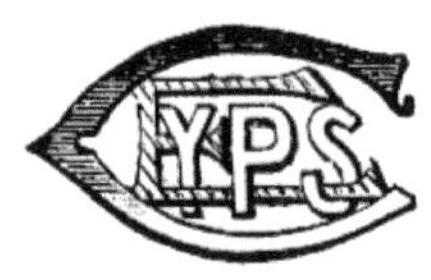

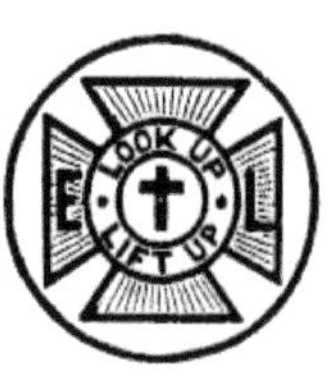

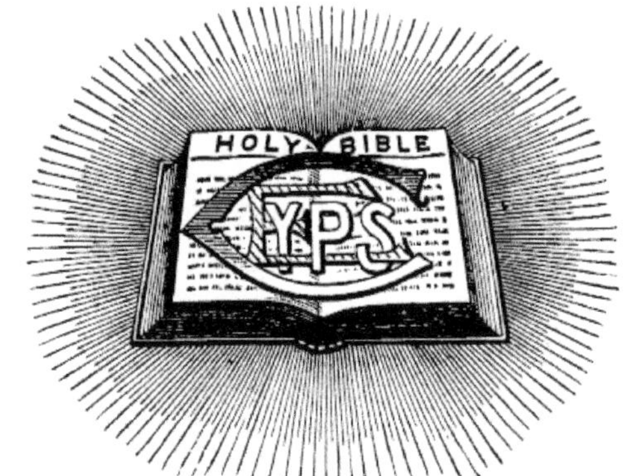

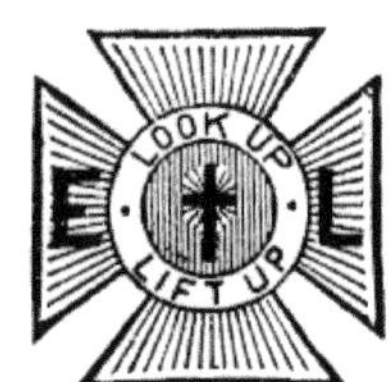

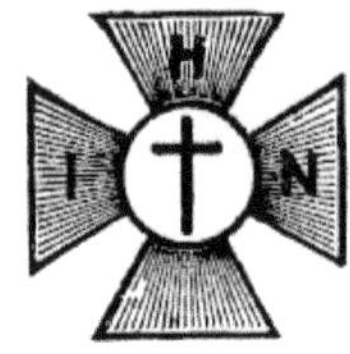

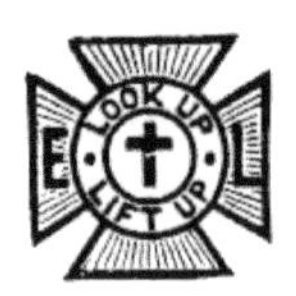

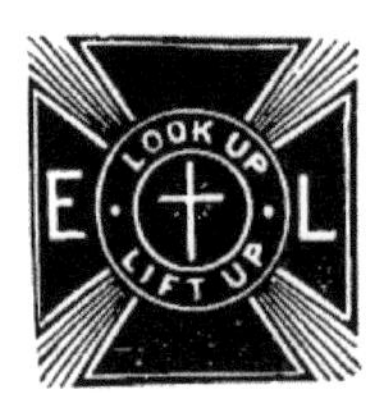

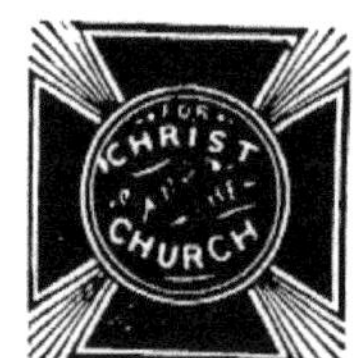

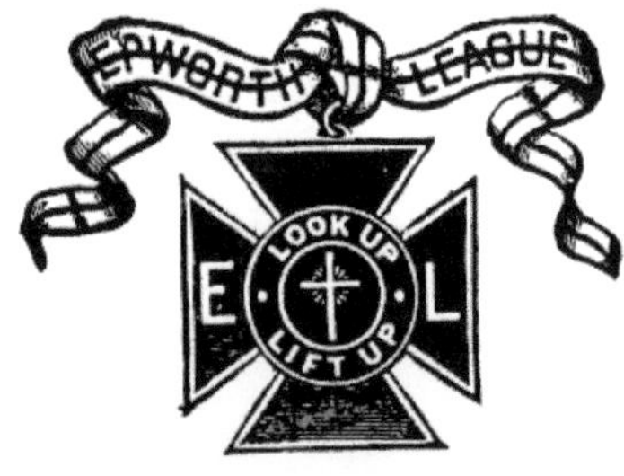

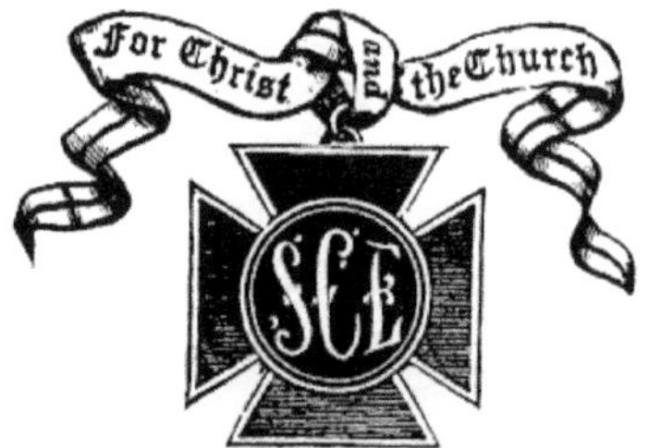

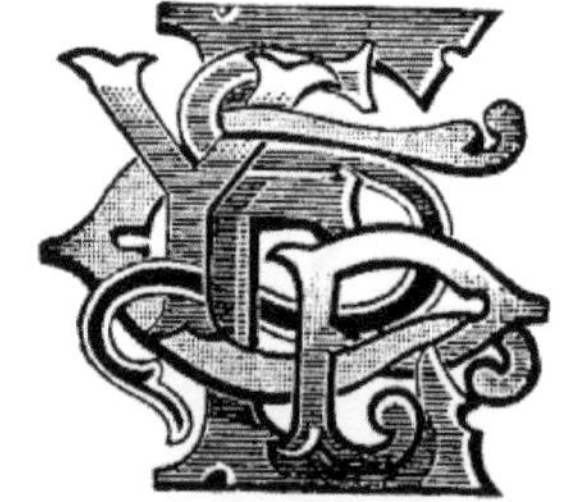

RELIGIOUS ICONOGRAPHY

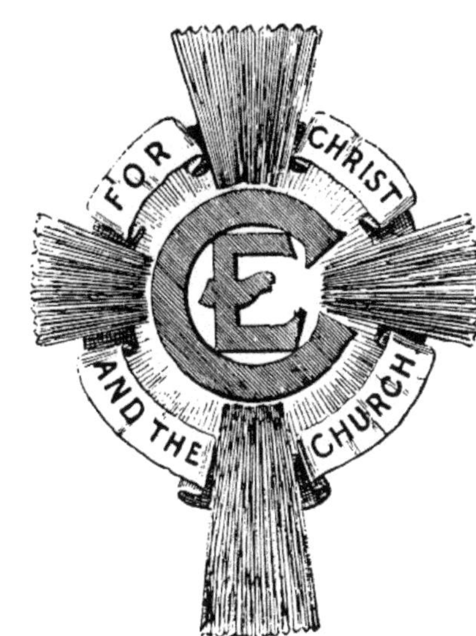
FOR CHRIST
AND THE CHURCH
CE

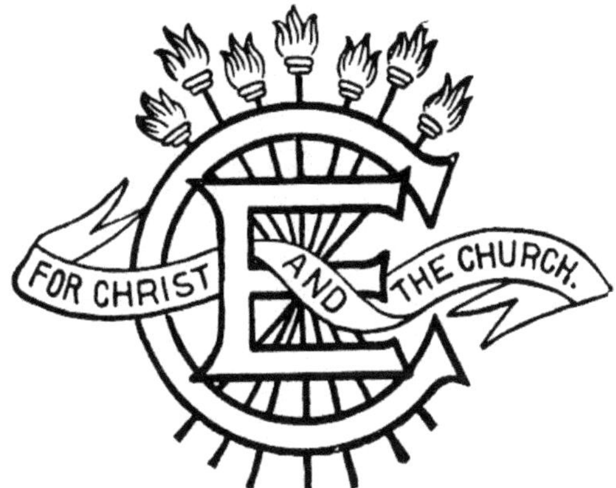
FOR CHRIST AND THE CHURCH.
CE

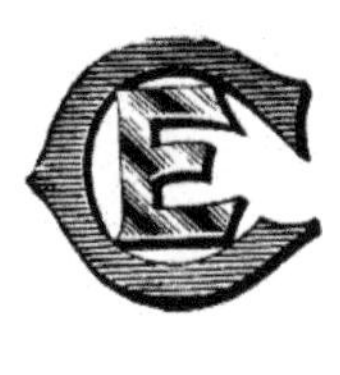

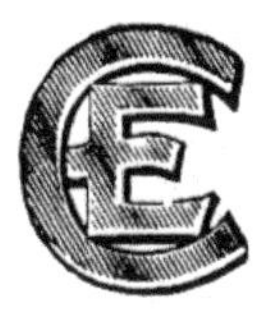

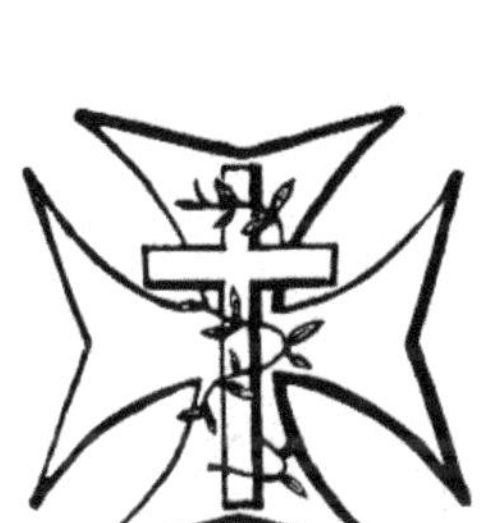
JUNIOR
CE

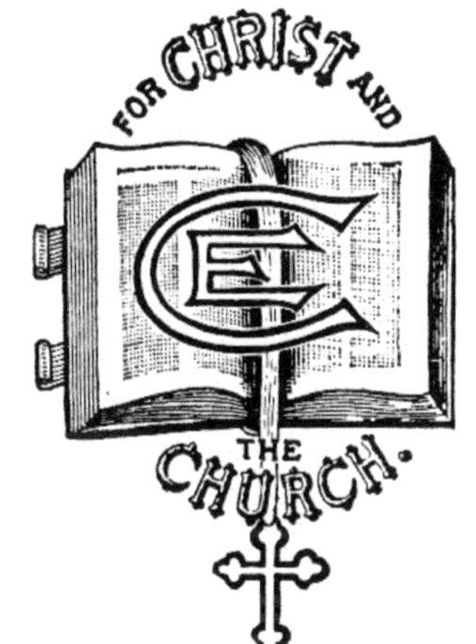
FOR CHRIST AND
THE
CHURCH.
CE

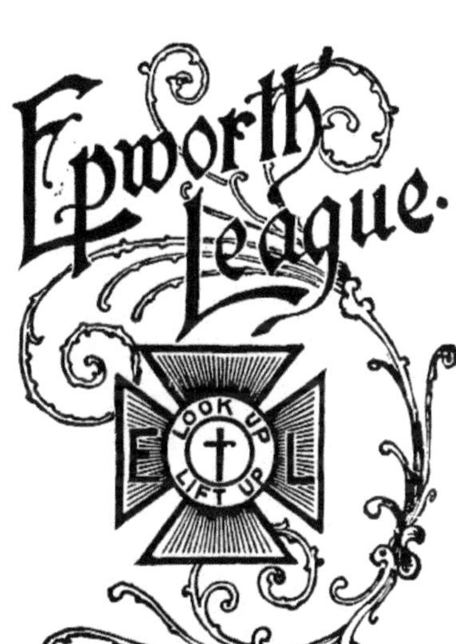
Epworth
League.
LOOK UP
LIFT UP
E
L

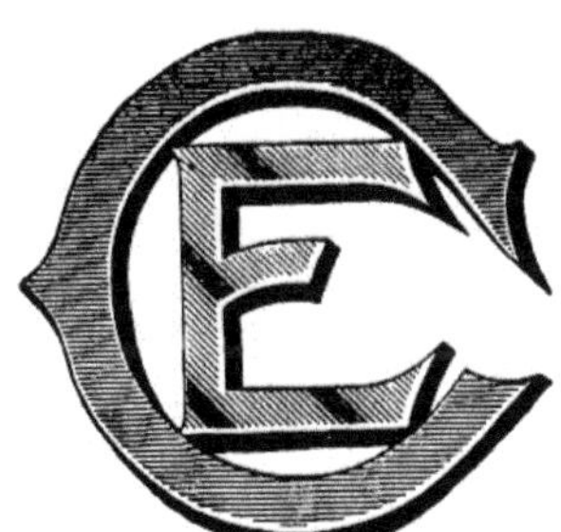

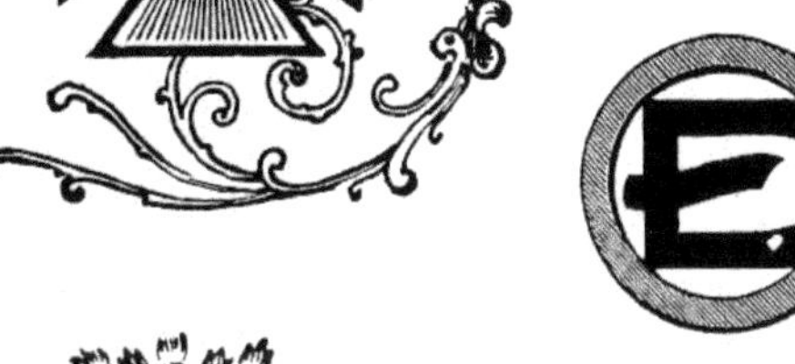

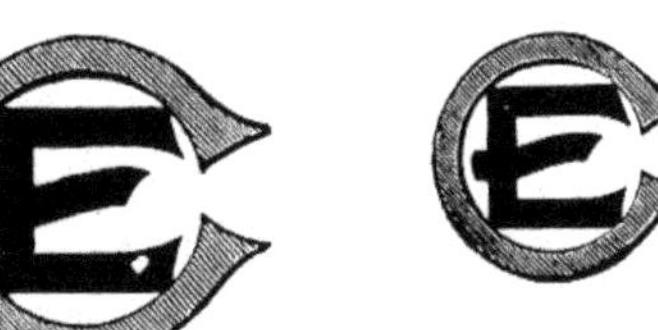

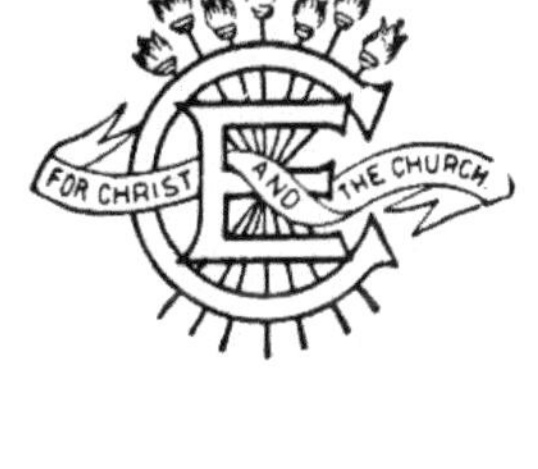
FOR CHRIST
AND
THE CHURCH

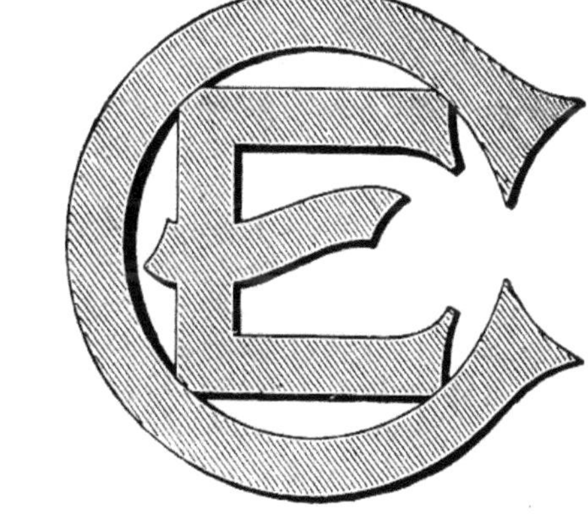

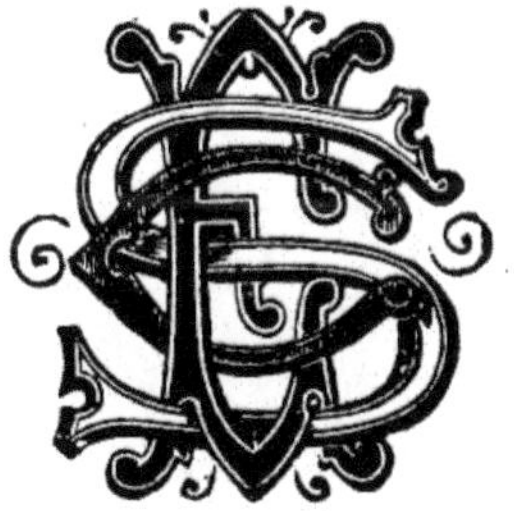

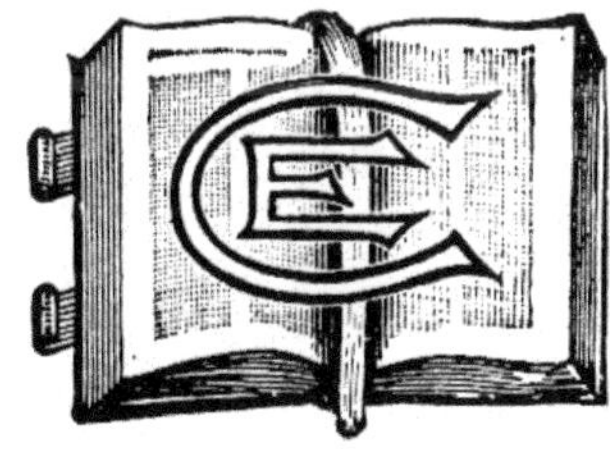

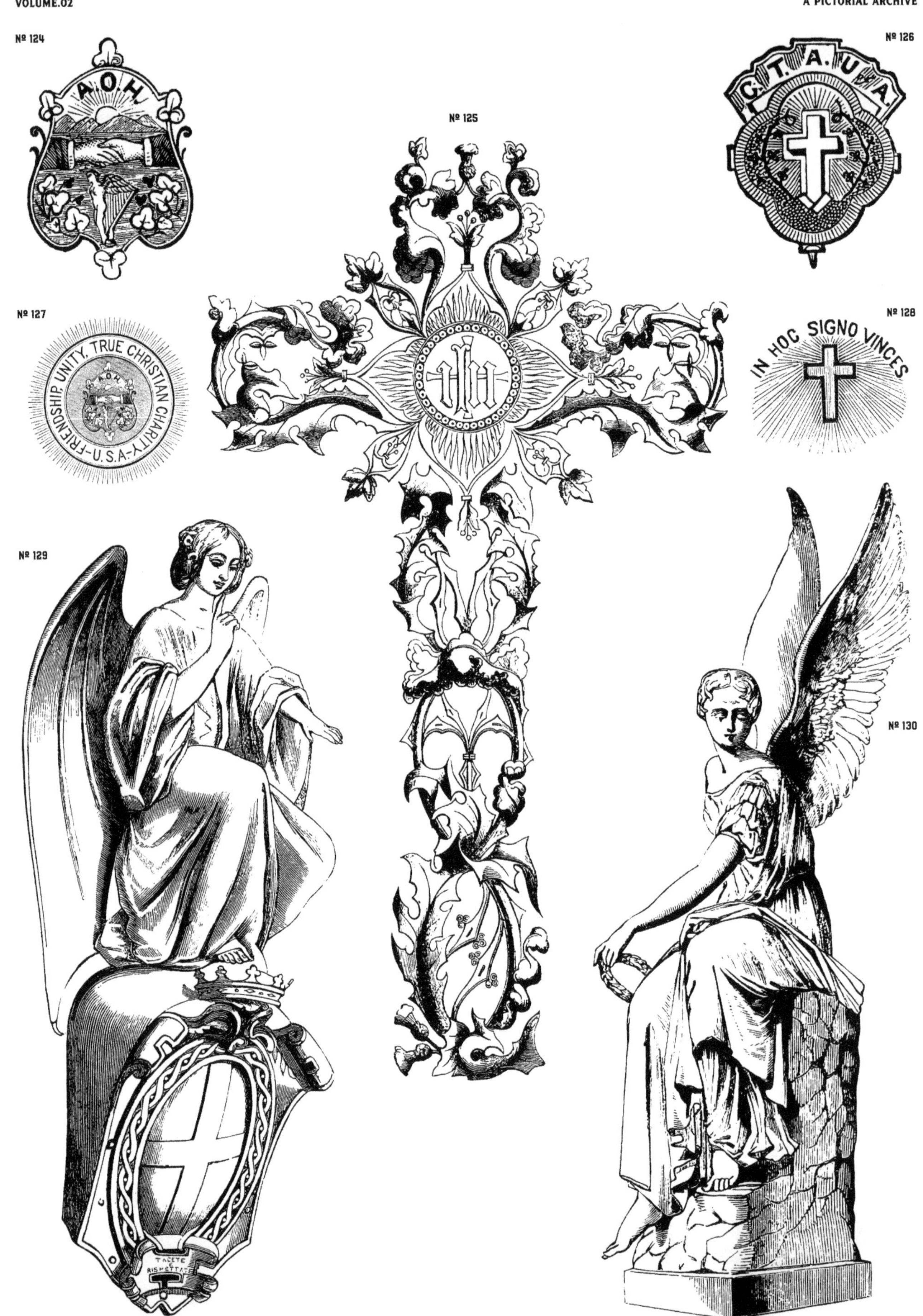

Nº 124
A.O.H.
Nº 125
Nº 126
C.T.A.U.A.
Nº 127
FRIENDSHIP, UNITY, TRUE CHRISTIAN CHARITY
-U.S.A.-
Nº 128
IN HOC SIGNO VINCES
Nº 129
TACETE RISPETTATE
Nº 130

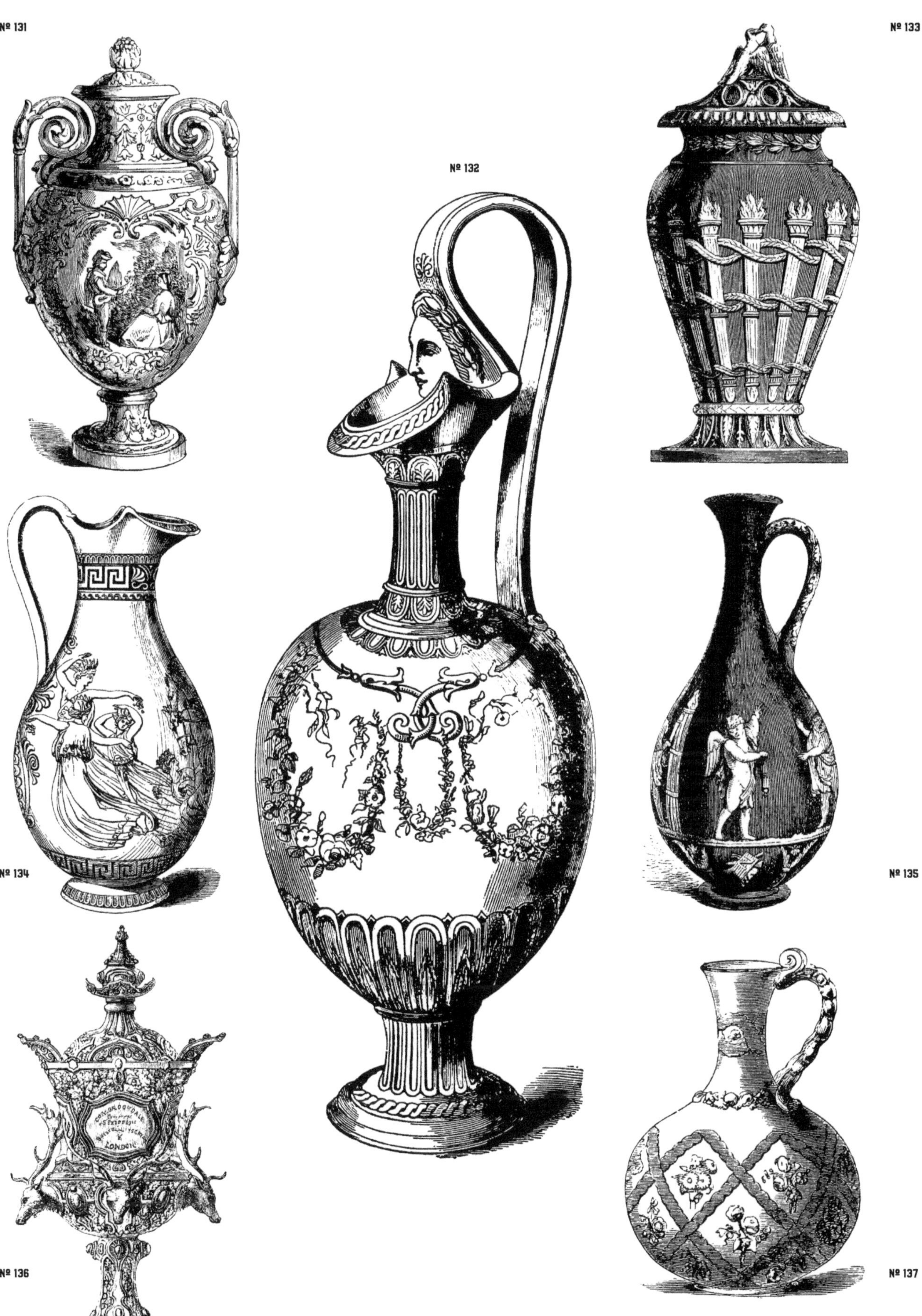

Nº 131

Nº 132

Nº 133

Nº 134

Nº 135

Nº 136

Nº 137

KEYS & LOCKS

Nº 138
Nº 139
Nº 140
Nº 141
Nº 142
Nº 143
Nº 144
Nº 145
Nº 146
Nº 147
Nº 148
Nº 149
Nº 150
Nº 151
Nº 152
BRANFORD, CT.

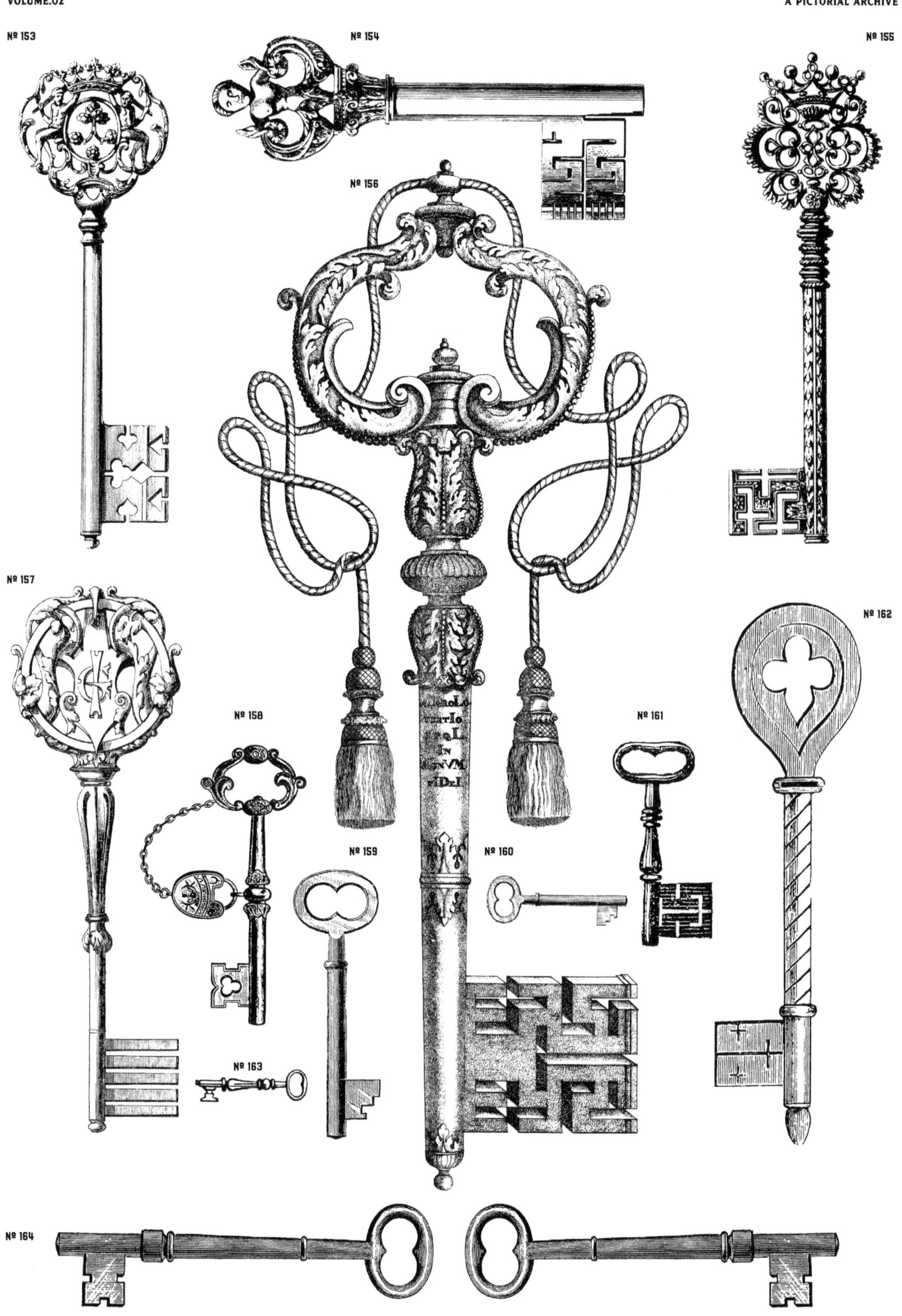
Nº 153
Nº 154
Nº 155
Nº 156
Nº 157
Nº 158
Nº 159
Nº 160
Nº 161
Nº 162
Nº 163
Nº 164

Nº 165

SNAKES

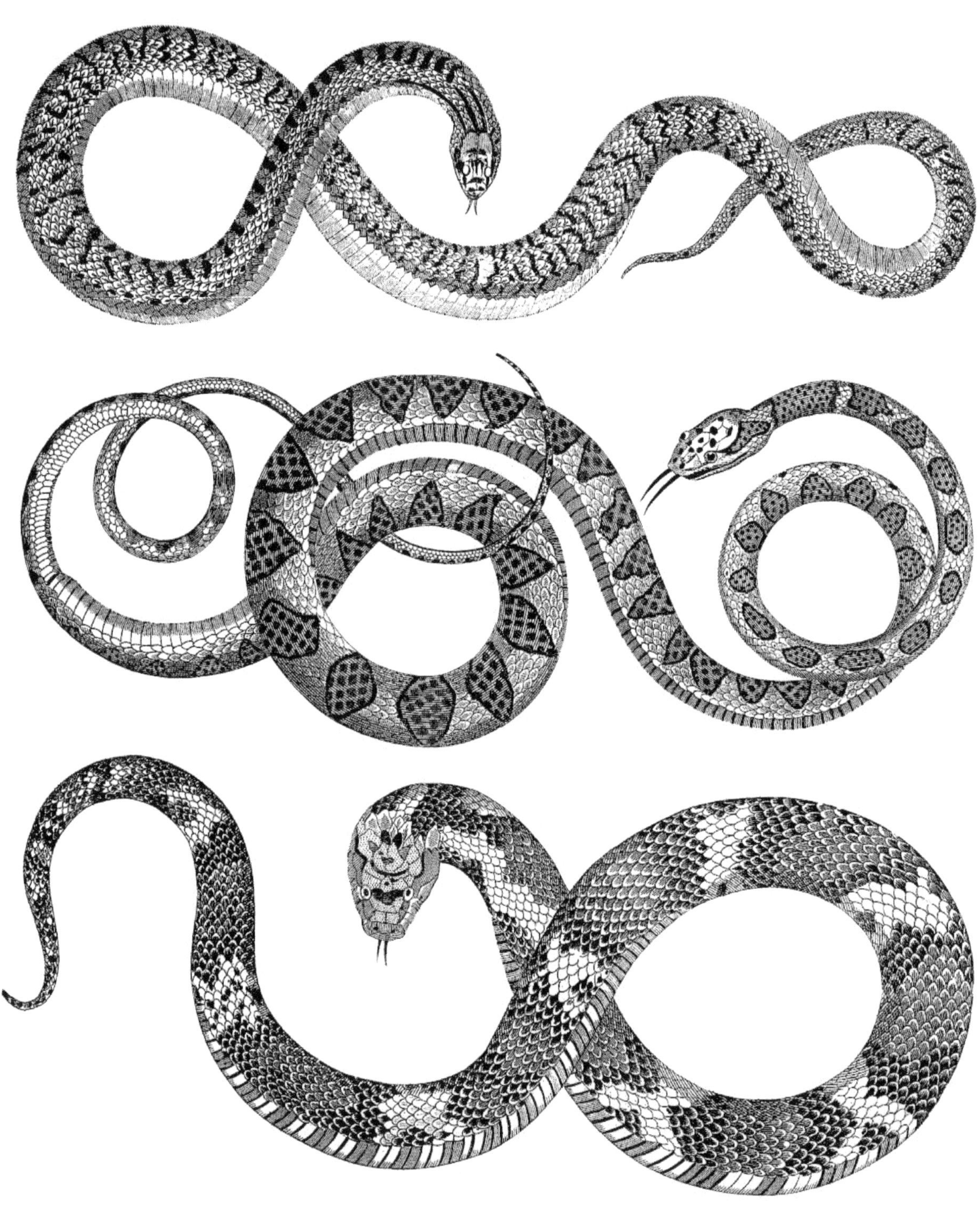

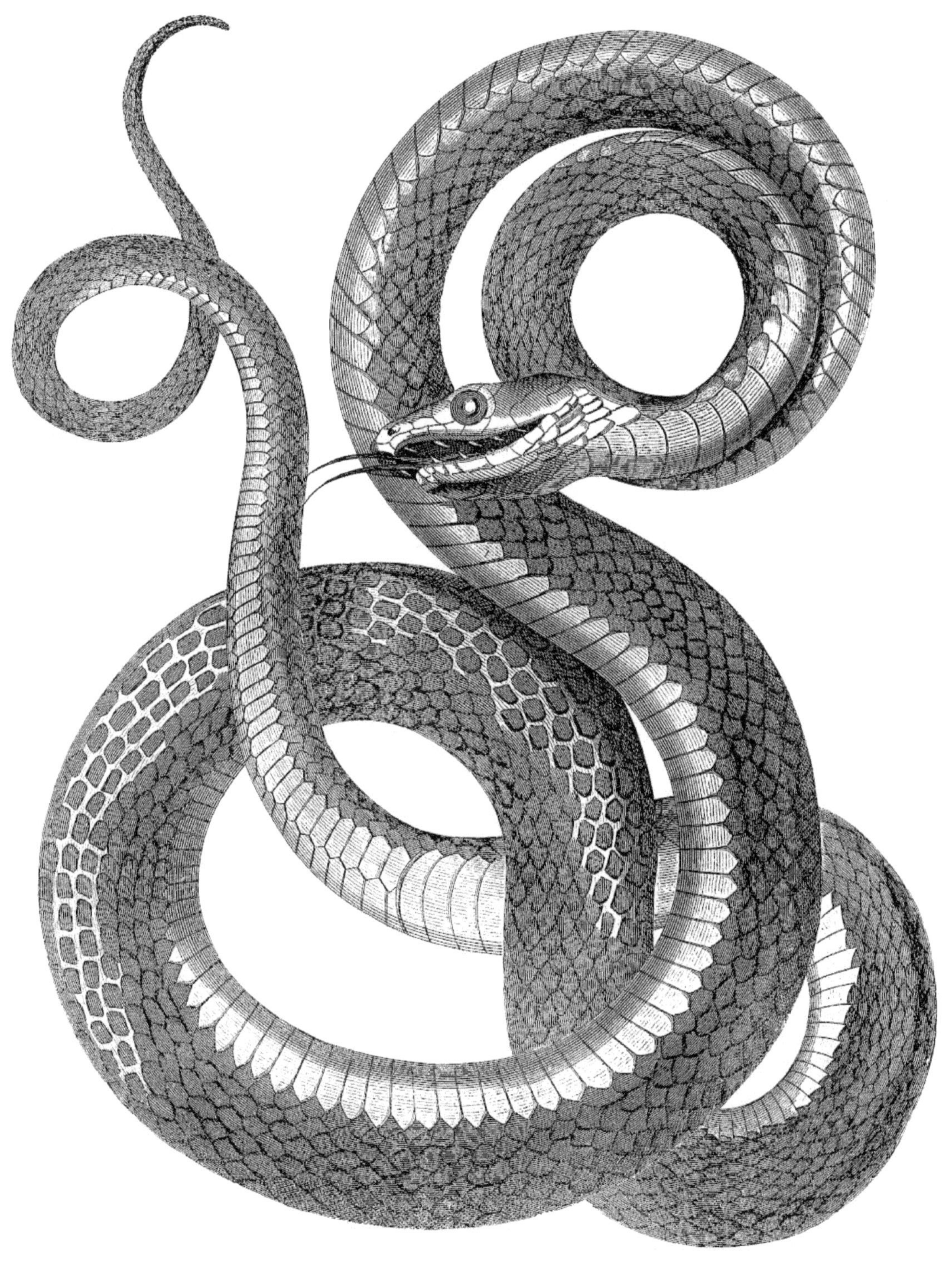

№ 167

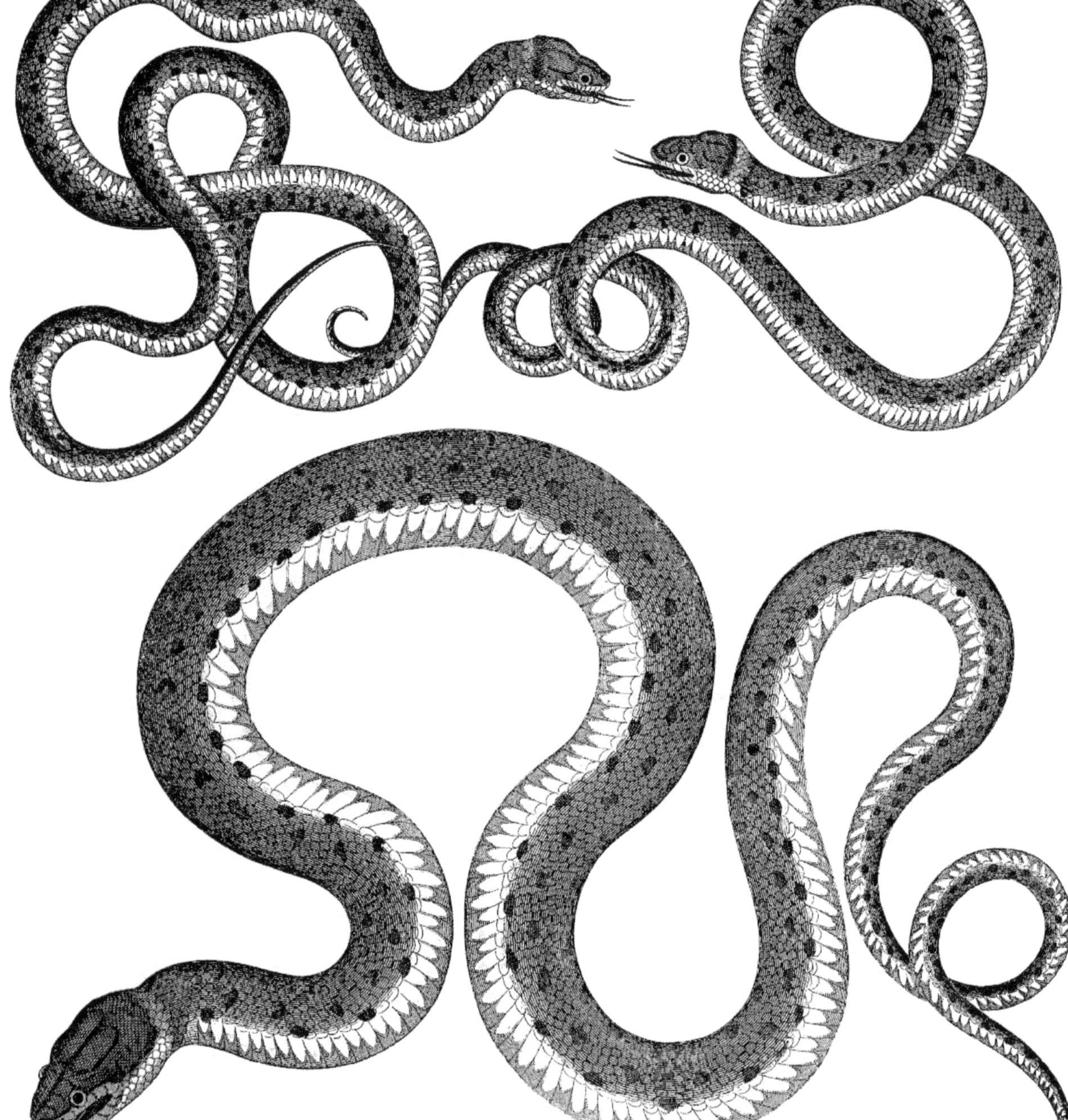

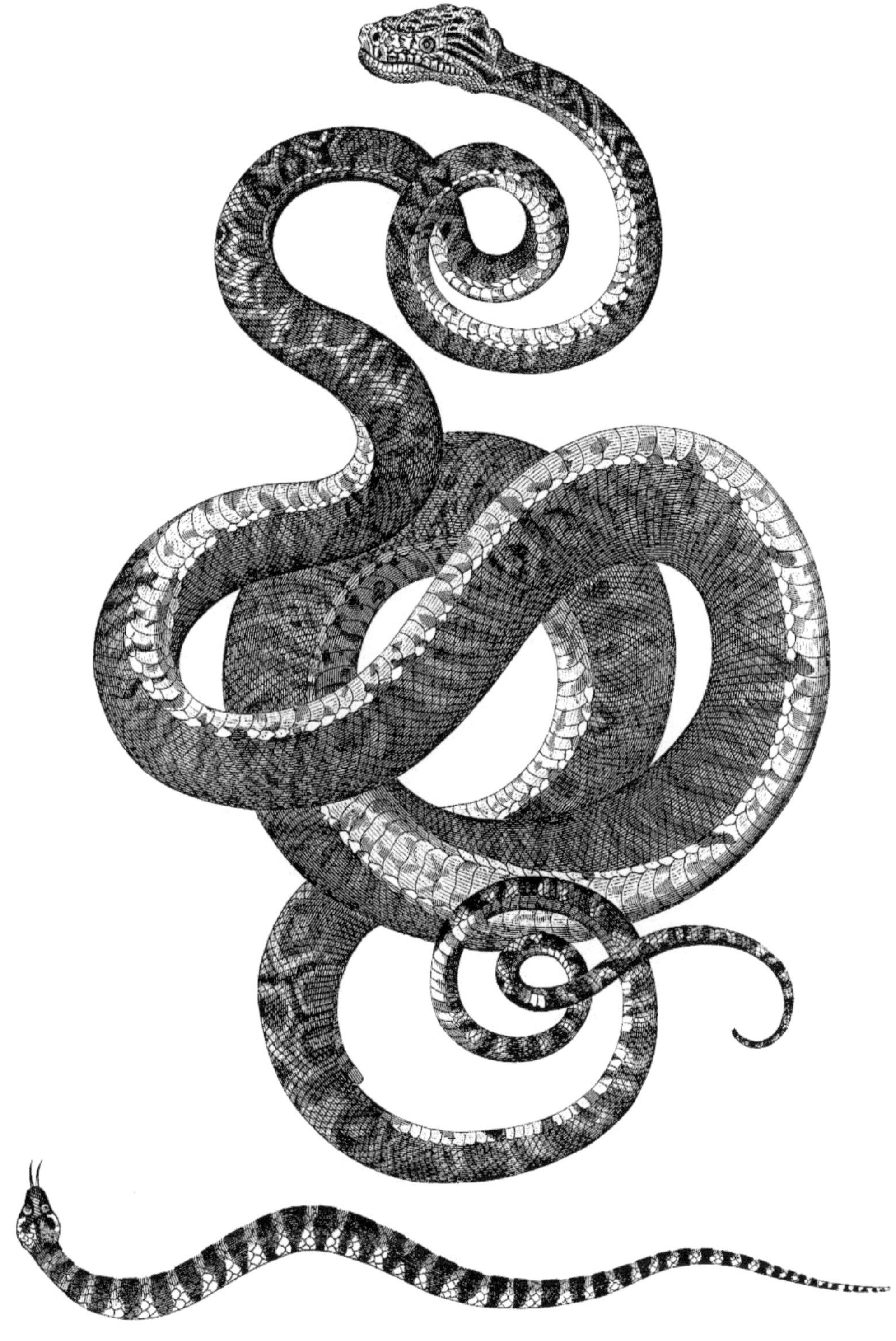

№ 169

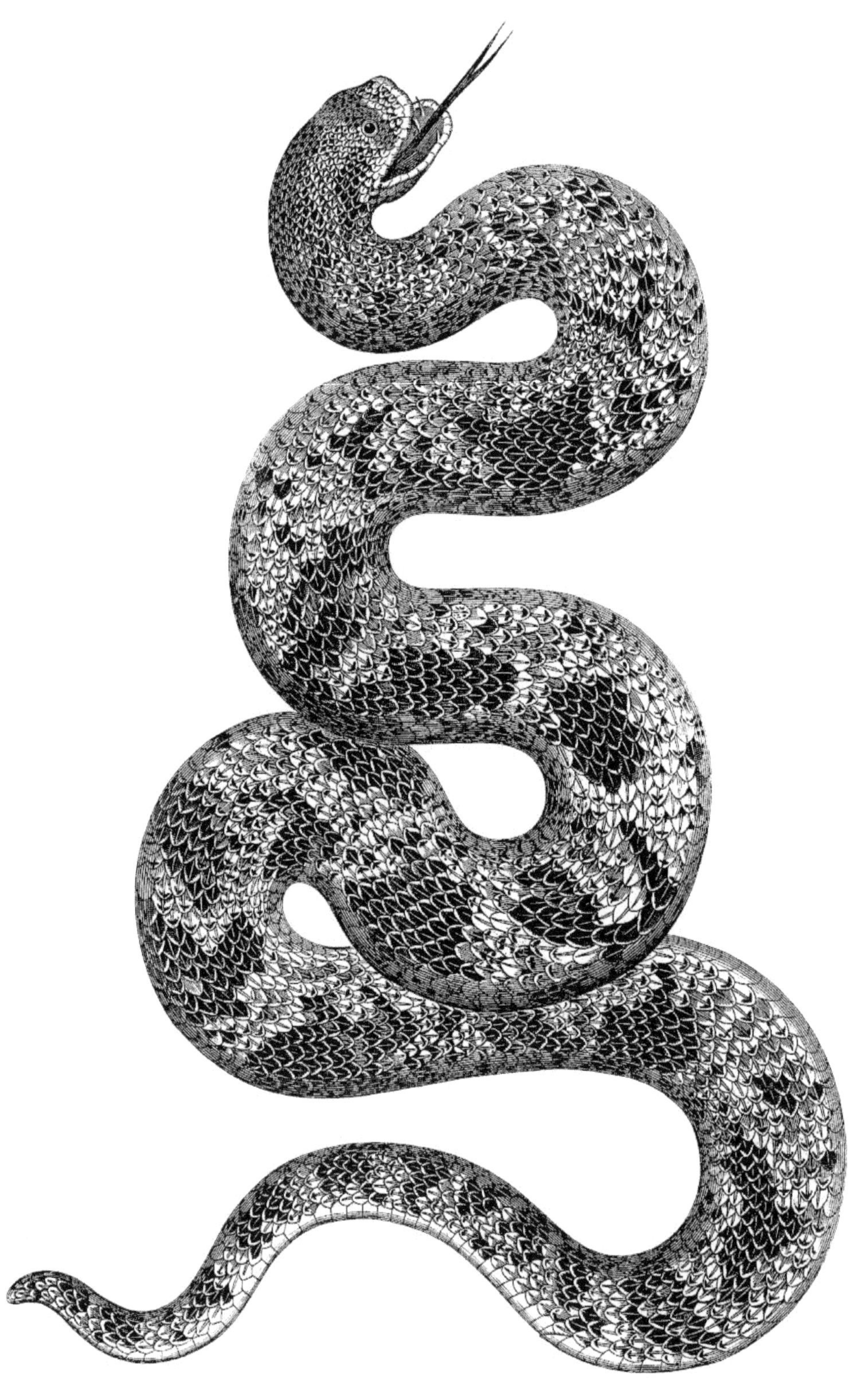

№ 170

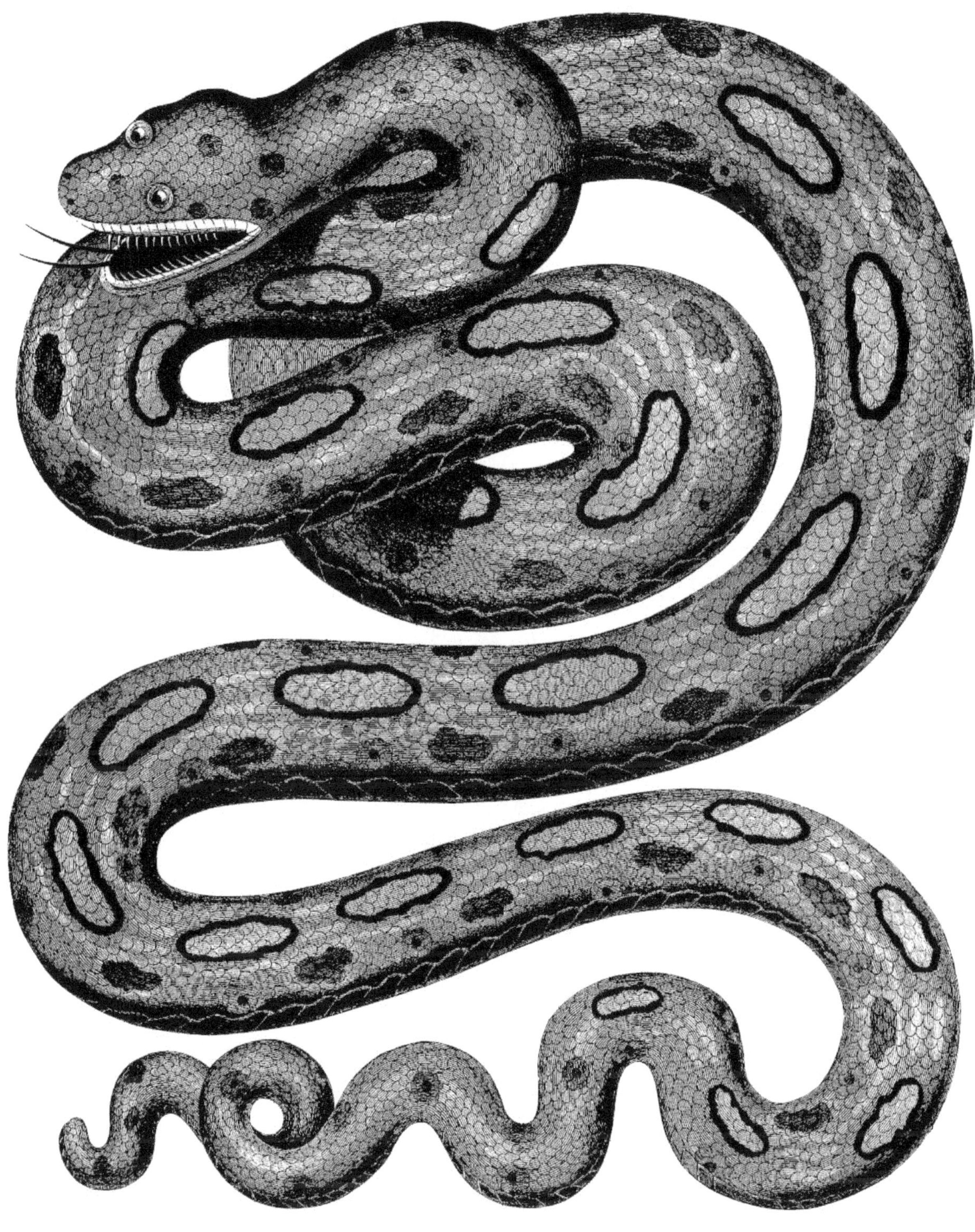

№ 171

№ 172

№ 173

№ 174

№ 175

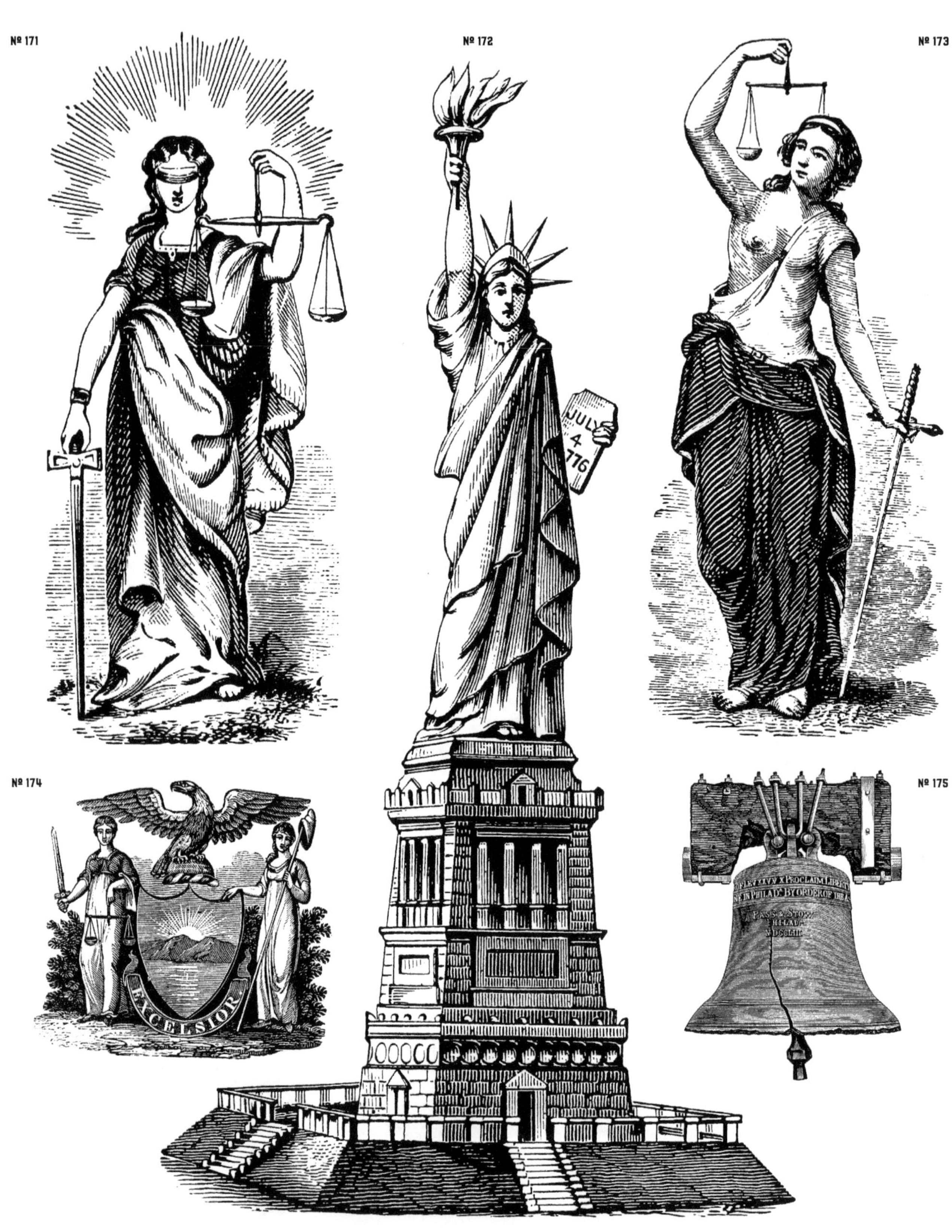

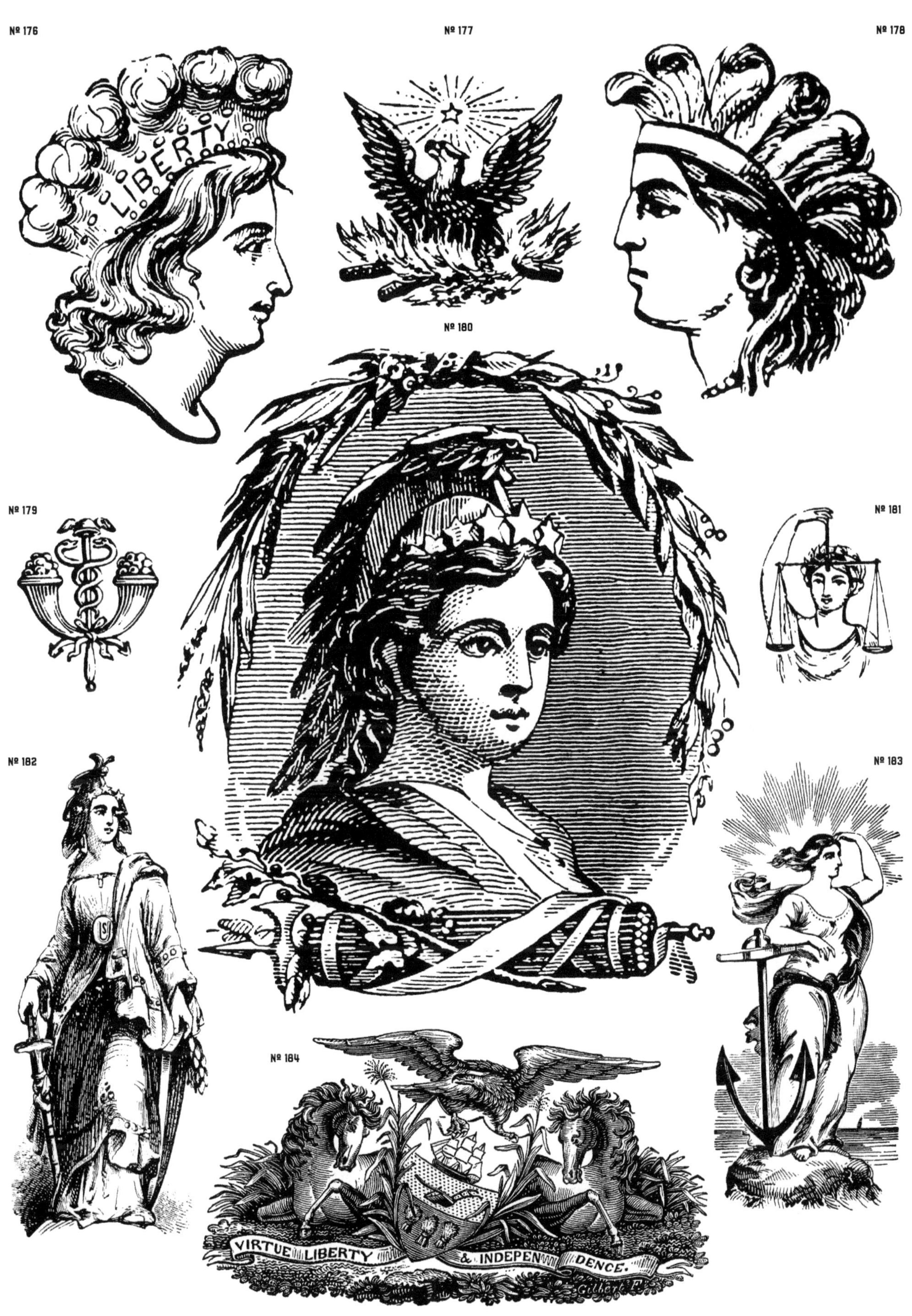
№ 176
№ 177
№ 178
LIBERTY
№ 180
№ 179
№ 181
№ 182
№ 183
№ 184
VIRTUE LIBERTY & INDEPEN DENCE.

AMERICANA

№ 185
№ 186
№ 187
№ 189
ESTADOS UNIDOS DO BRAZIL
15 DE NOVEMBRO DE 1889.
№ 188
№ 190
TOTE
FREEDOM CHARITY
FRIENDSHIP
№ 191
№ 192
I.O.R.M.
№ 193
EUREKA.

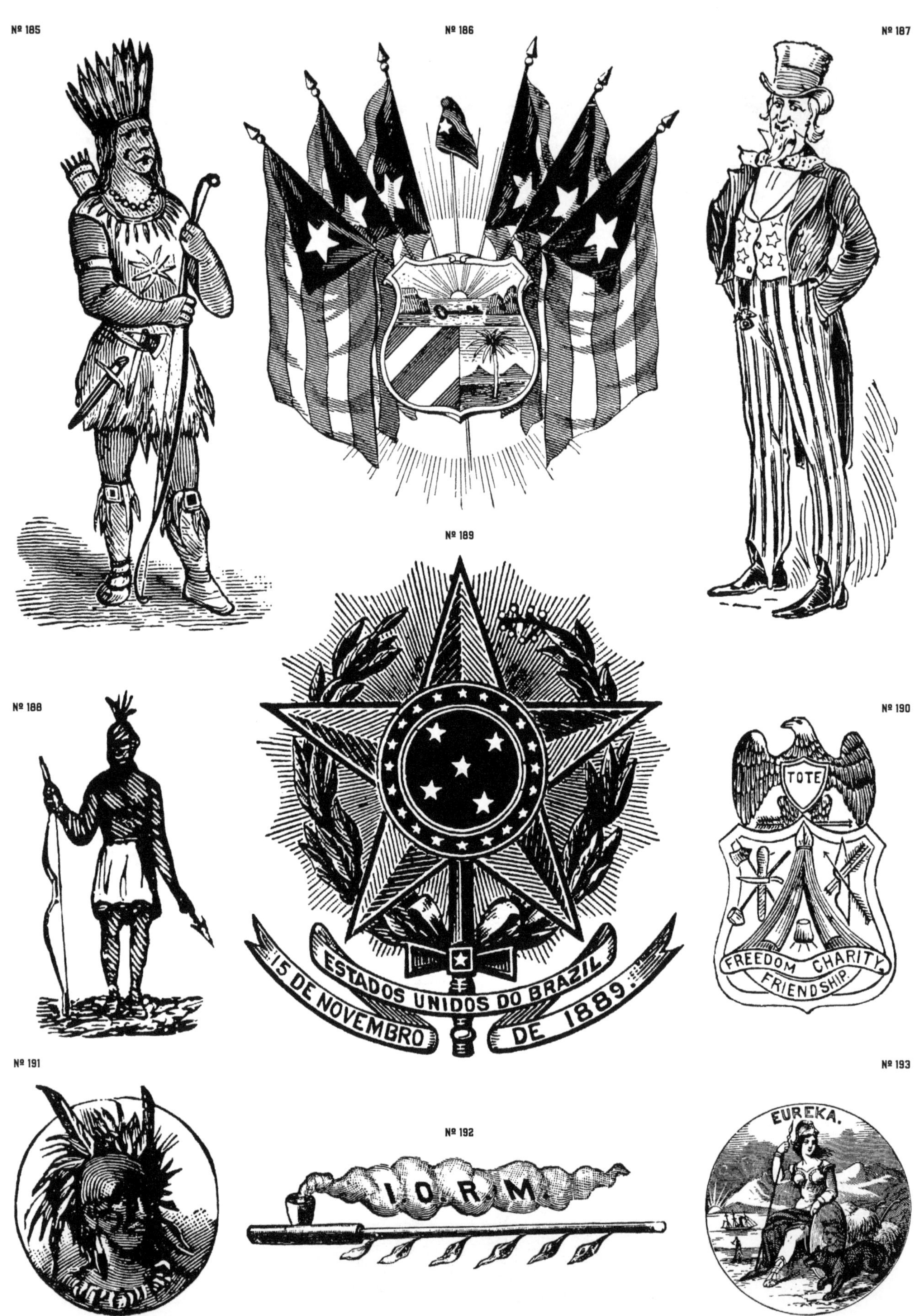

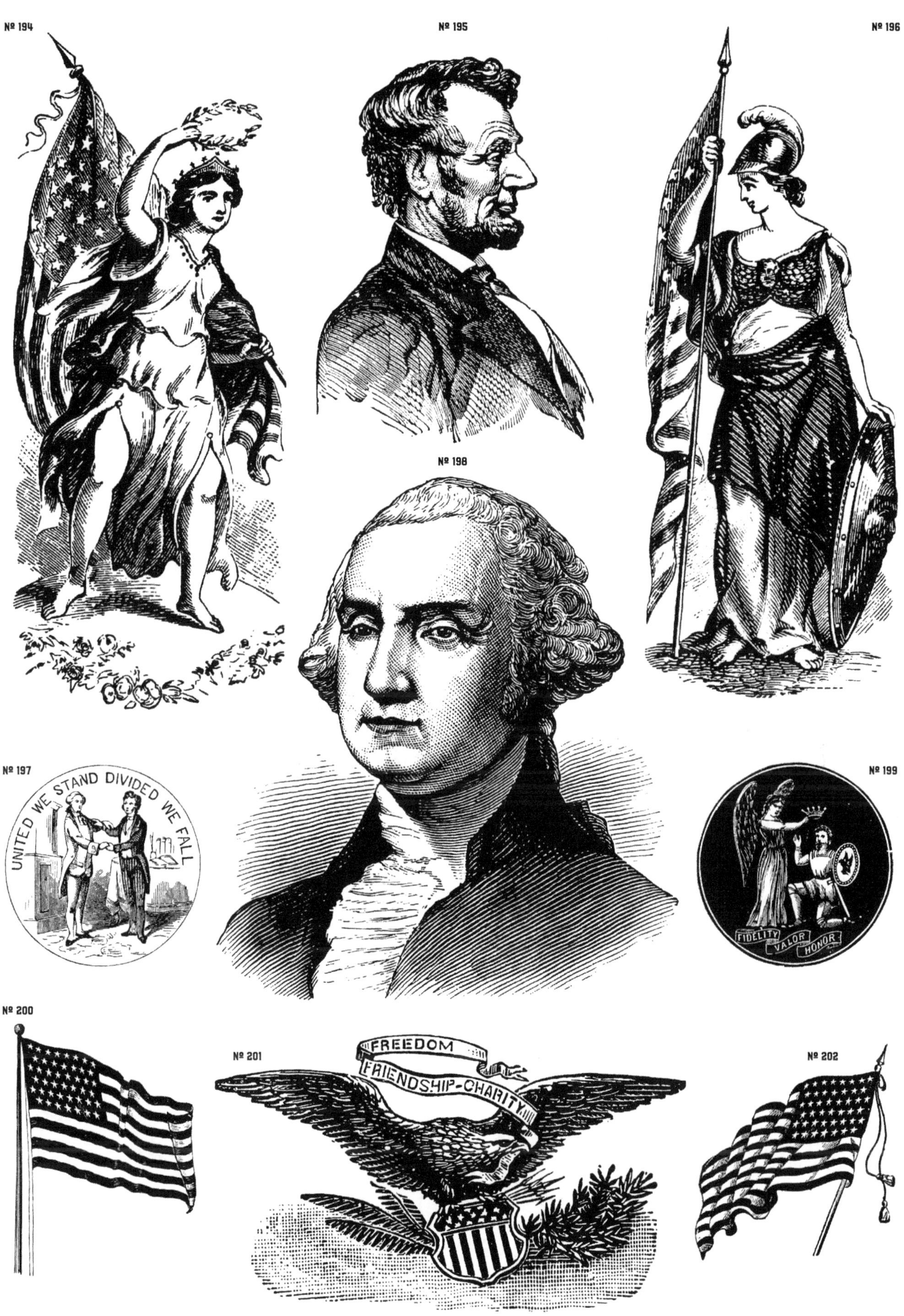

Nº 194
Nº 195
Nº 196
Nº 198
Nº 197
UNITED WE STAND DIVIDED WE FALL
Nº 199
FIDELITY VALOR HONOR
Nº 200
Nº 201
FREEDOM
FRIENDSHIP-CHARITY
Nº 202

№ 203

№ 204

№ 205

№ 206

№ 207

№ 208

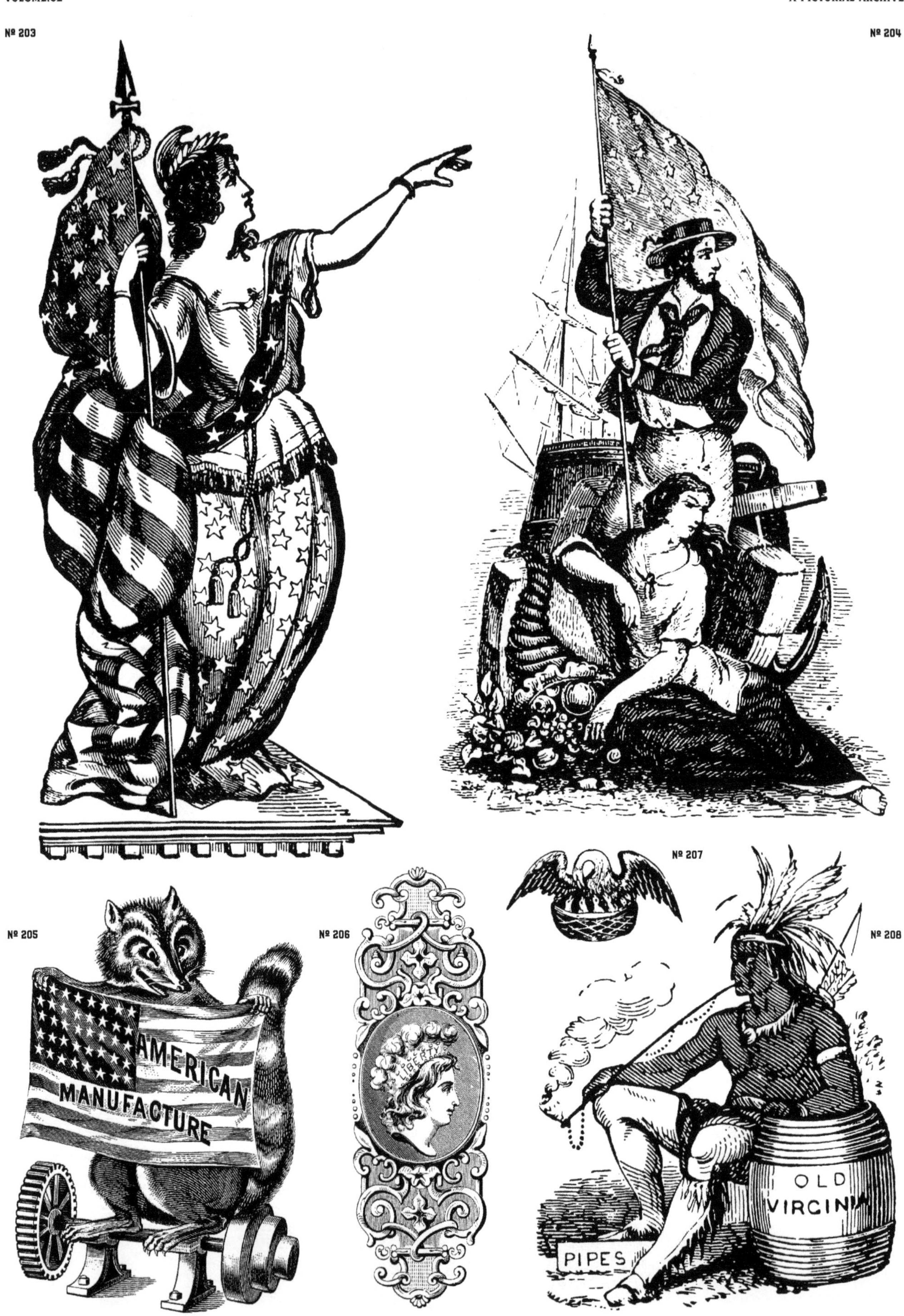

AMERICANA

CLOCKS & WATCHES

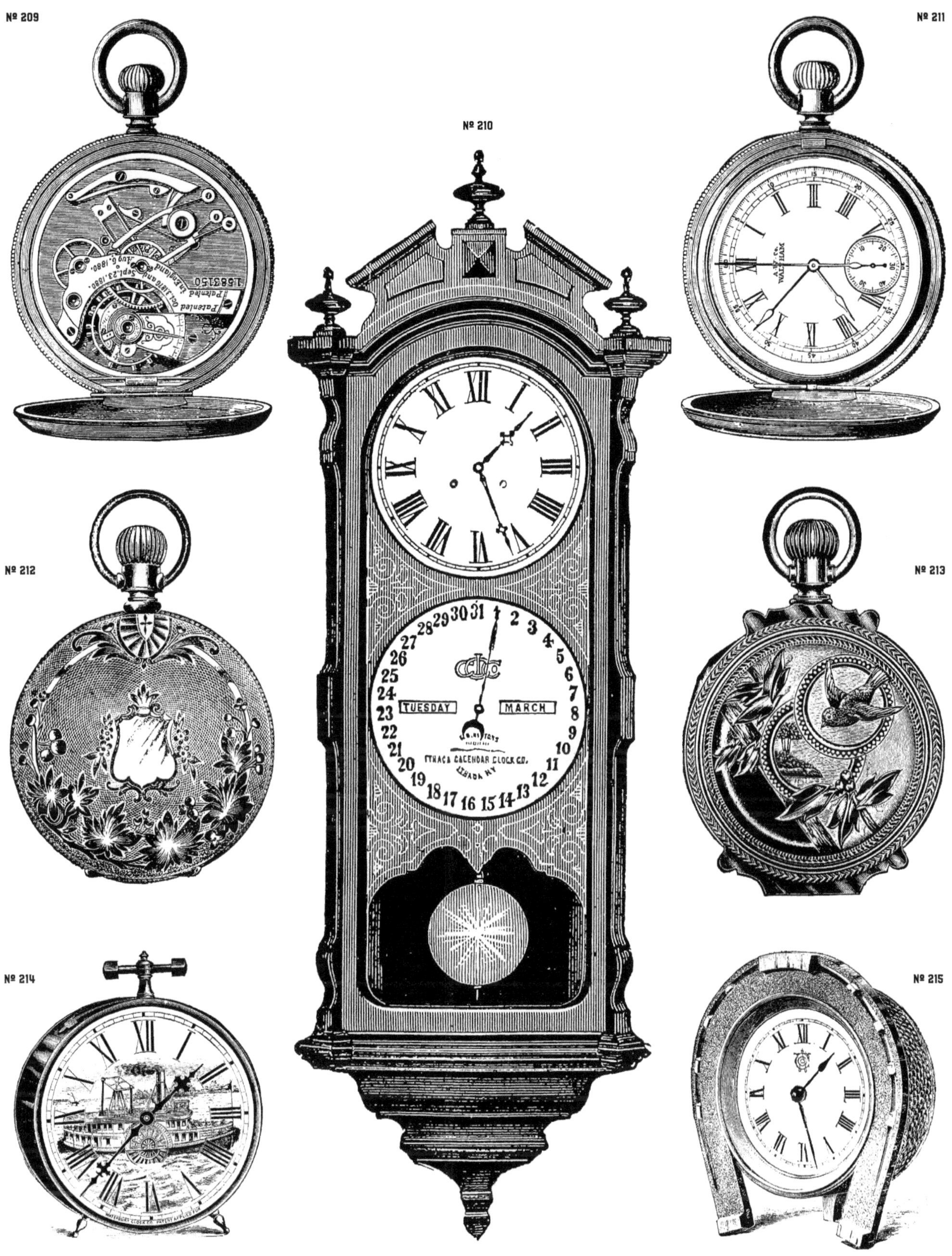

MILITARY MEDALS

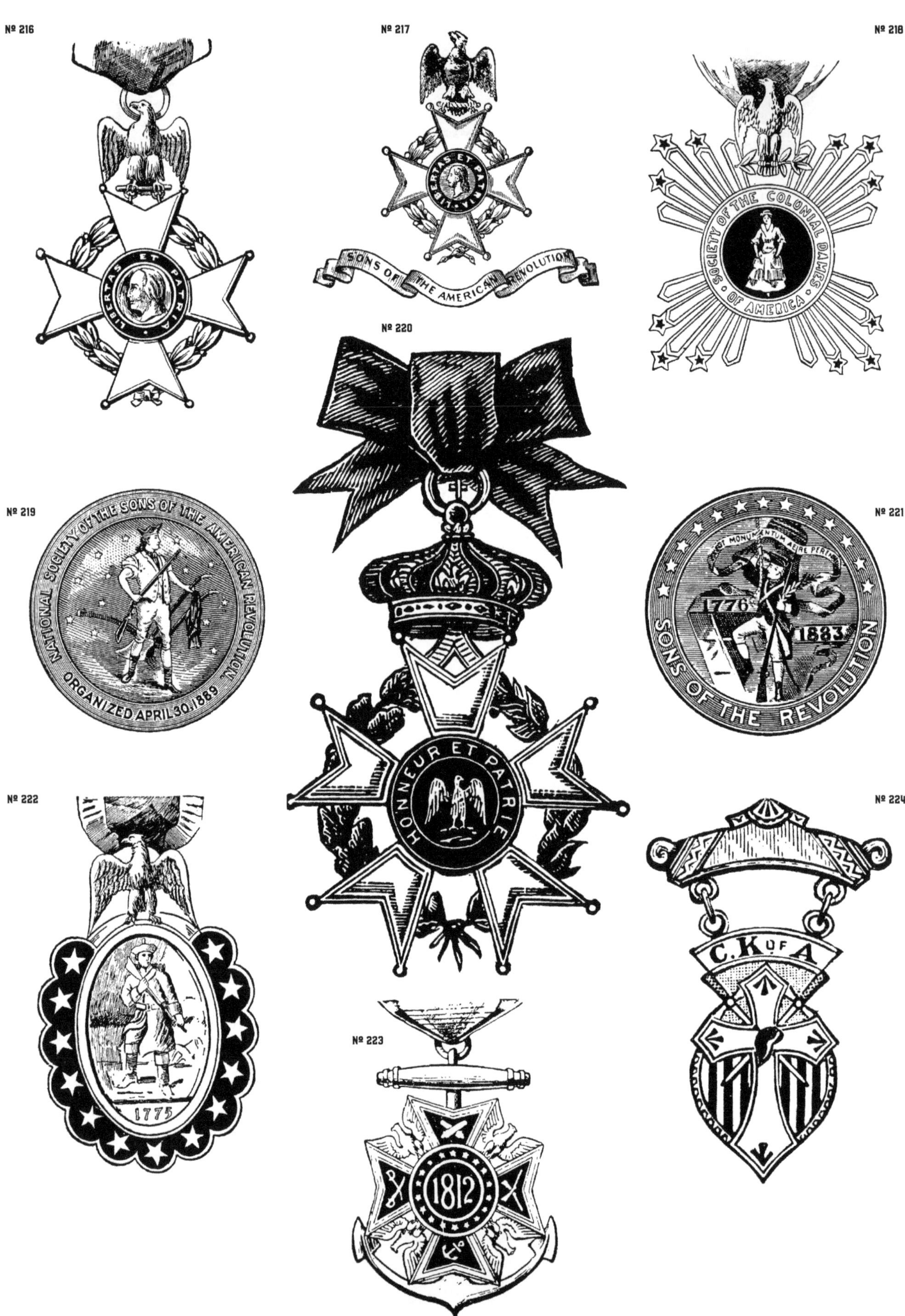

Nº 216
Nº 217
Nº 218
Nº 219
Nº 220
Nº 221
Nº 222
Nº 223
Nº 224

№ 225

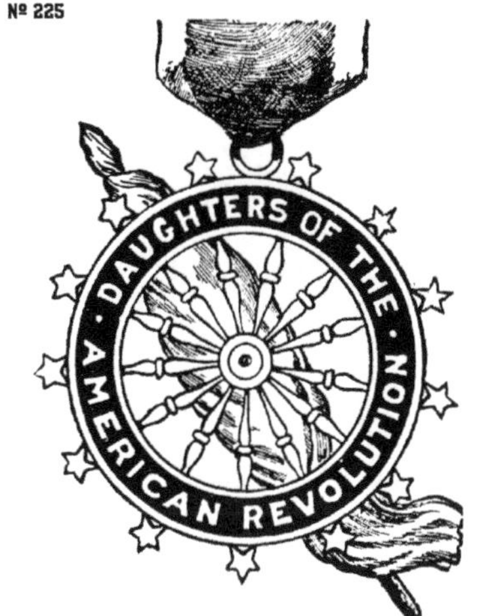

№ 226

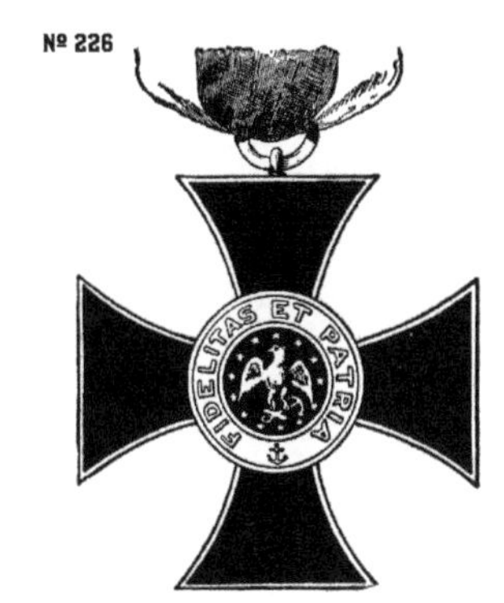

№ 227

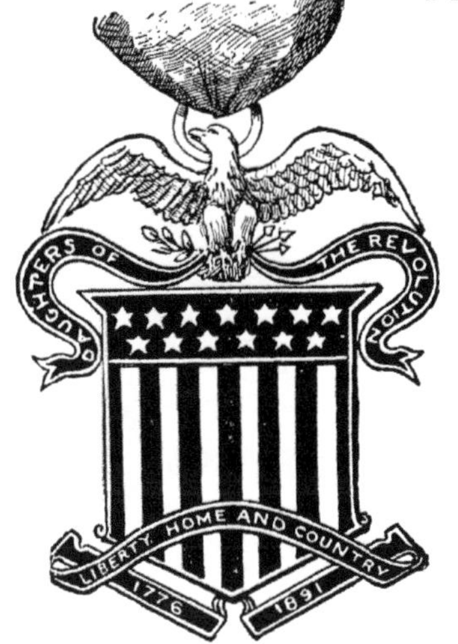

№ 228

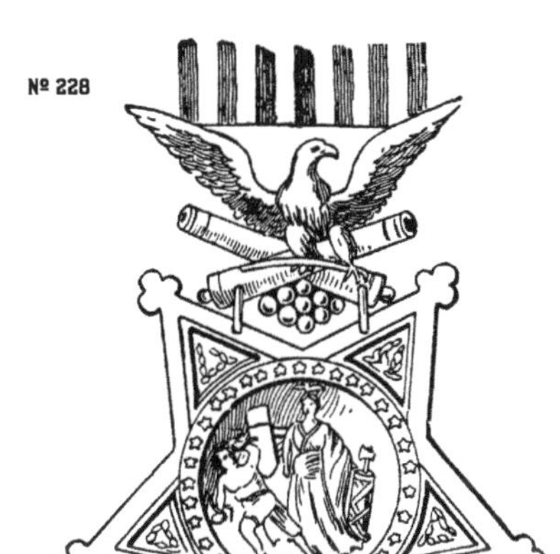

№ 229

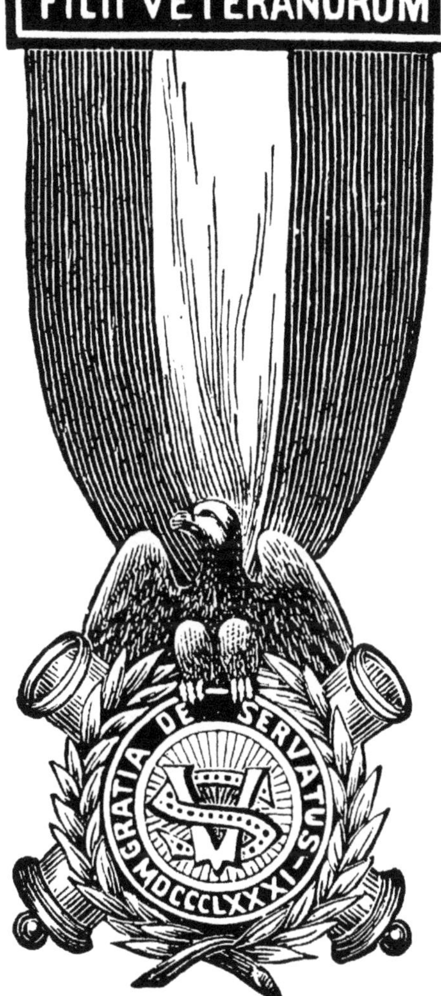

№ 230

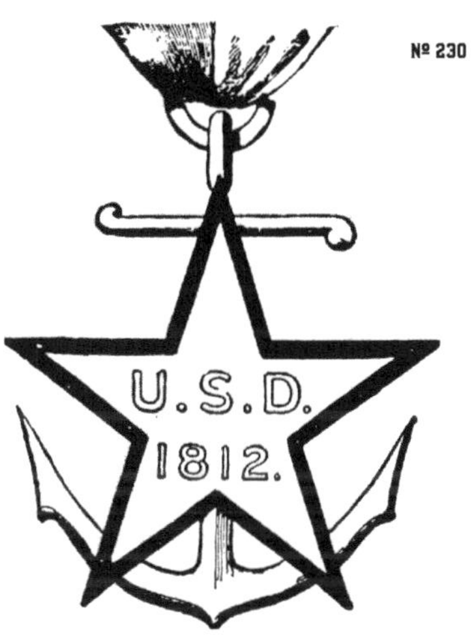

№ 231

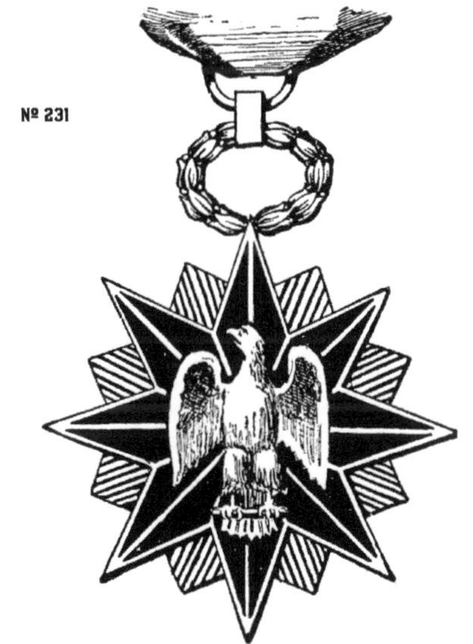

№ 232

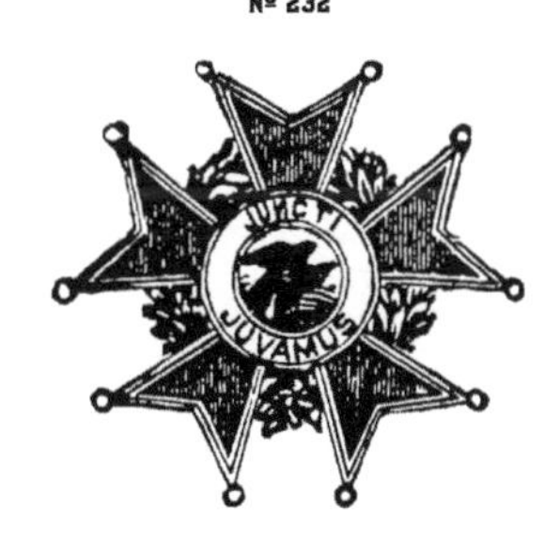

№ 233

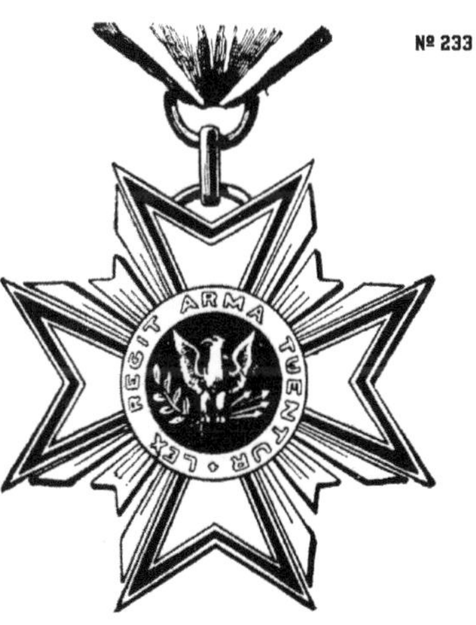

№ 234

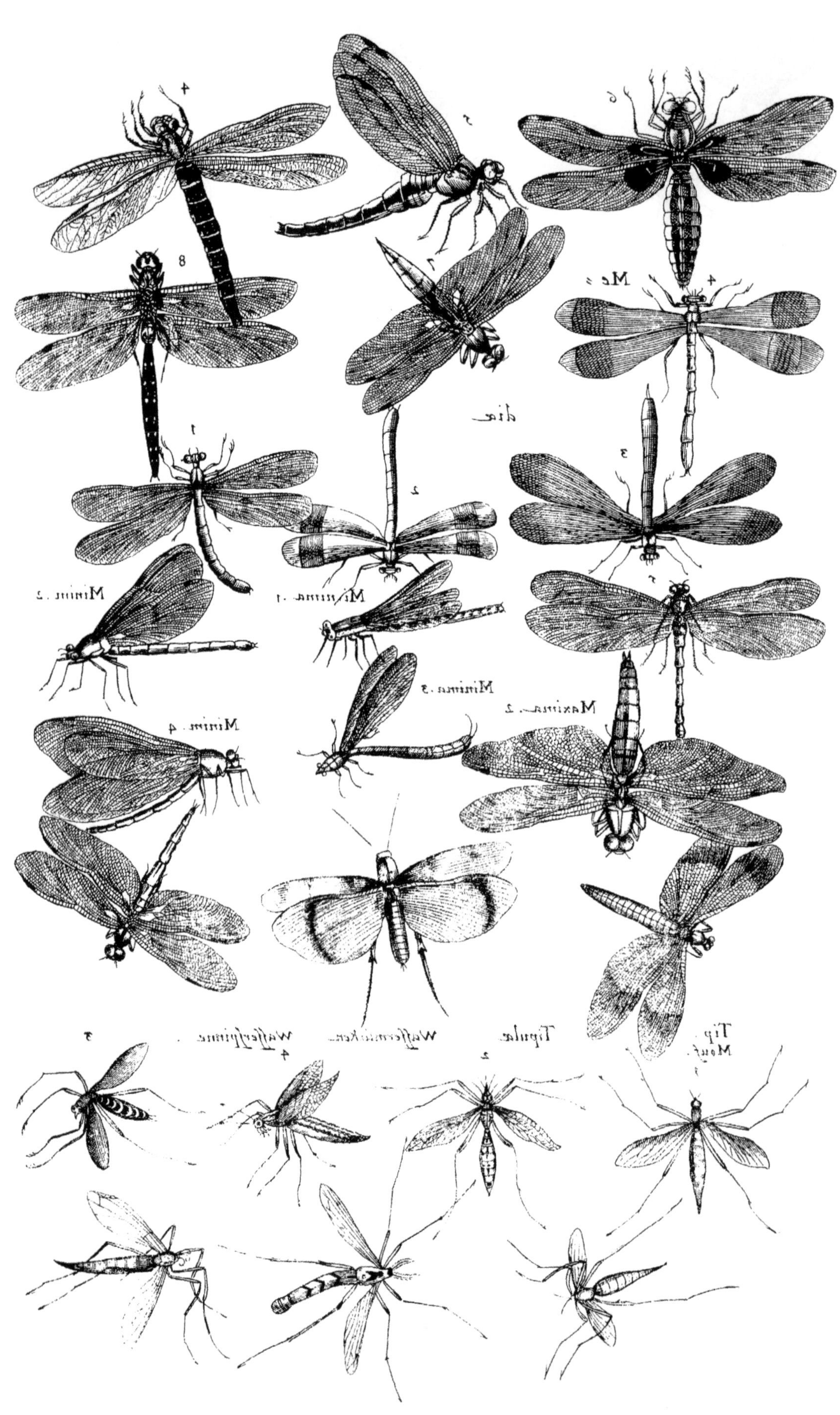

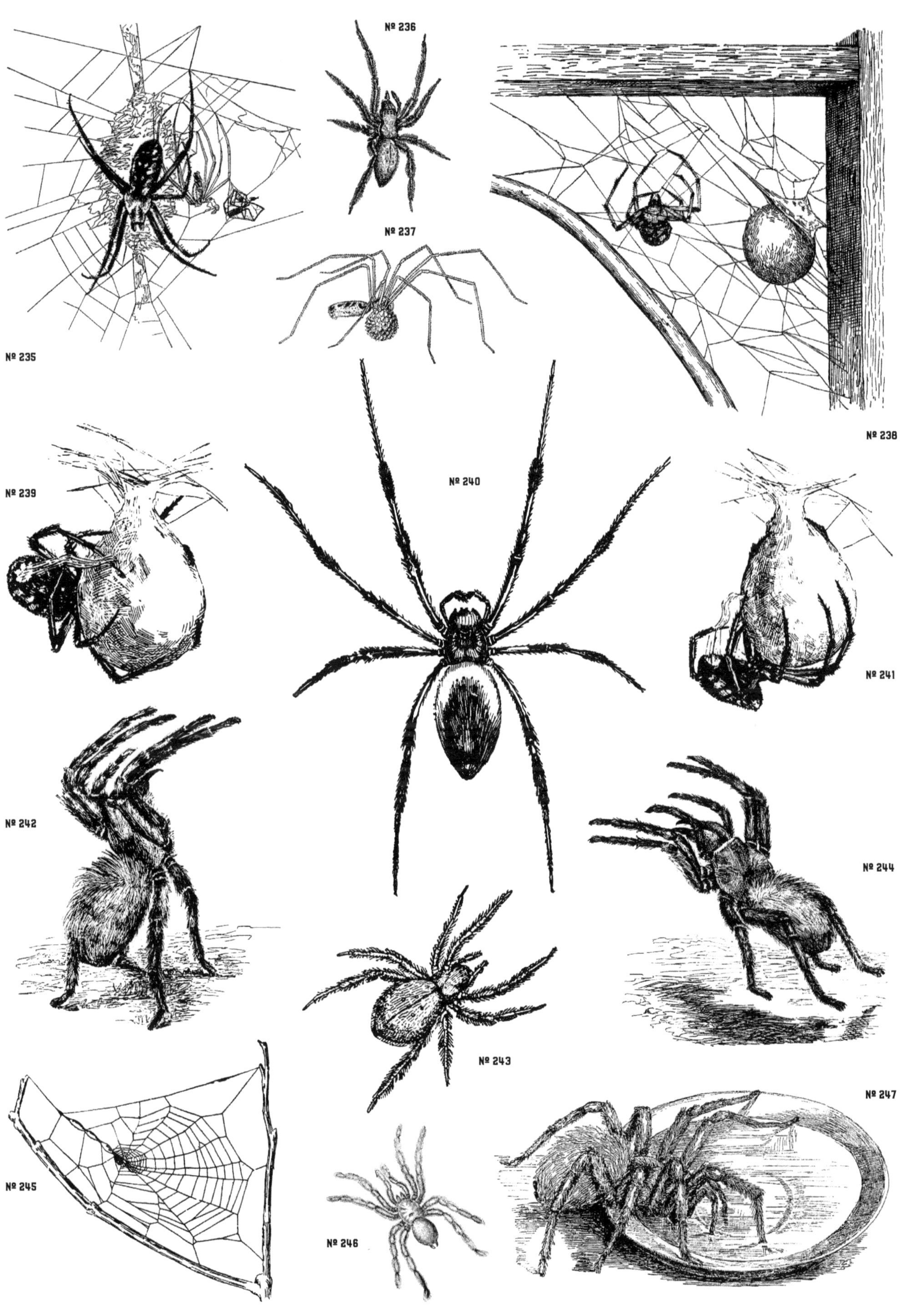
Nº 236
Nº 237
Nº 235
Nº 238
Nº 239
Nº 240
Nº 241
Nº 242
Nº 244
Nº 243
Nº 247
Nº 245
Nº 246

№ 248

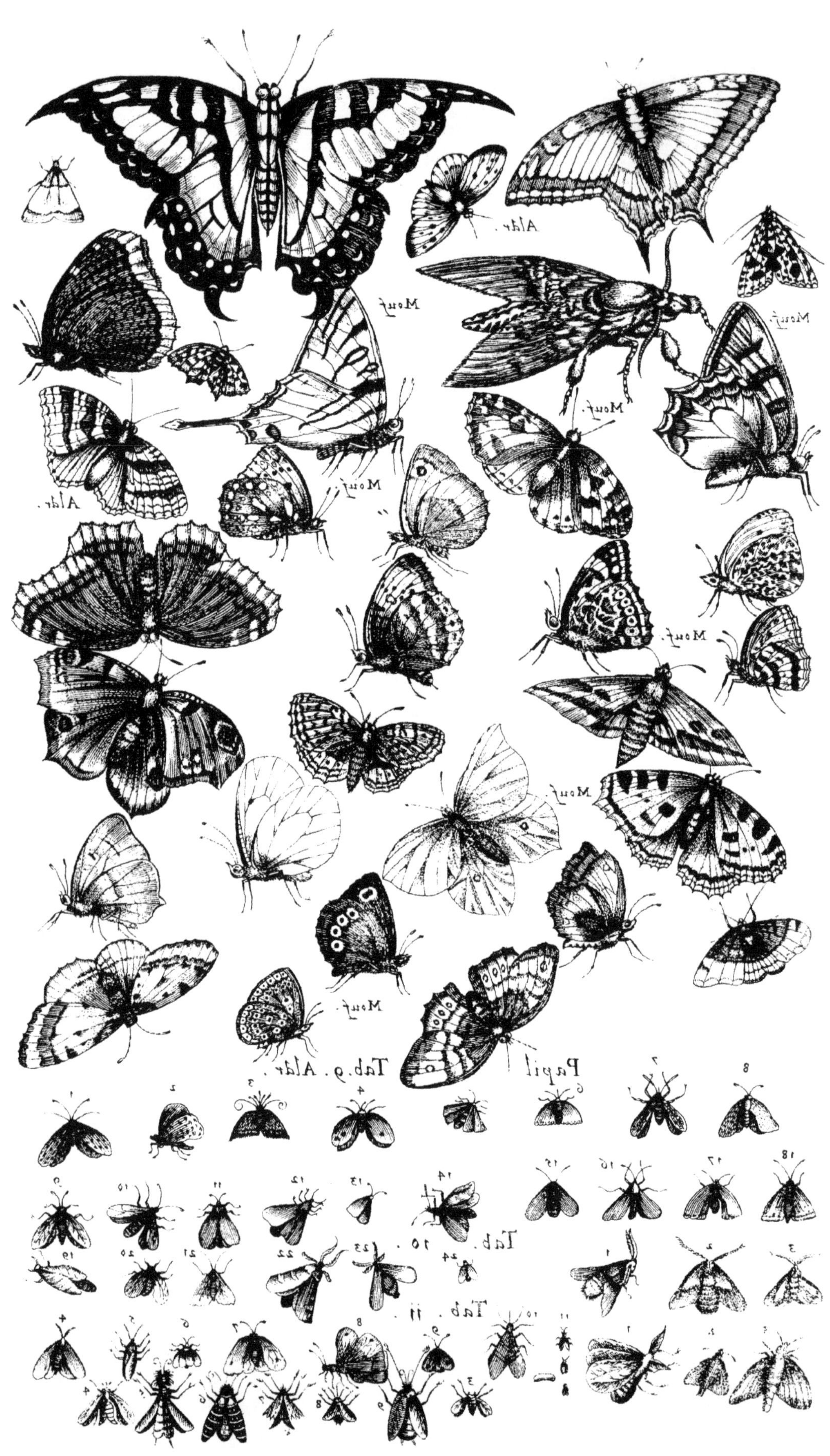

Nº 249 Nº 227

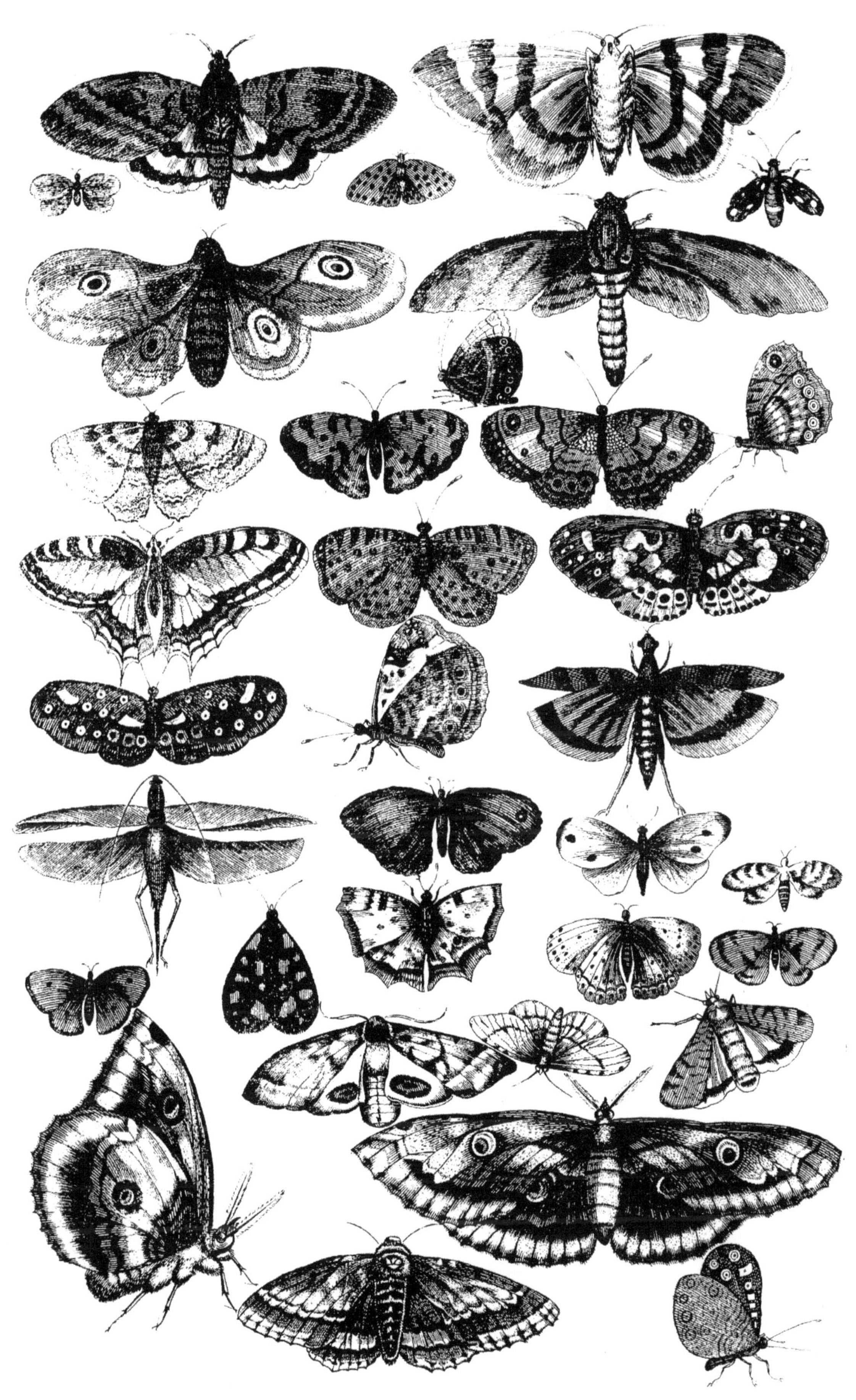

№ 250

INSECTS

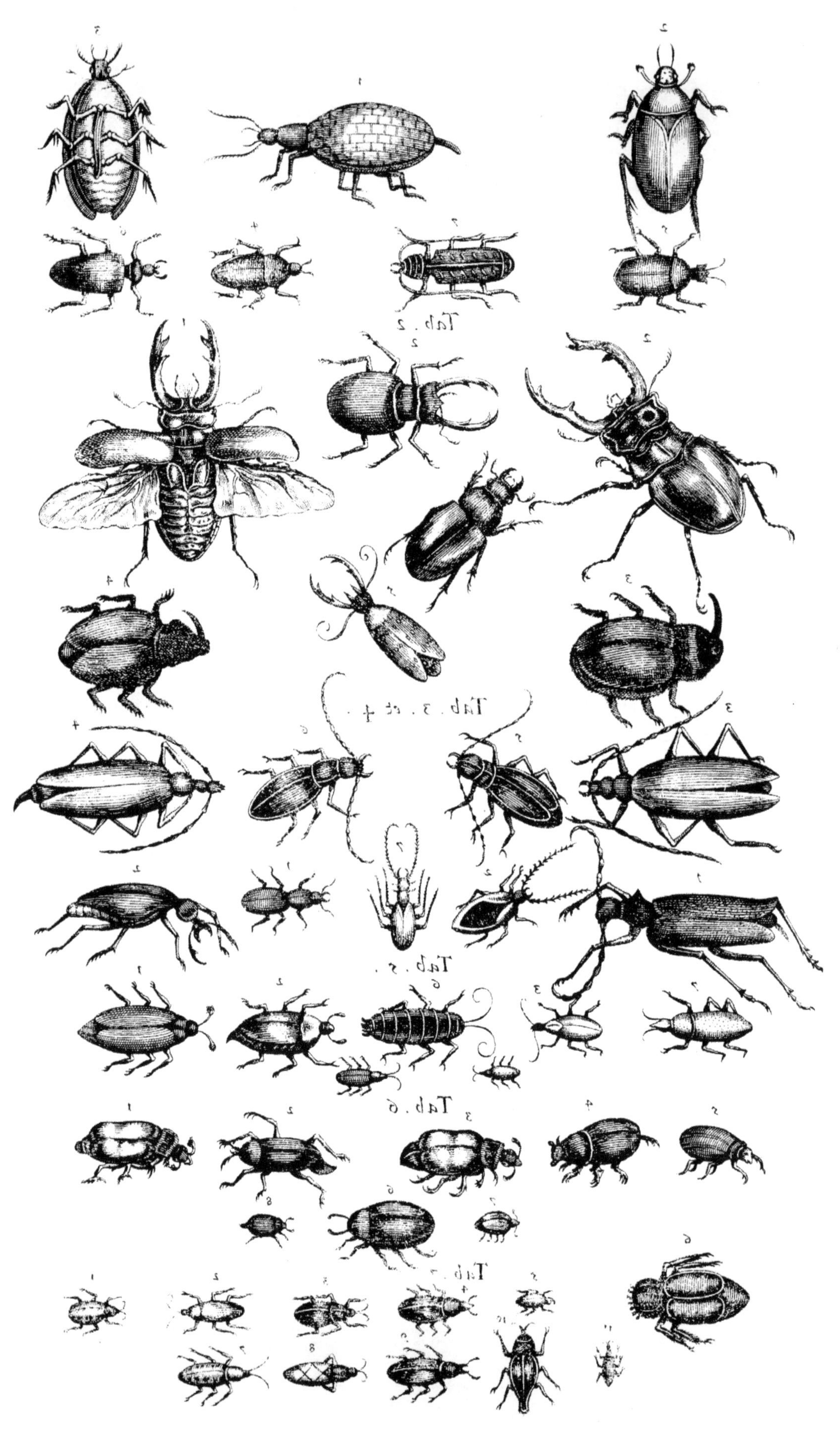

№ 251

№ 227

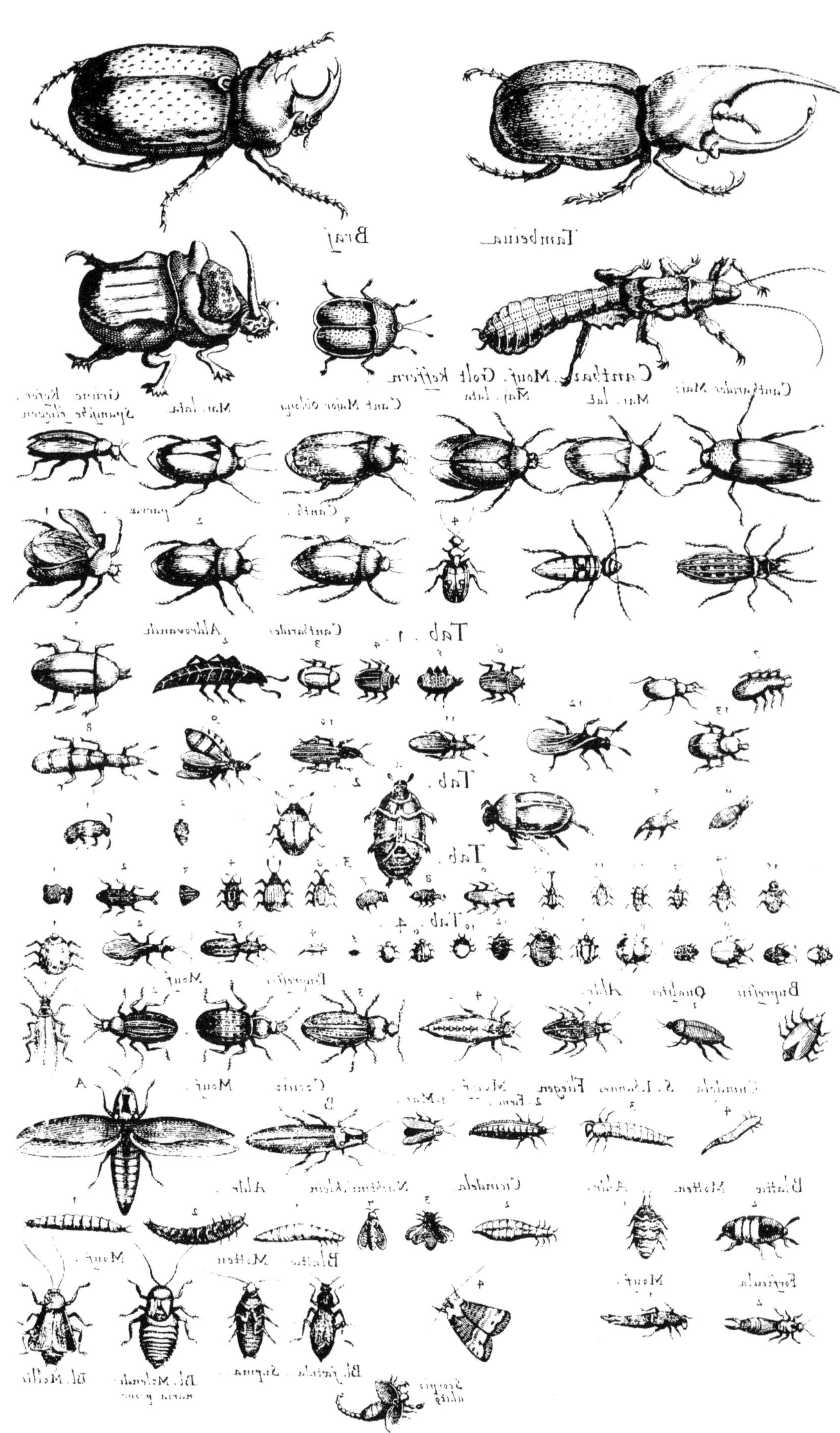

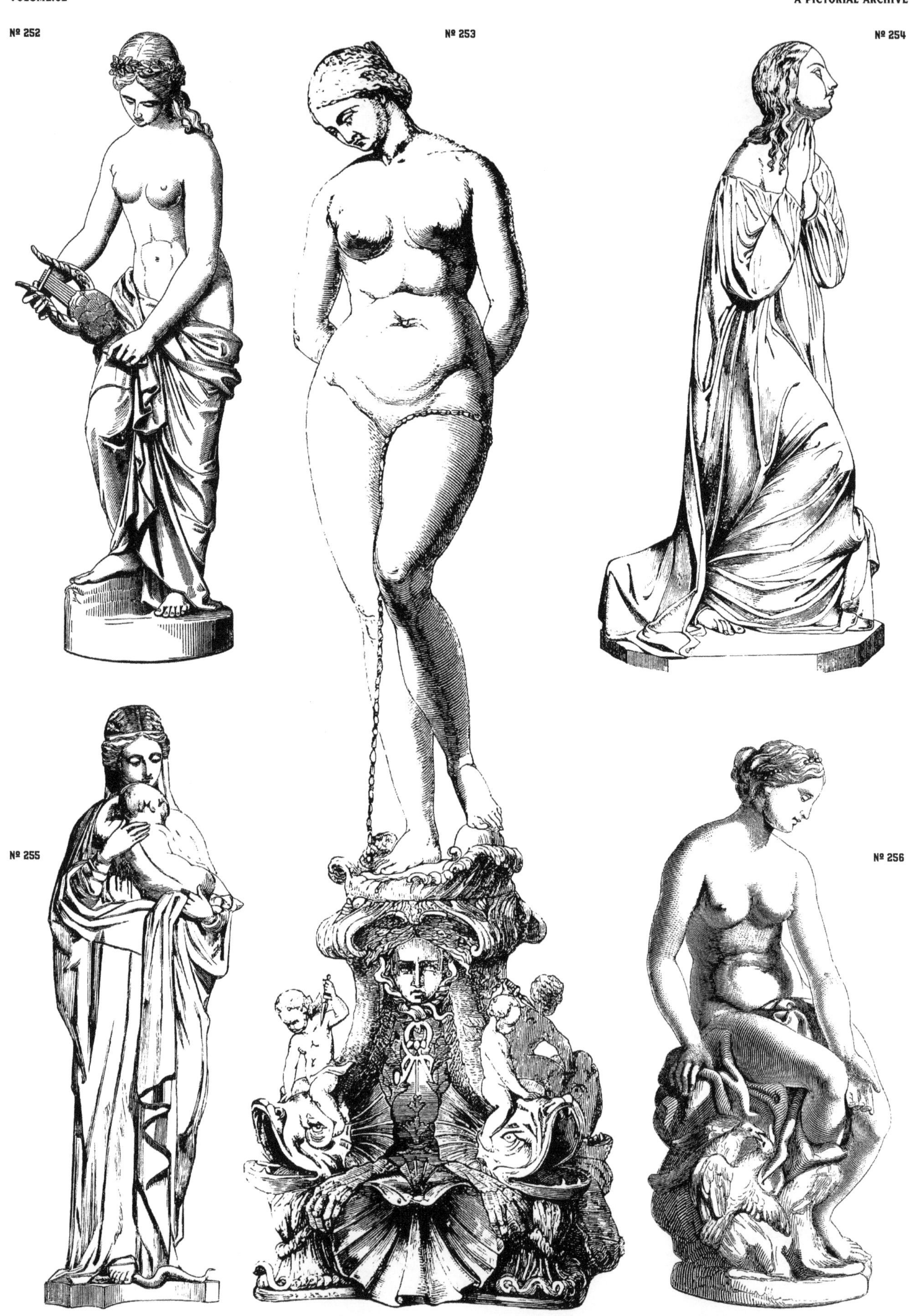
№ 252
№ 253
№ 254
№ 255
№ 256

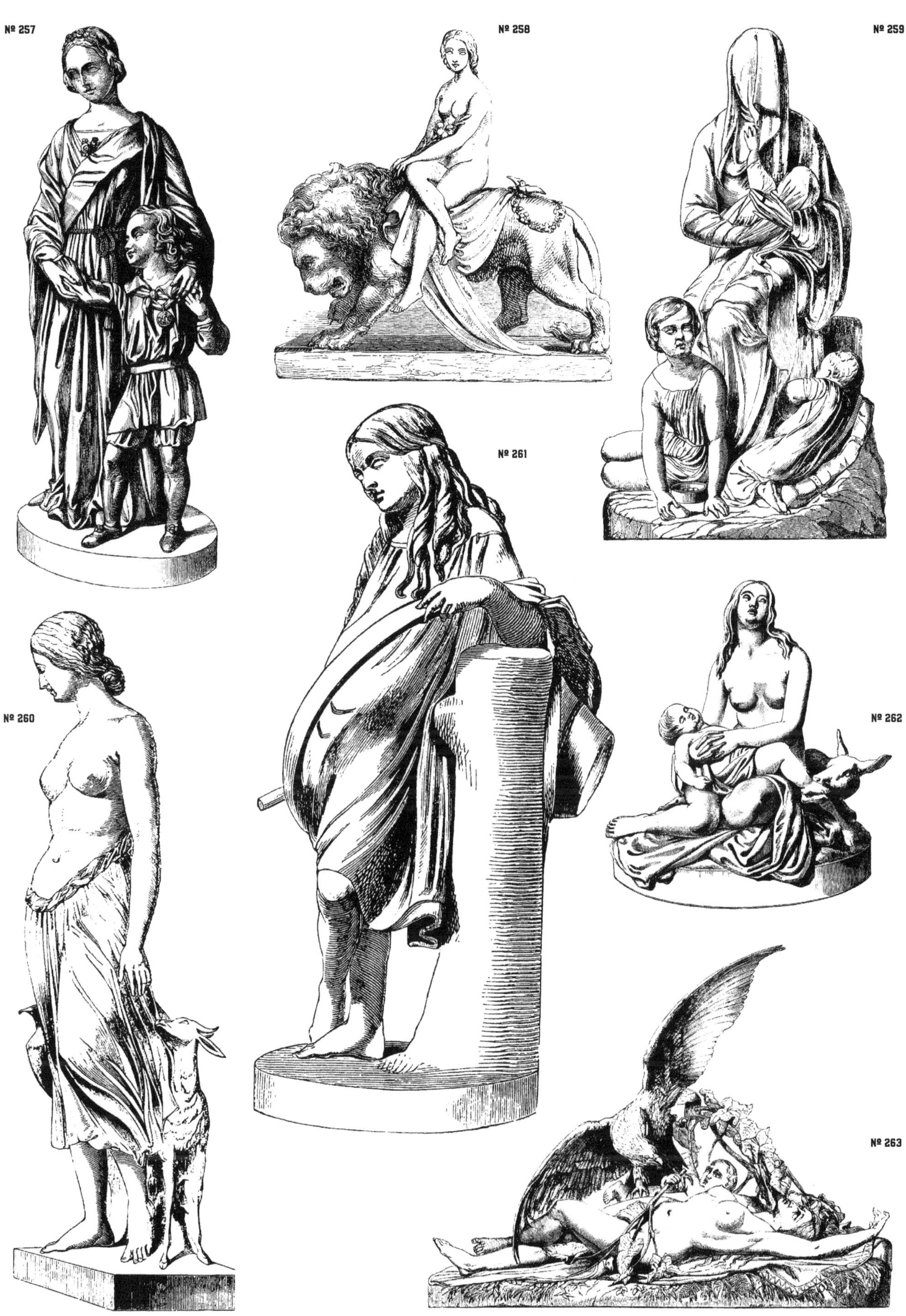
№ 257
№ 258
№ 259
№ 261
№ 260
№ 262
№ 263

WOMEN

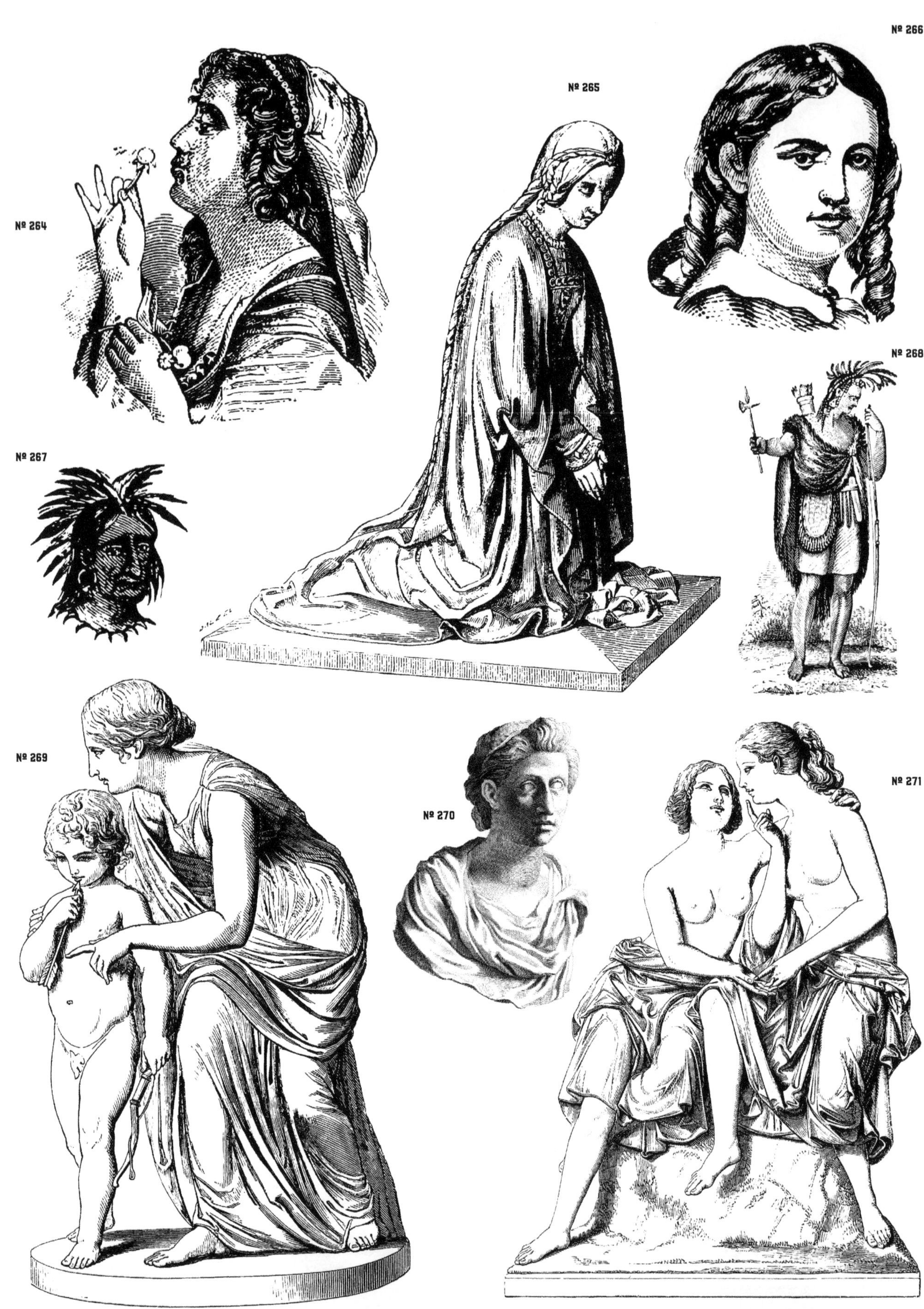

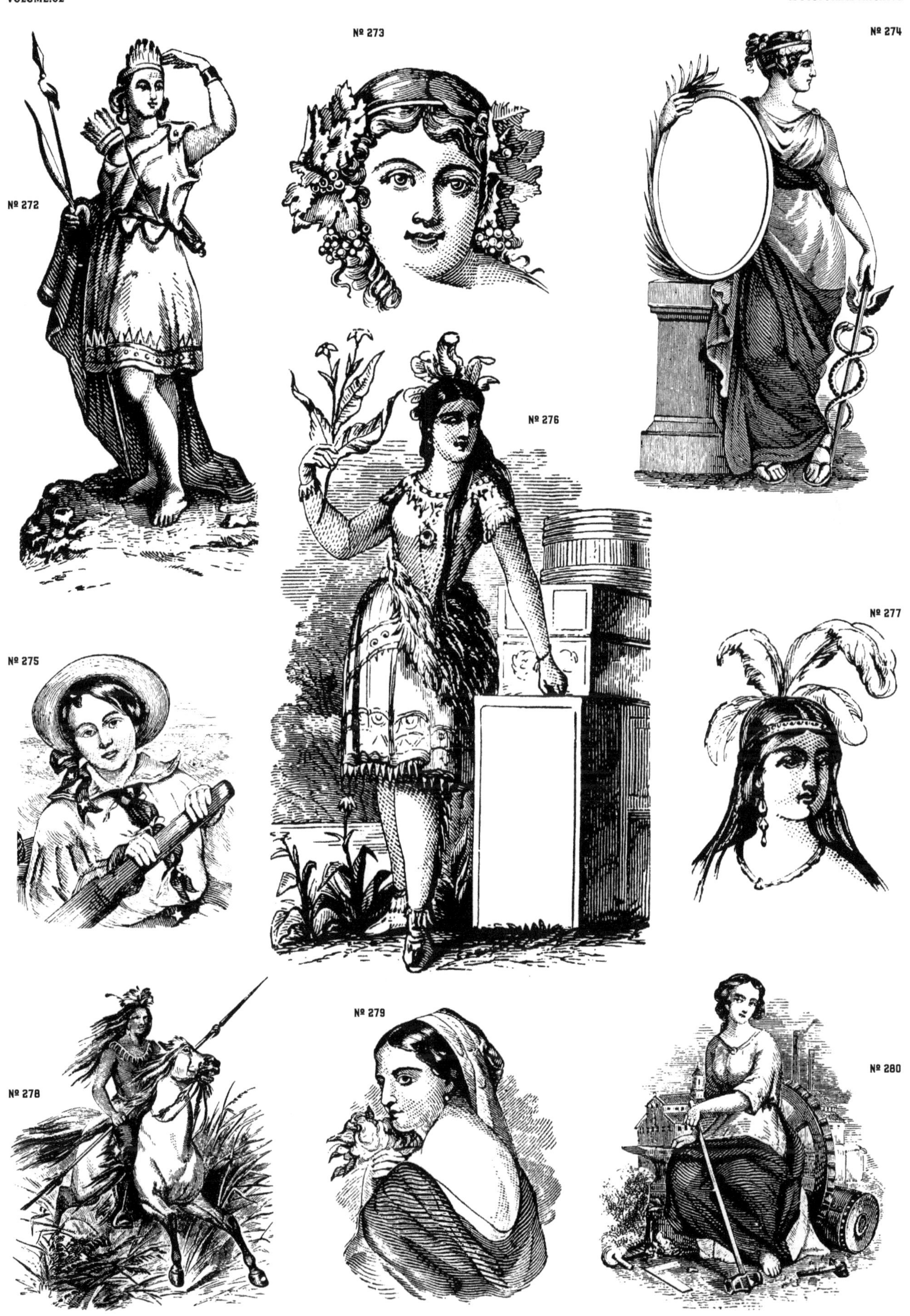

WOMEN

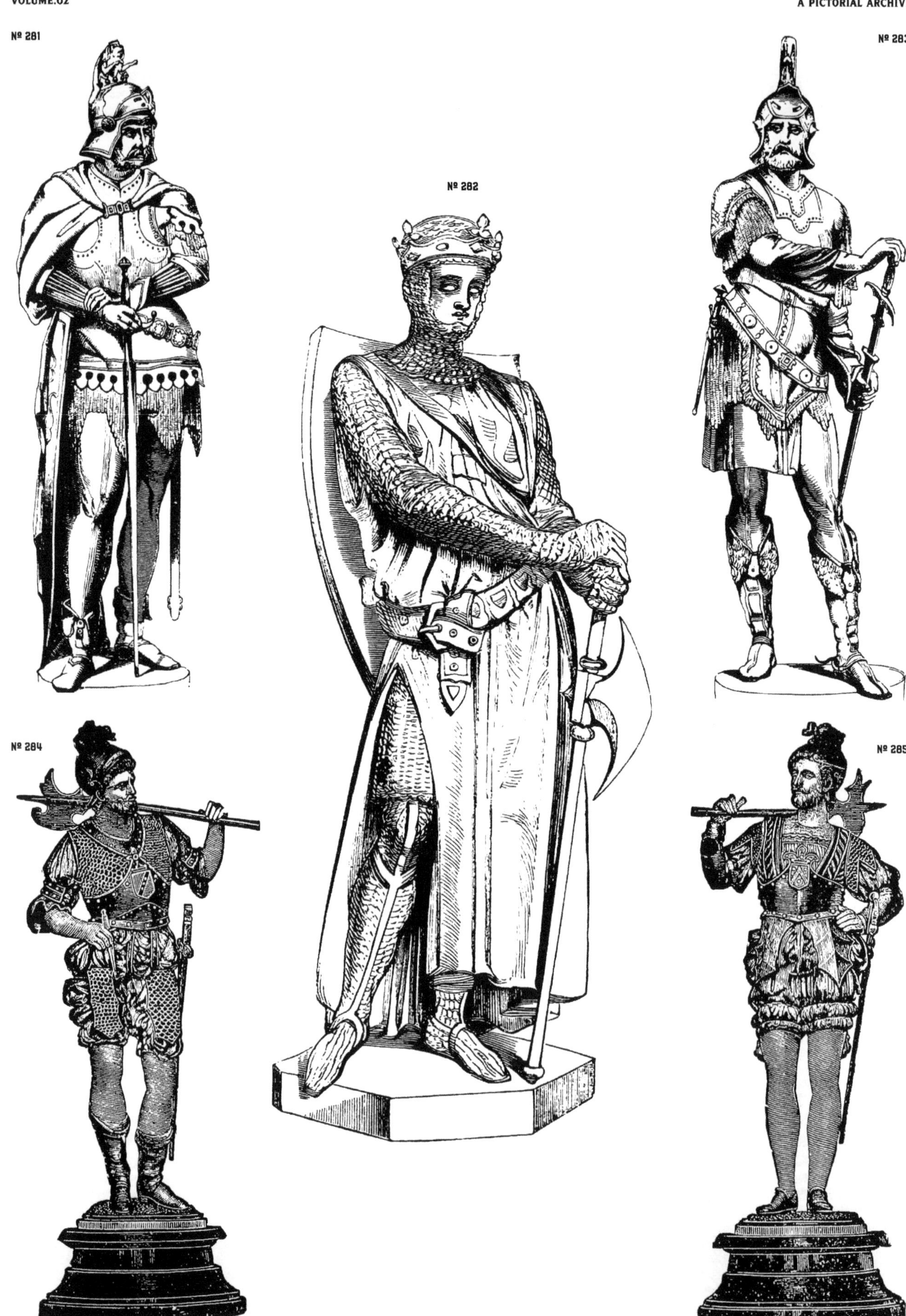

№ 281
№ 282
№ 283
№ 284
№ 285

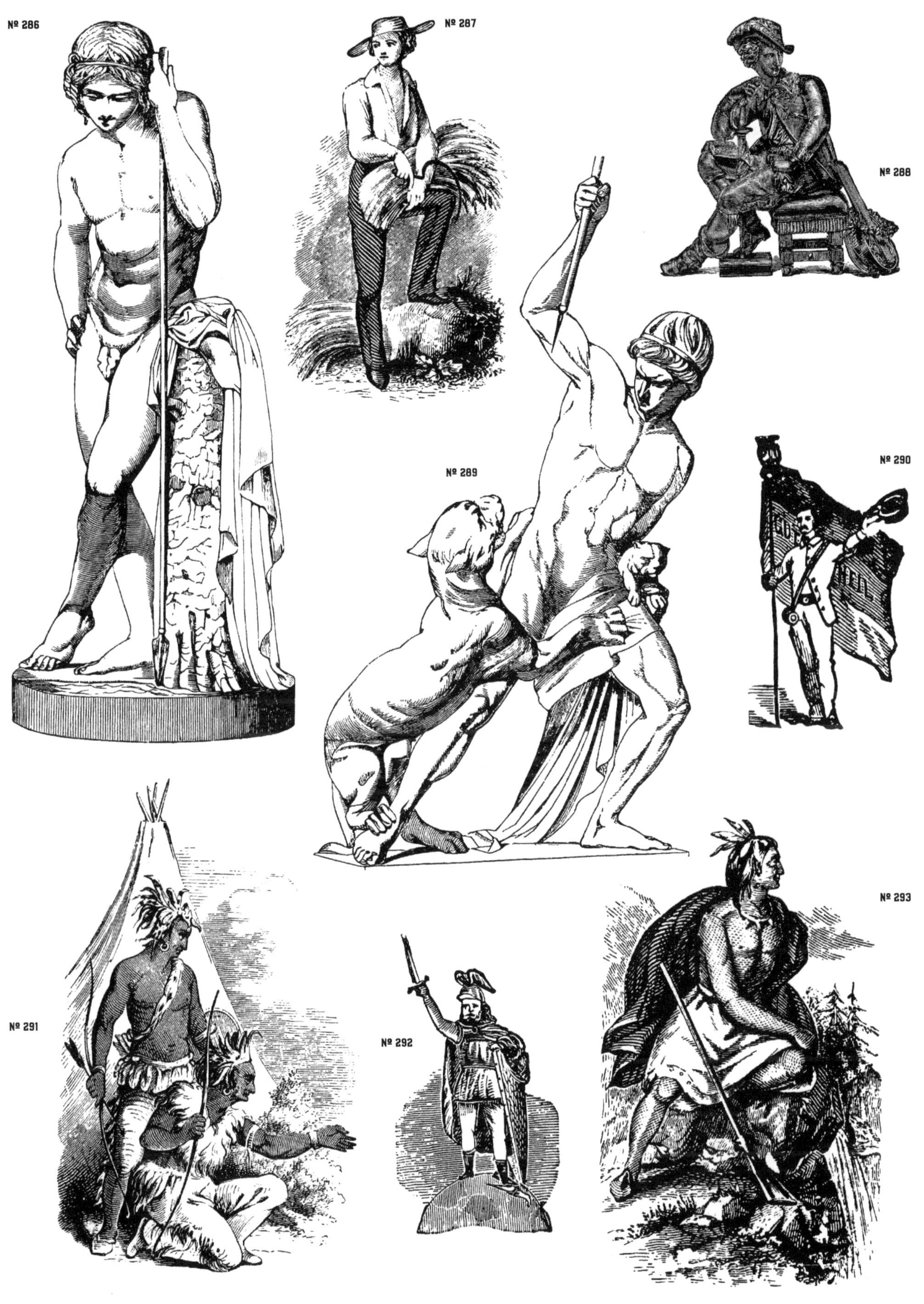

№ 286

№ 287

№ 288

№ 289

№ 290

№ 291

№ 292

№ 293

MEN

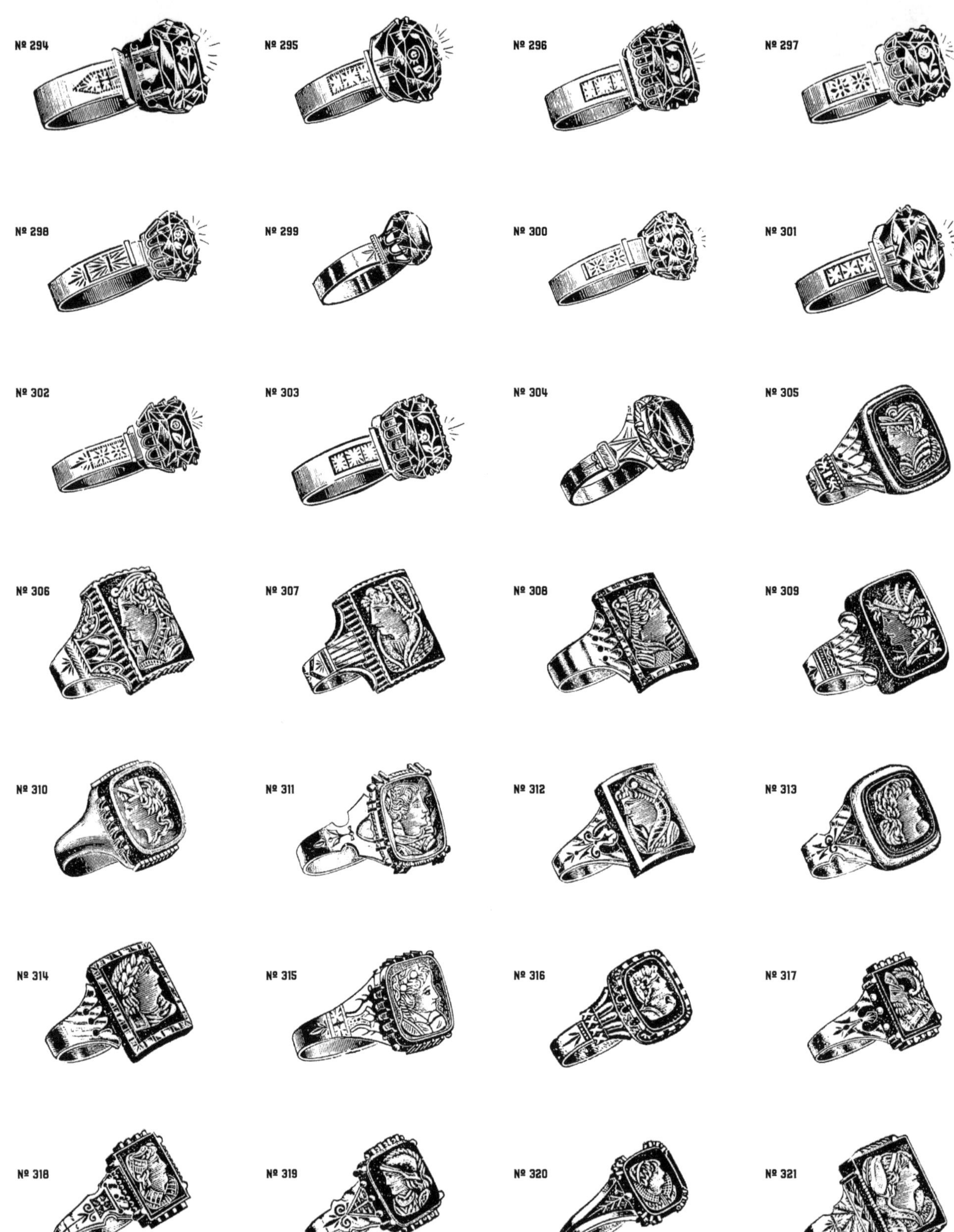

№ 294
№ 295
№ 296
№ 297
№ 298
№ 299
№ 300
№ 301
№ 302
№ 303
№ 304
№ 305
№ 306
№ 307
№ 308
№ 309
№ 310
№ 311
№ 312
№ 313
№ 314
№ 315
№ 316
№ 317
№ 318
№ 319
№ 320
№ 321

№ 322
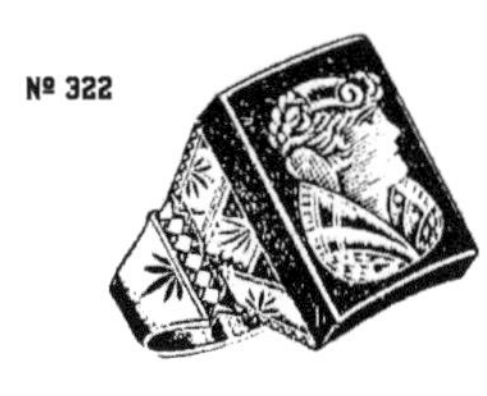

№ 323
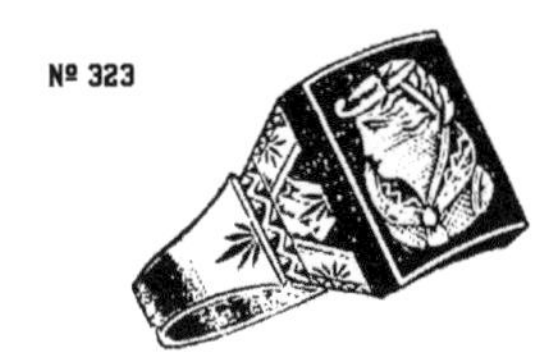

№ 324
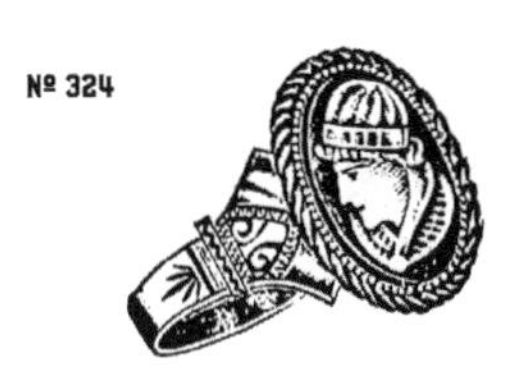

№ 325
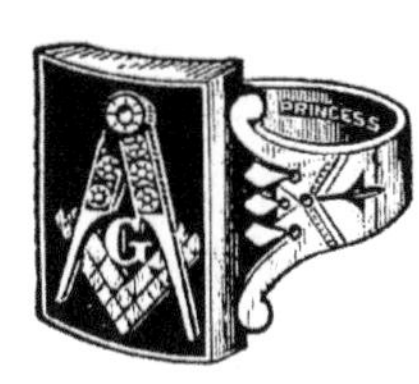

№ 326
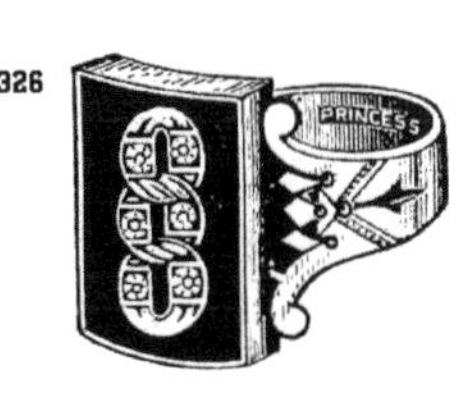

№ 327
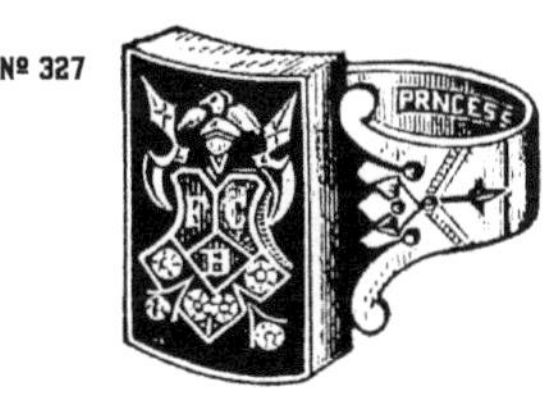

№ 328
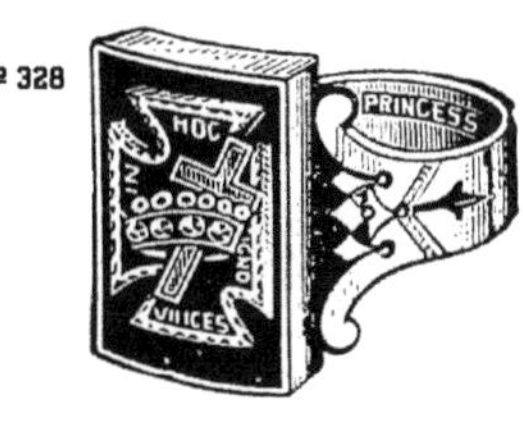

№ 329
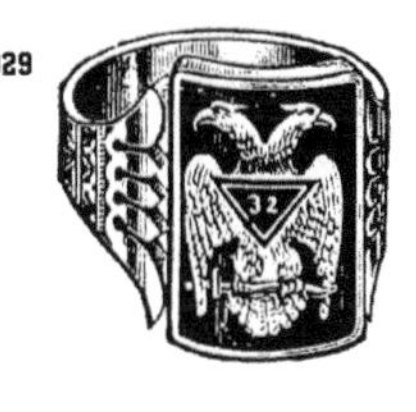

№ 330
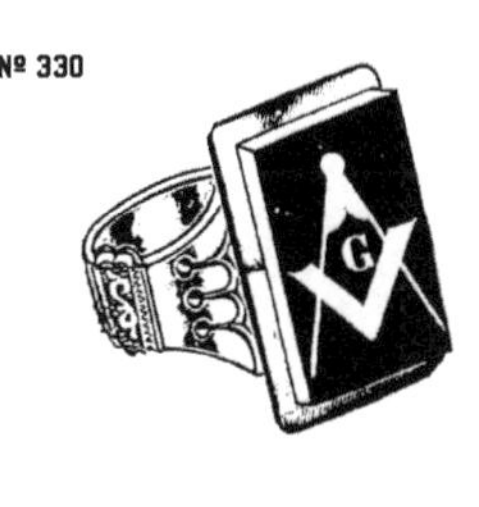

№ 331
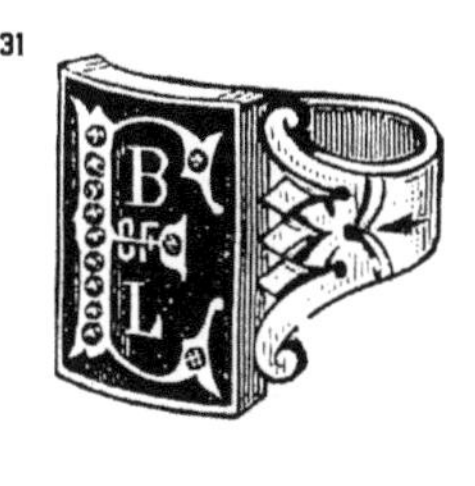

№ 332
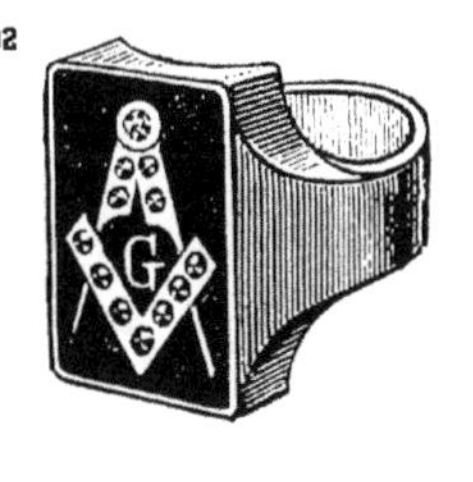

№ 333
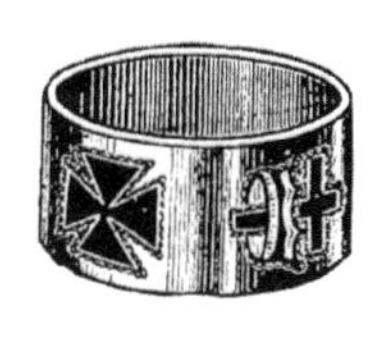

№ 334
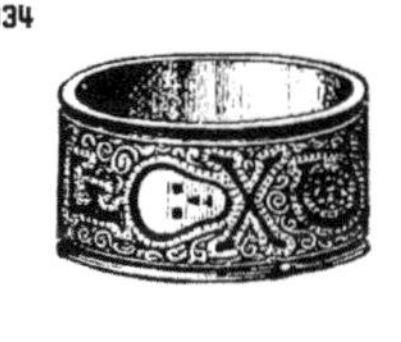

№ 335
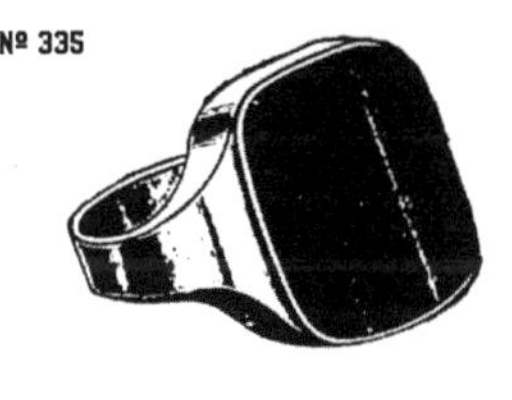

№ 336
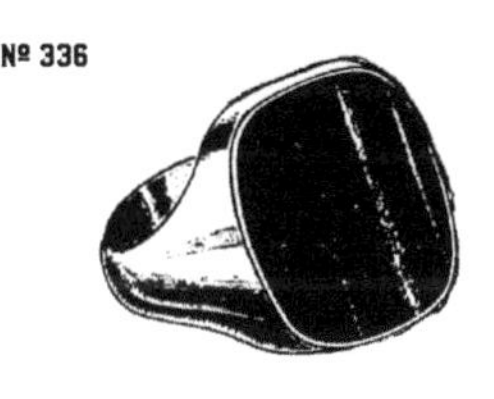

№ 337
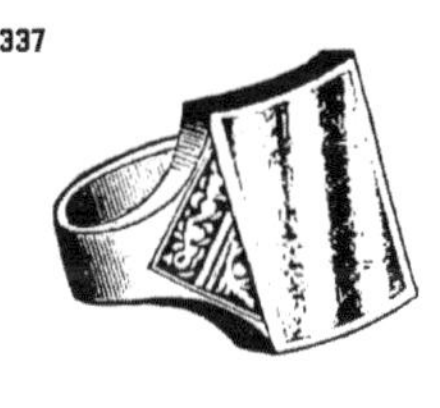

№ 338
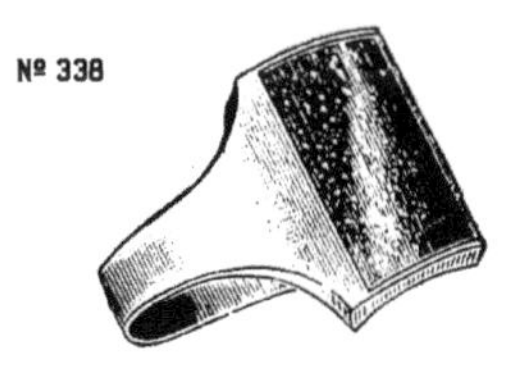

№ 339
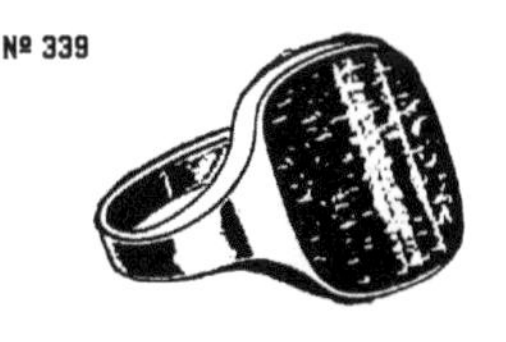

№ 340
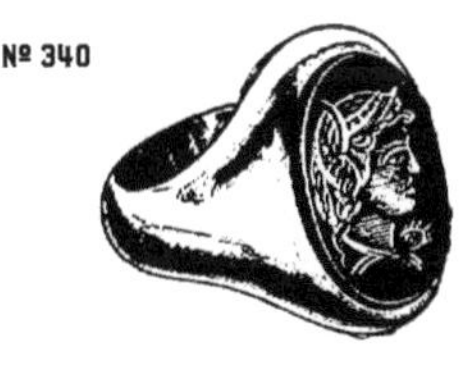

№ 341
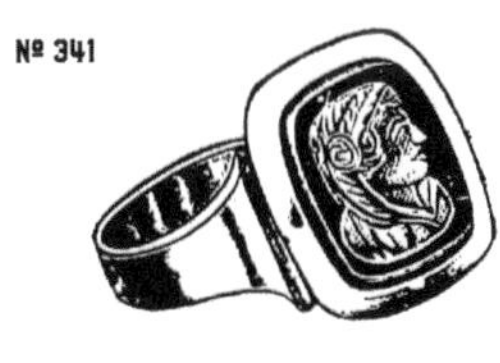

№ 342
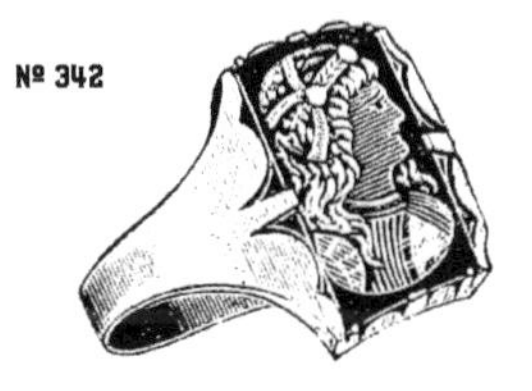

№ 343
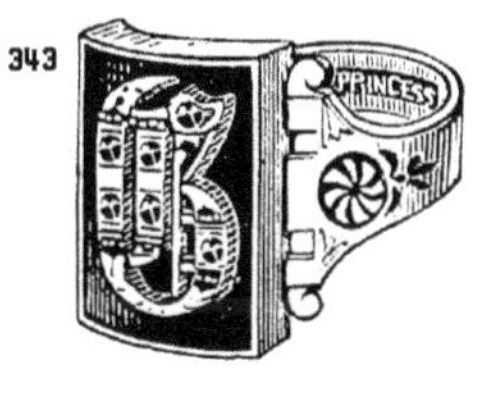

№ 344
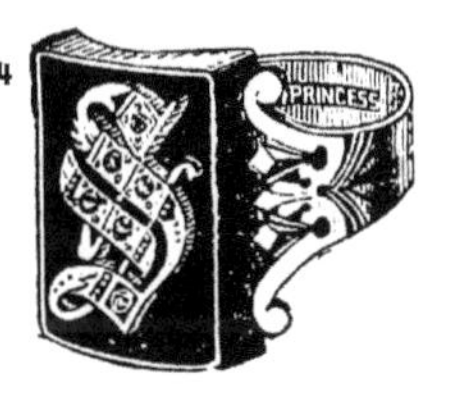

№ 345
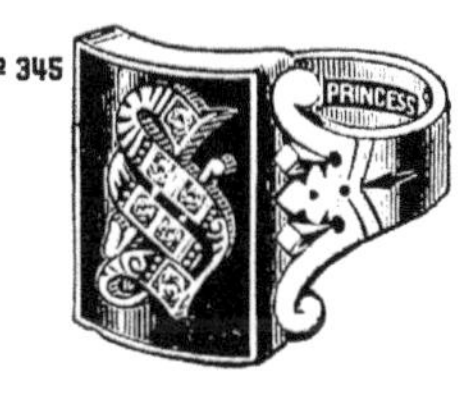

№ 346
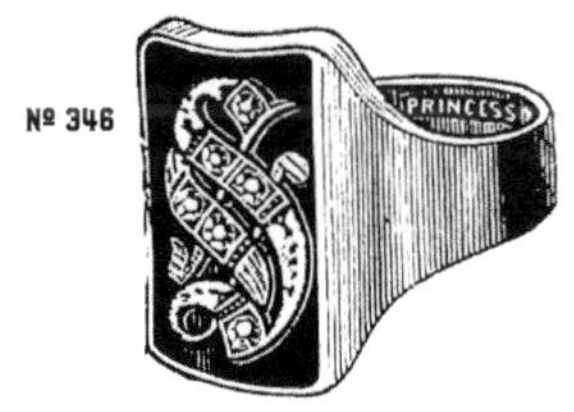

№ 347
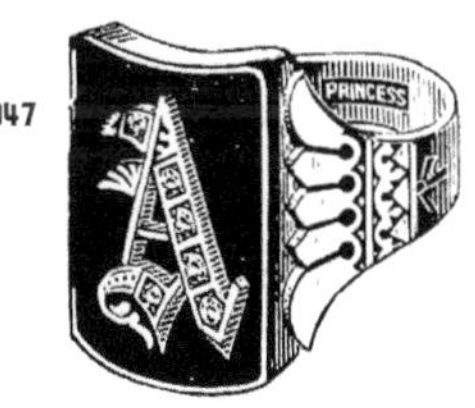

№ 348
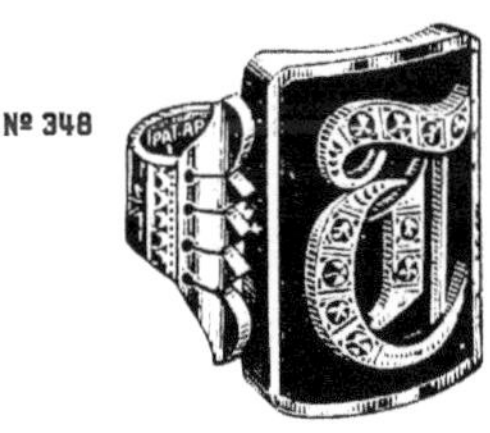

№ 349
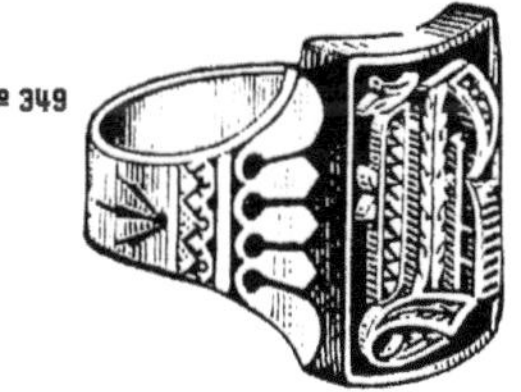

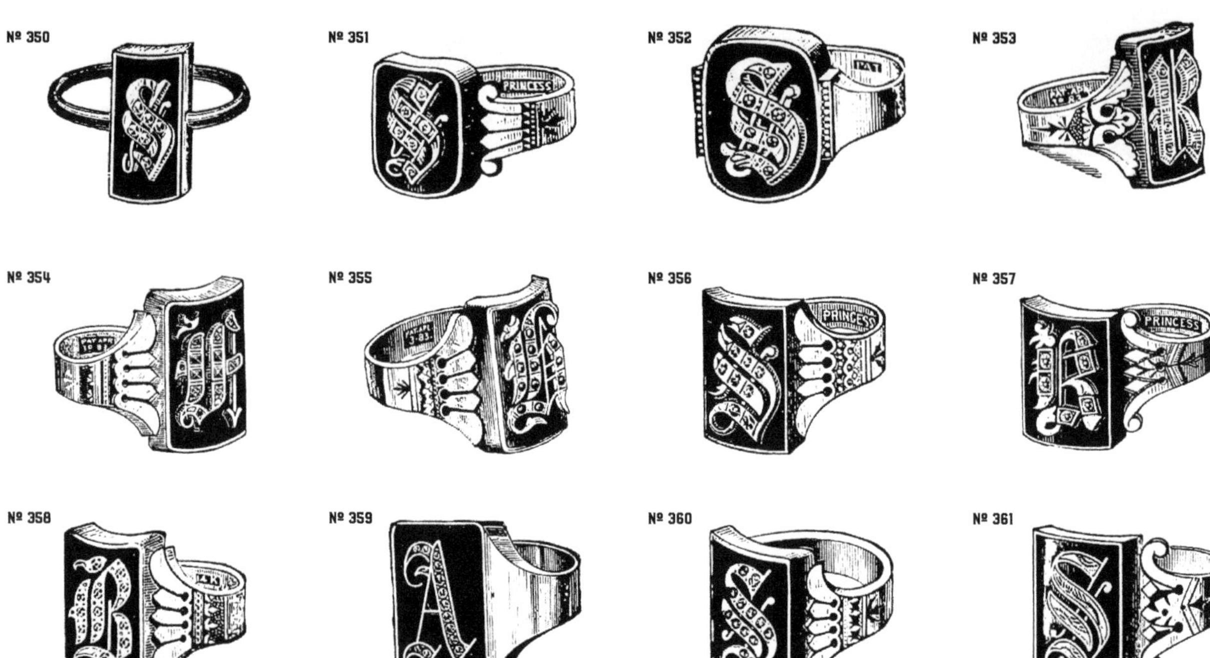

№ 350 № 351 № 352 № 353

№ 354 № 355 № 356 № 357

№ 358 № 359 № 360 № 361

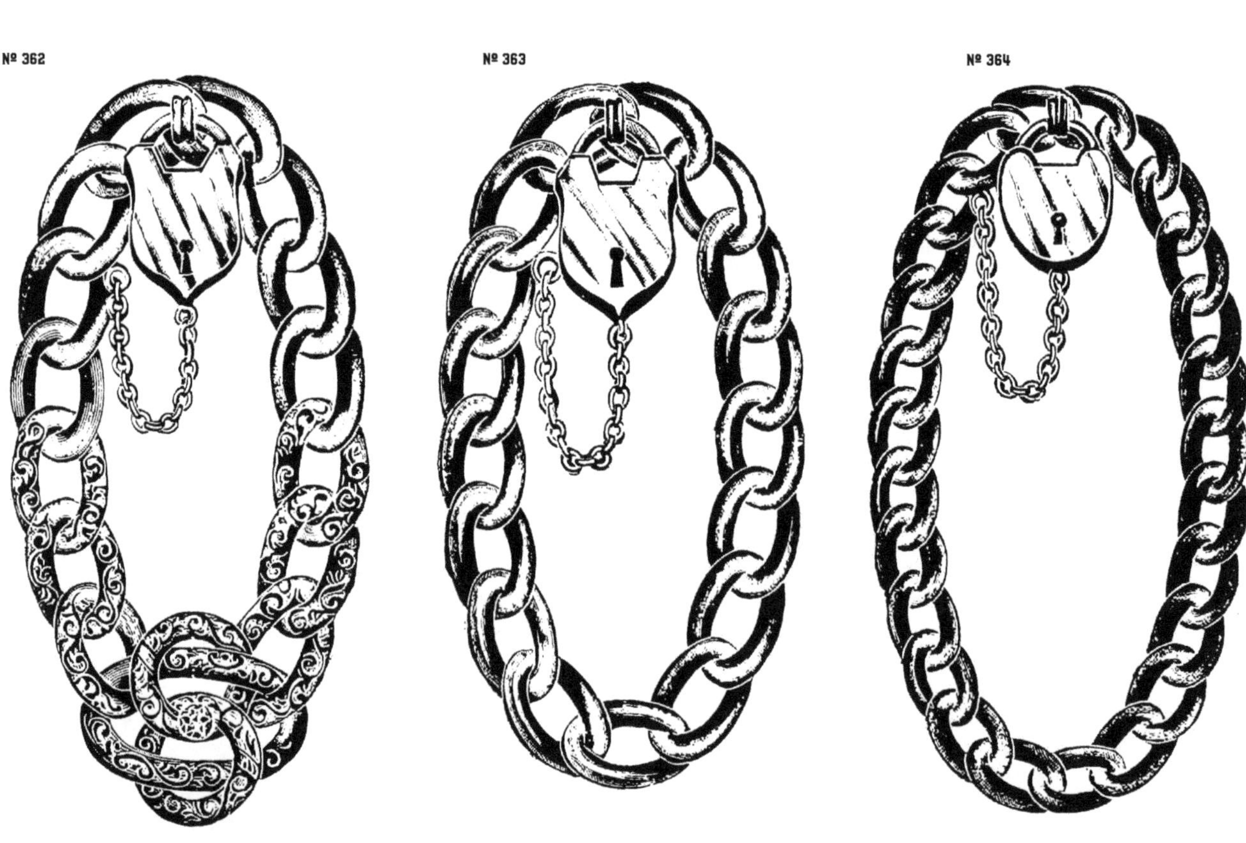

№ 362 № 363 № 364

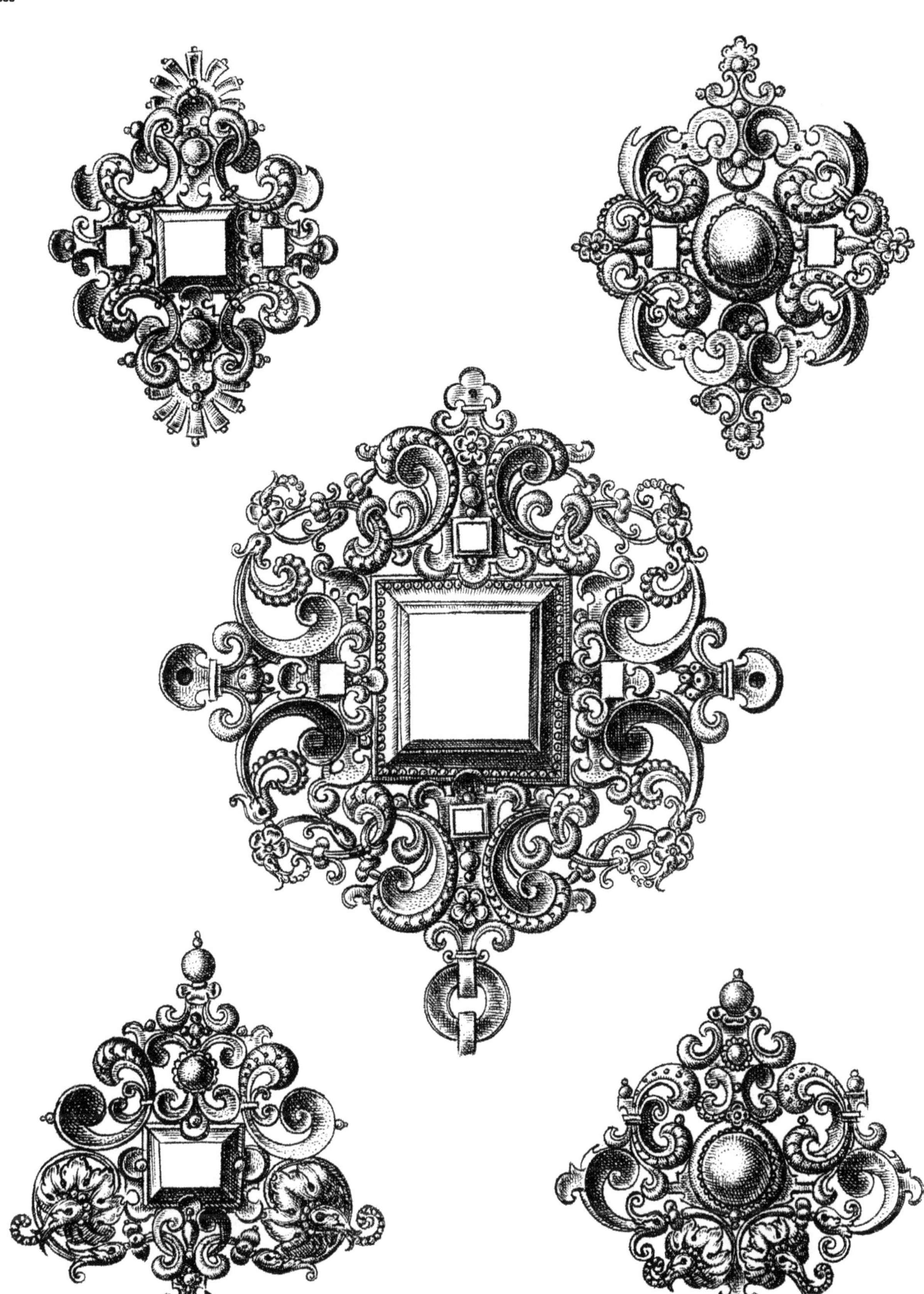

Nº 366

HANDS

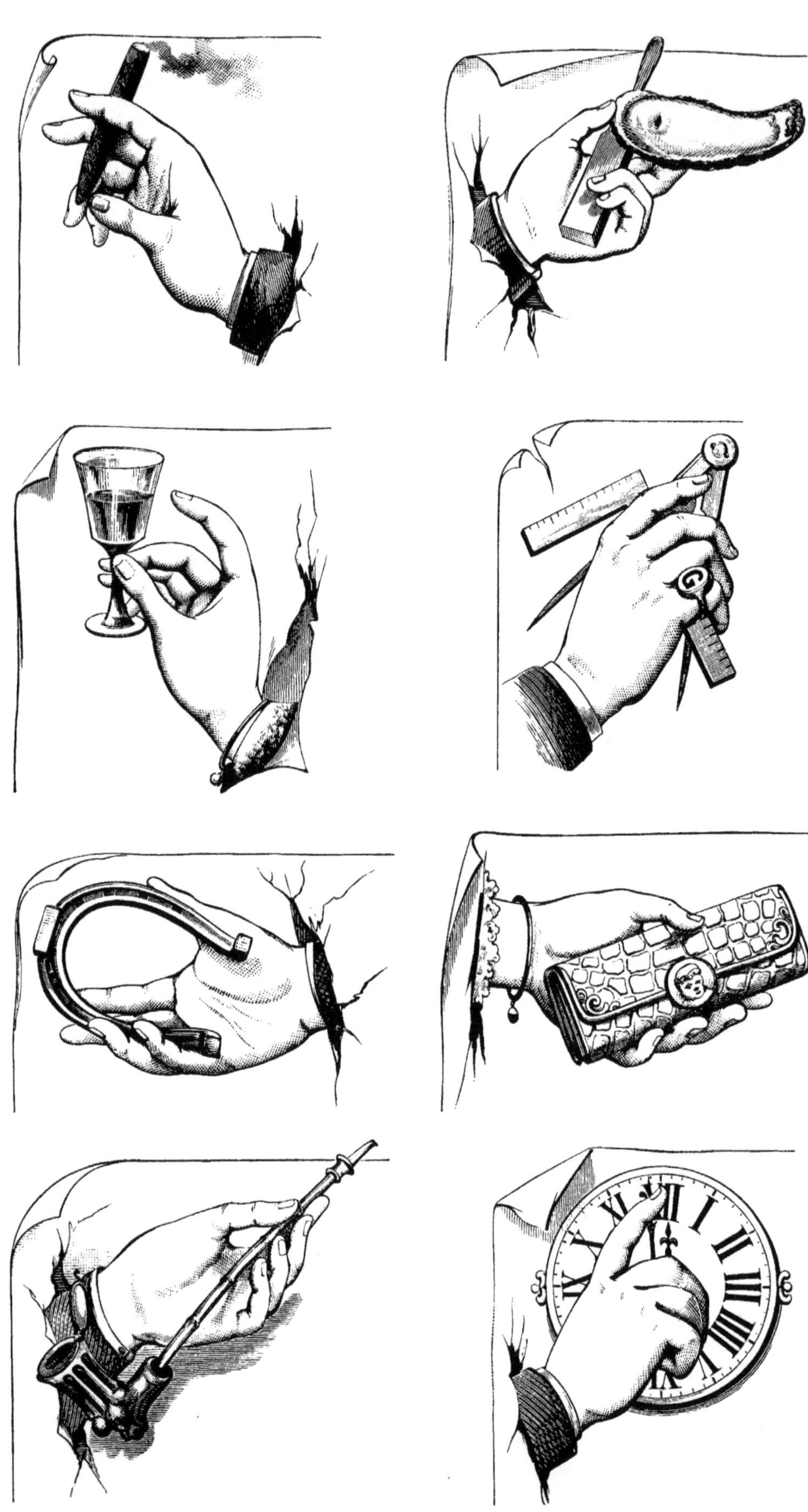

№ 367

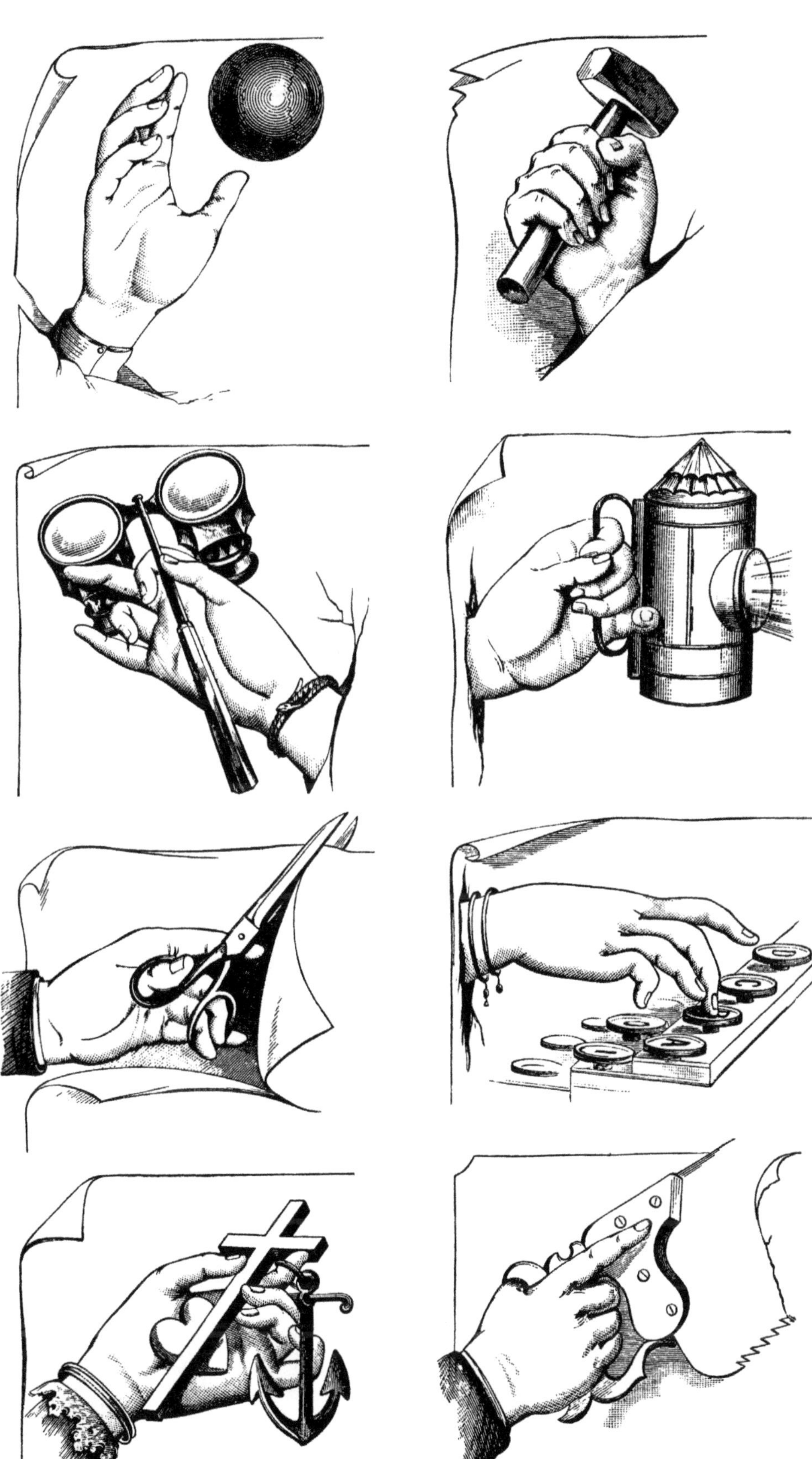

Nº 368

HANDS

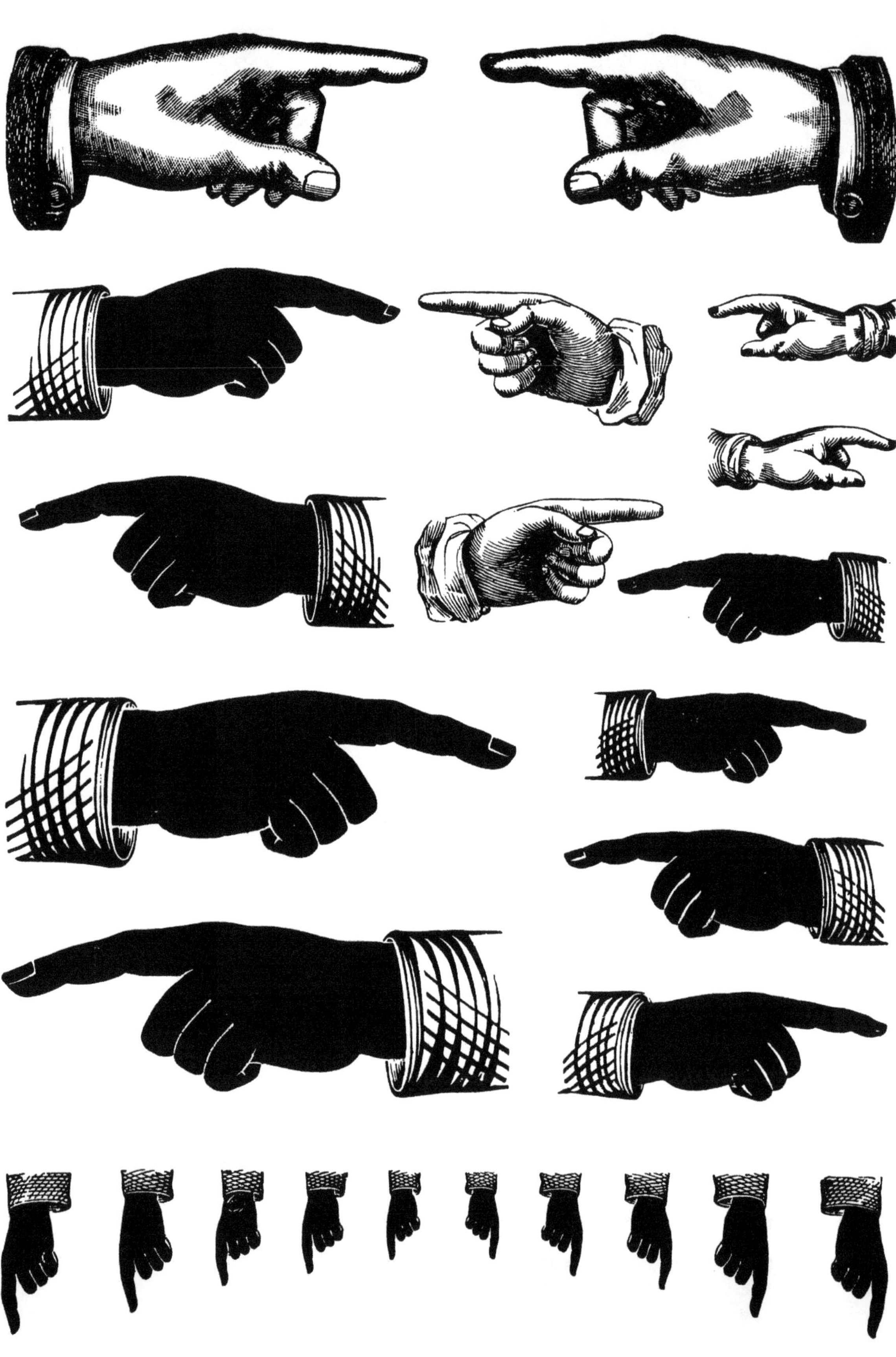

№ 369

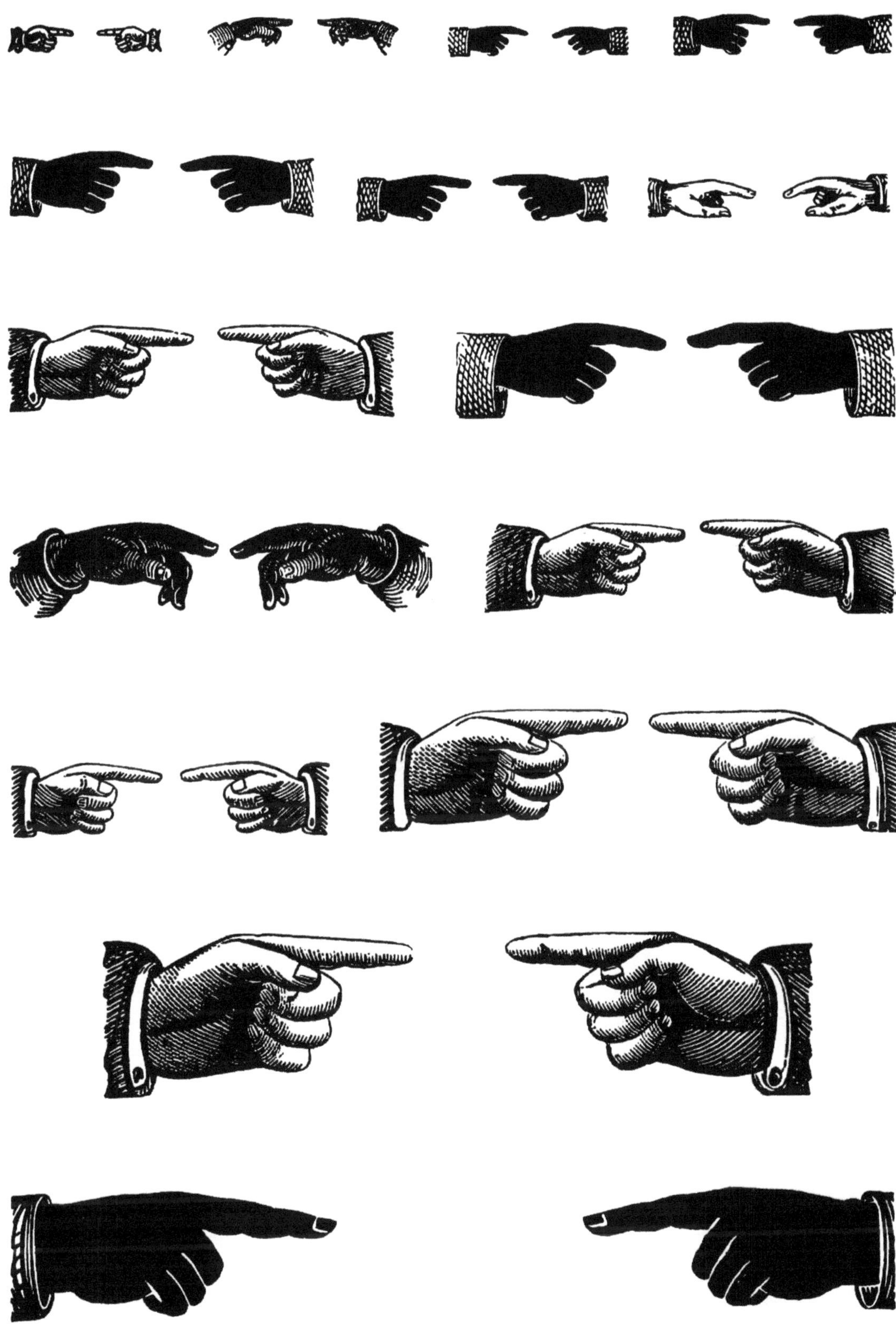

Nº 370

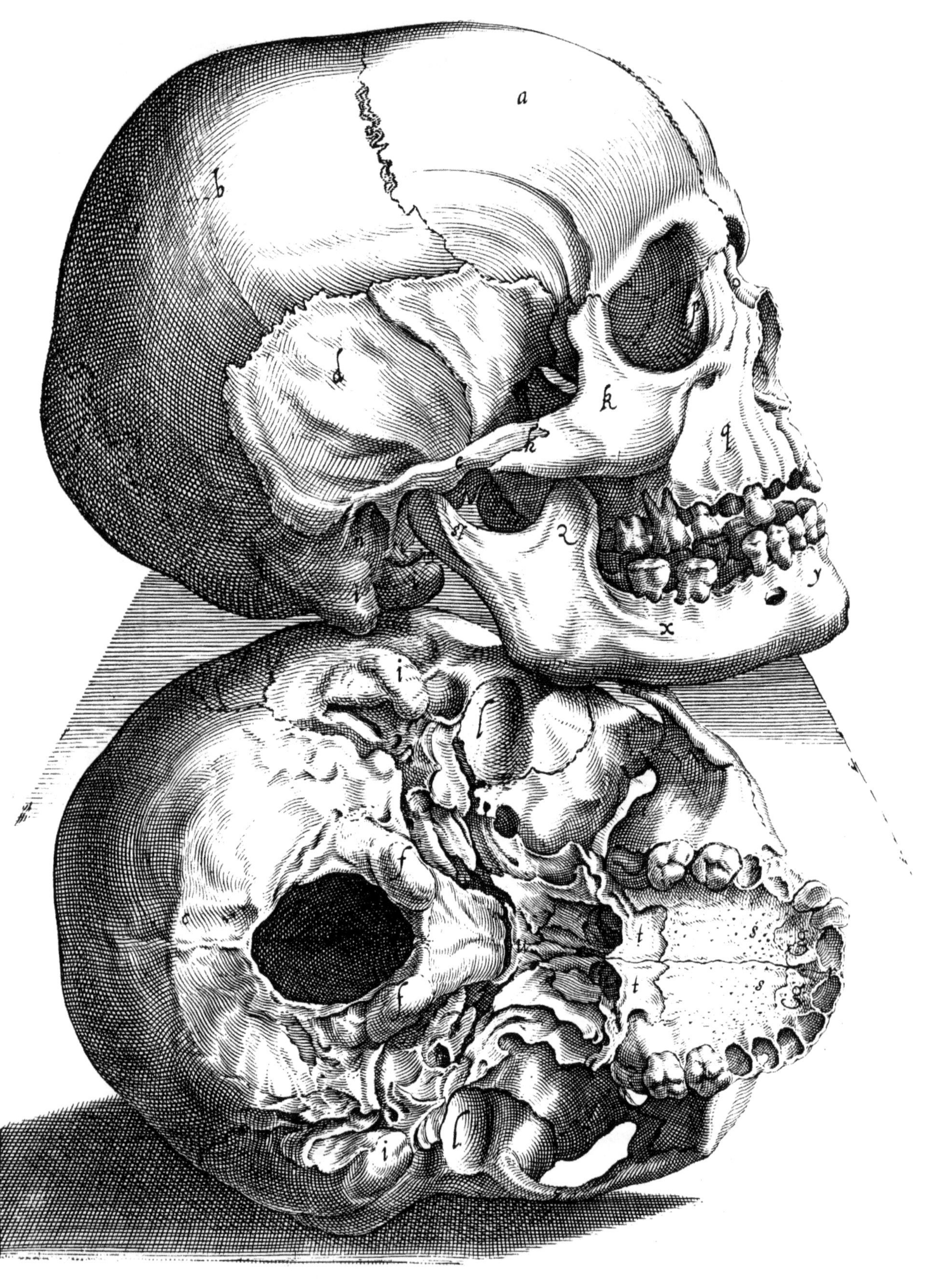

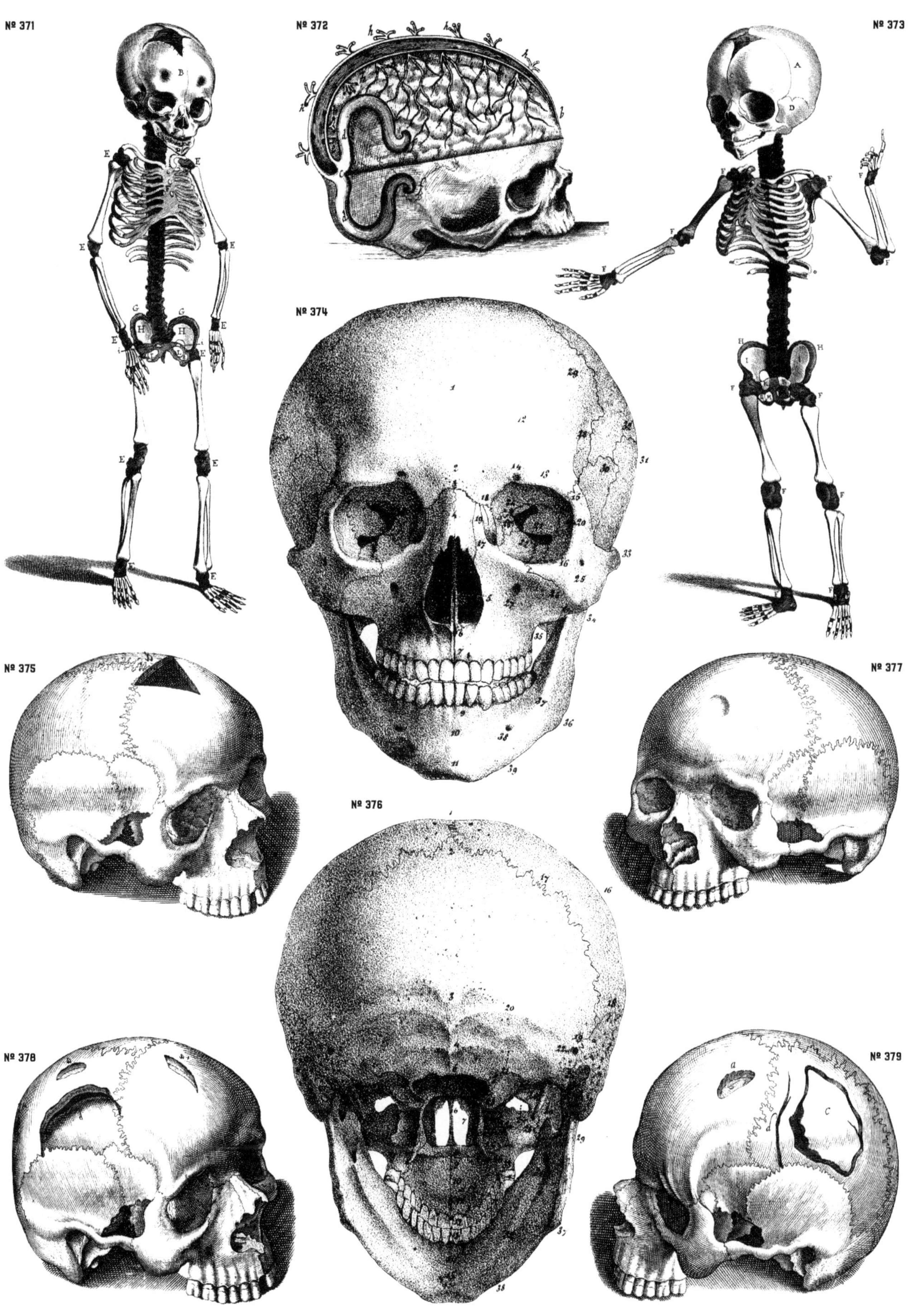

SKULLS & SKELETONS

№ 380

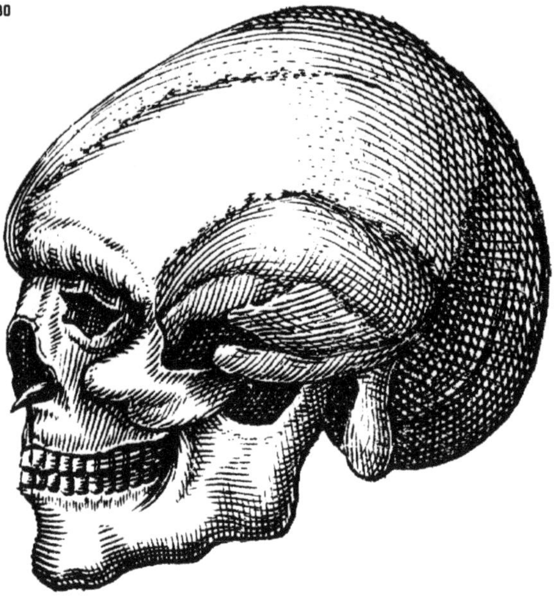

№ 381

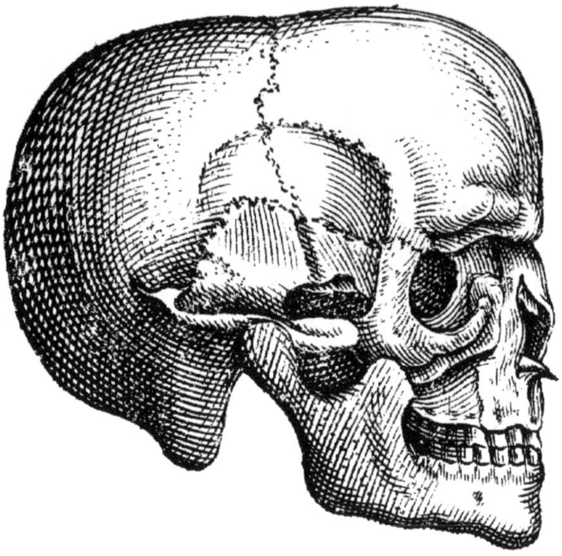

№ 382

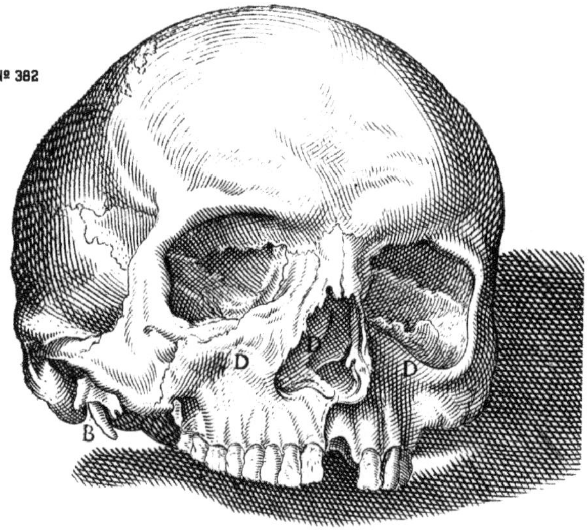

№ 383

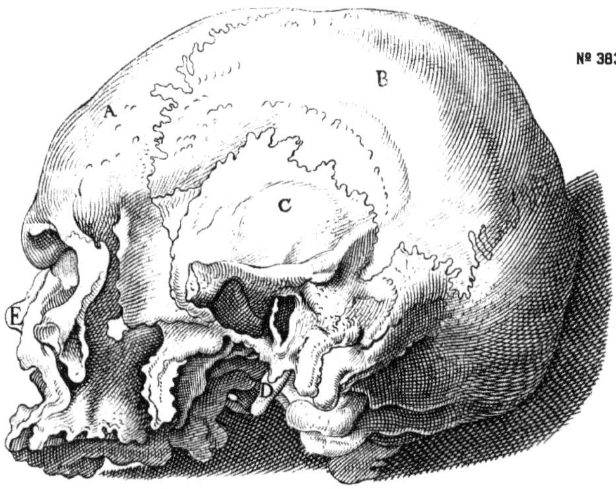

№ 384

№ 385

№ 386

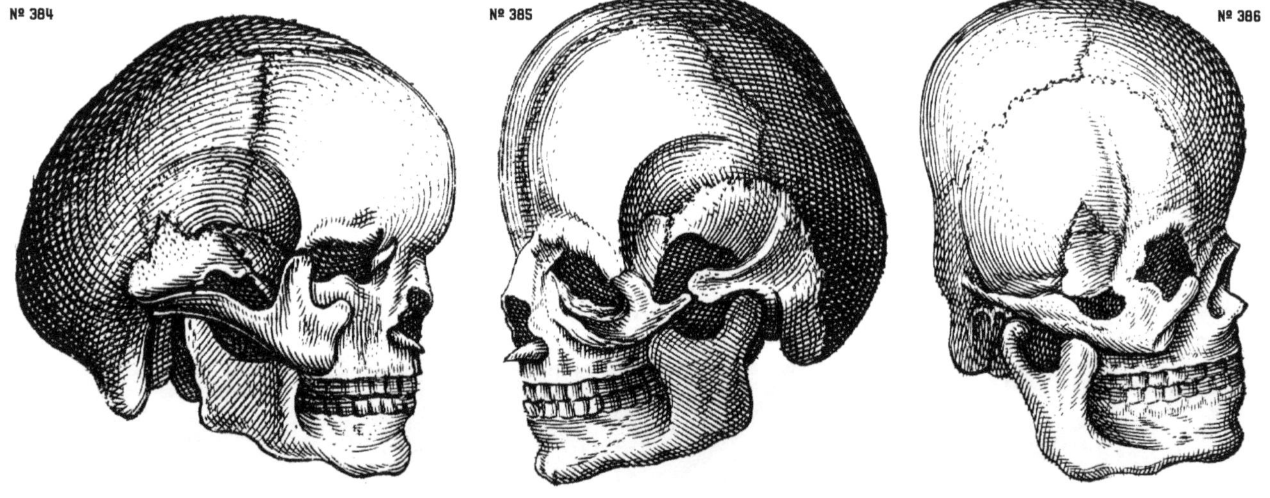

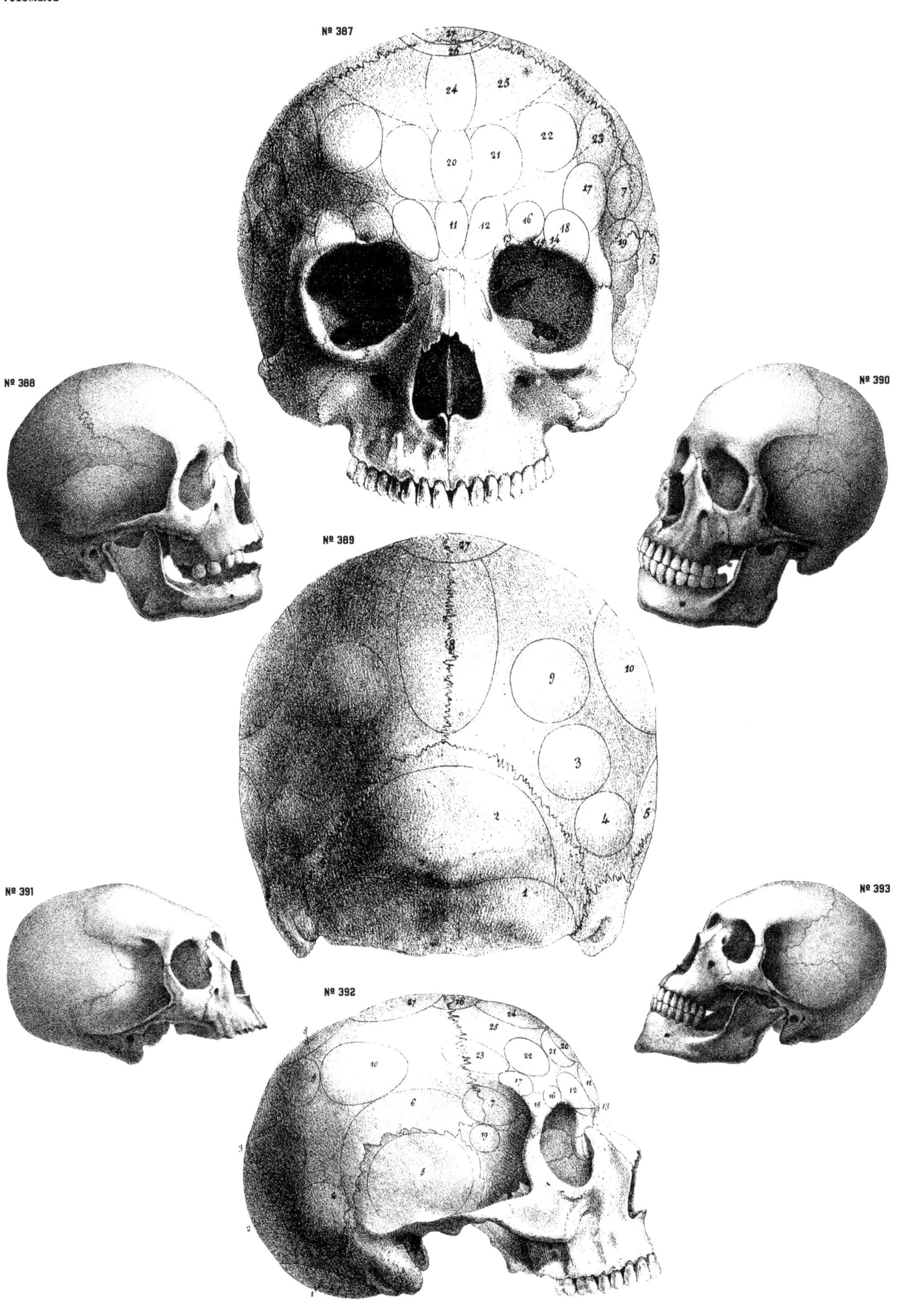
№ 387
№ 388
№ 390
№ 389
№ 391
№ 393
№ 392

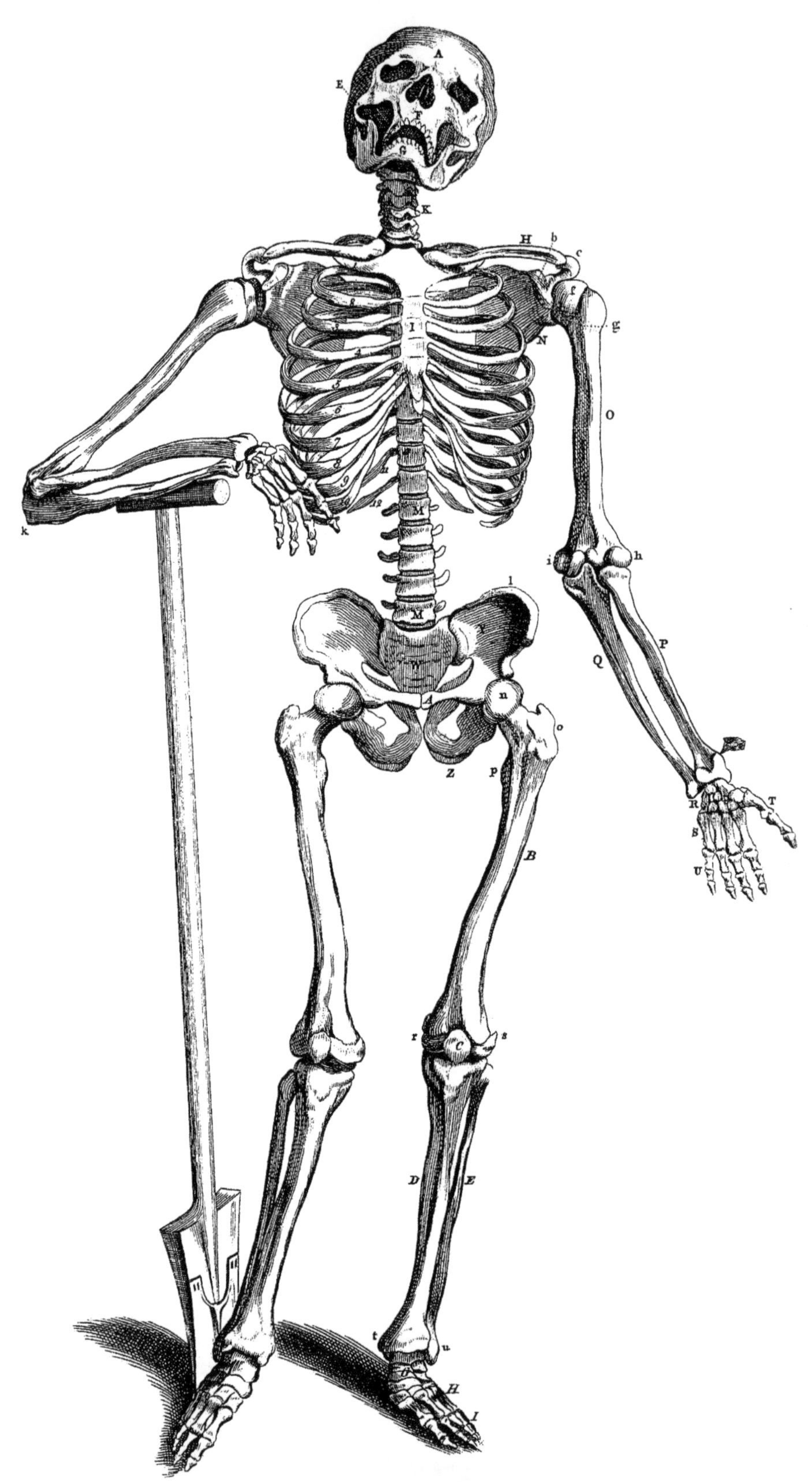

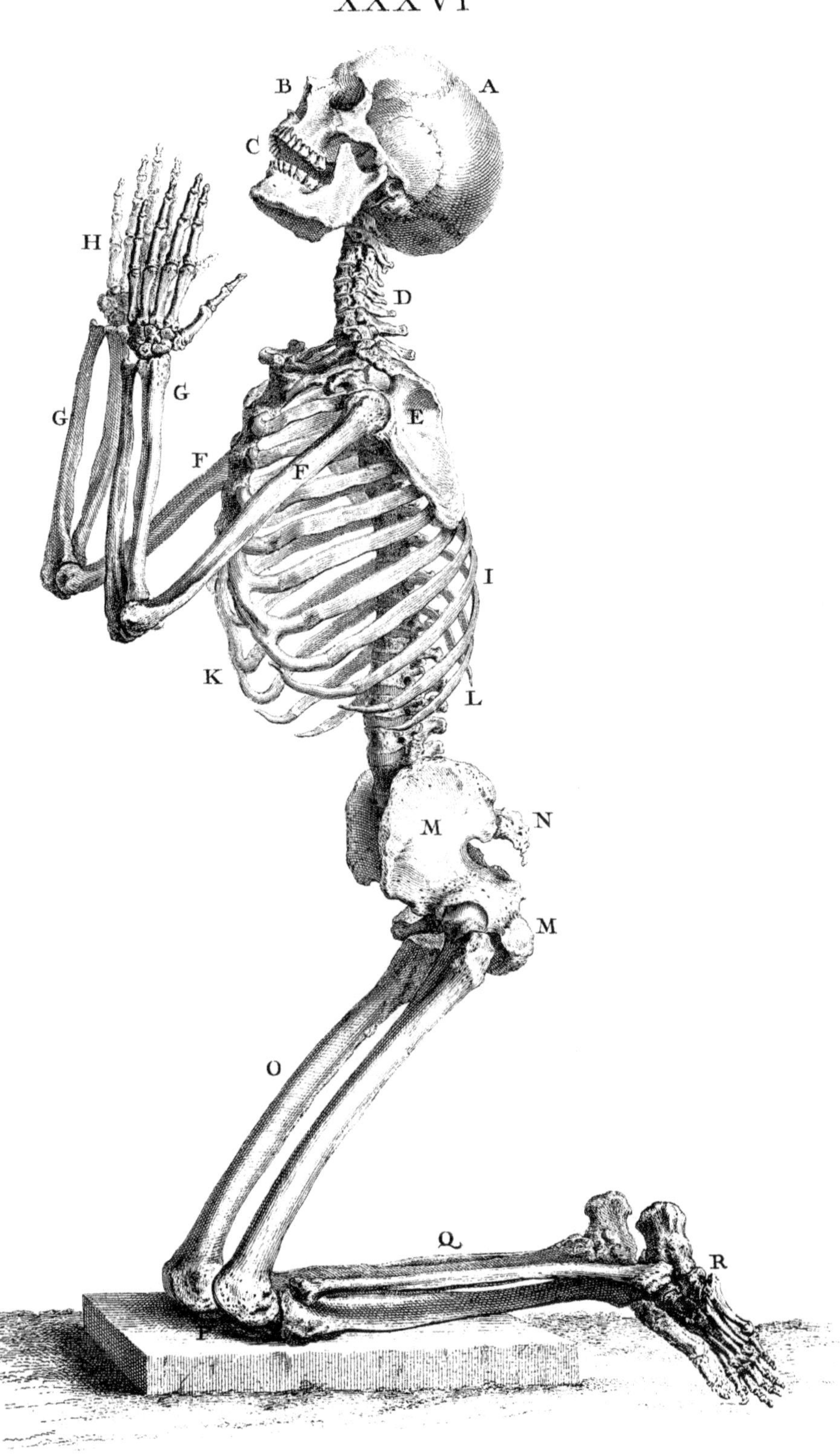
XXXVI
A
B
C
D
E
F
F
G
G
H
I
K
L
M
N
M
O
Q
R

№ 396

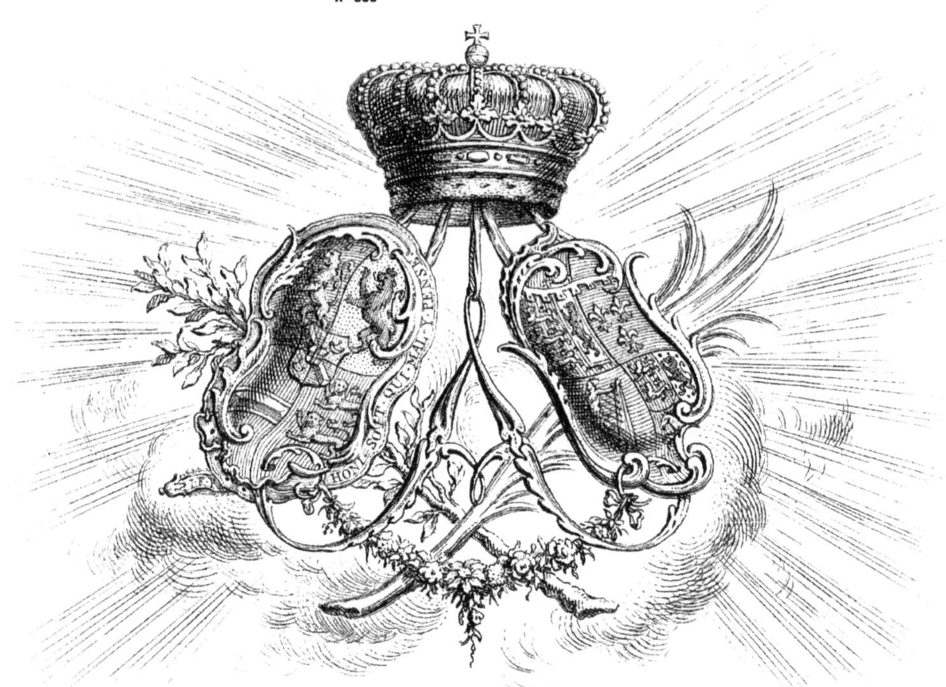

№ 397

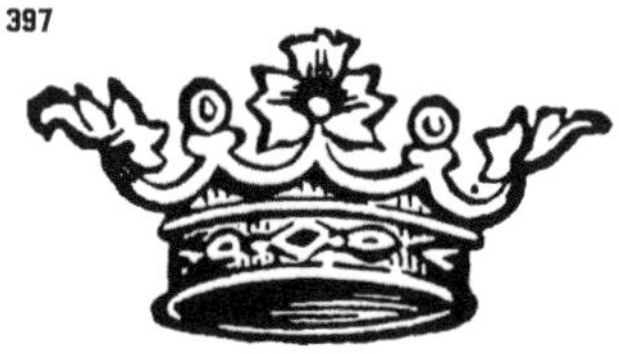

№ 398

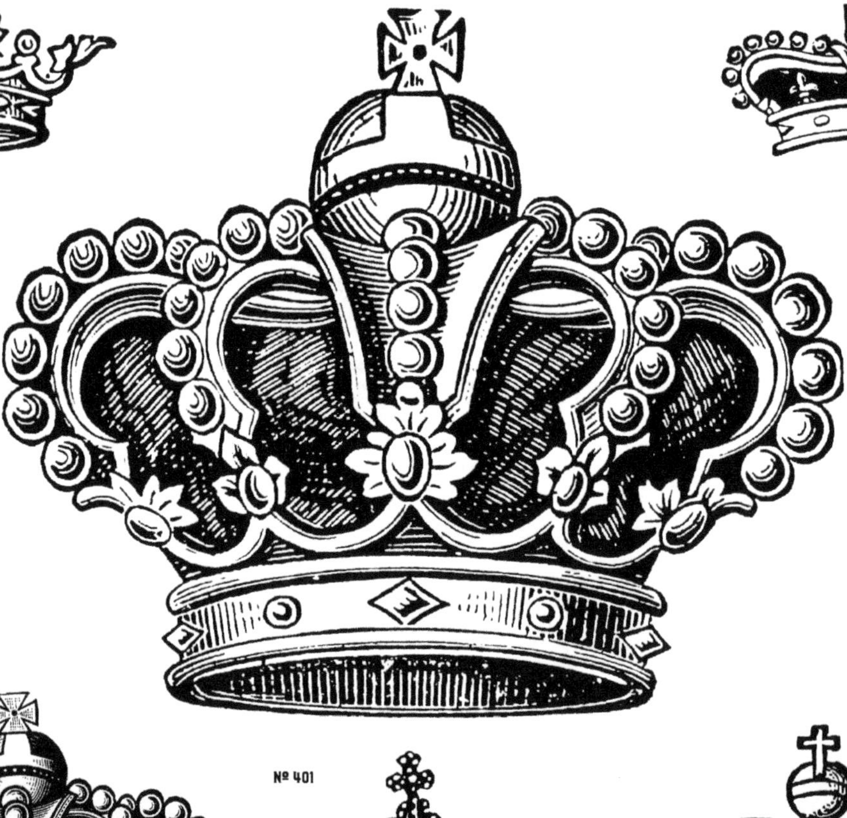

№ 399

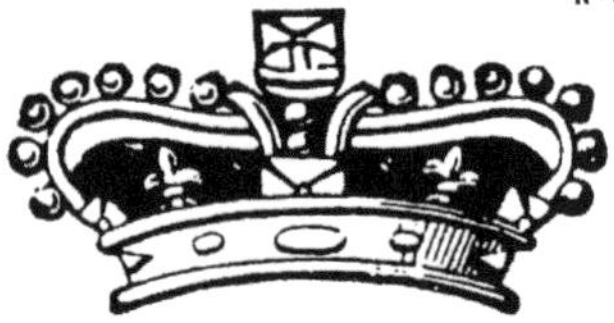

CROWNS

№ 400

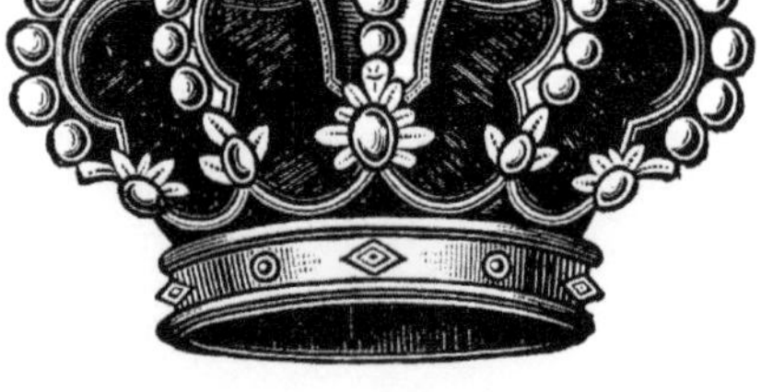

№ 401

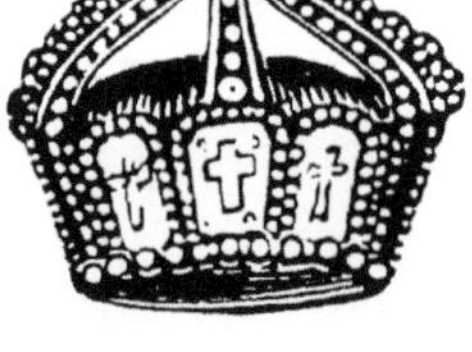

№ 402

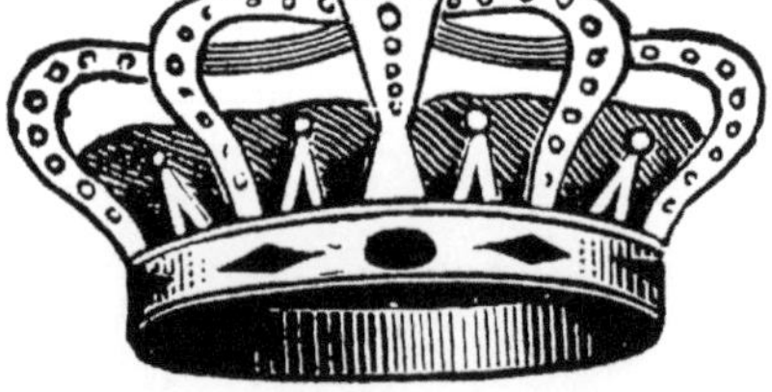

Nº 403
Nº 404
Nº 406
Nº 405
Nº 407
Nº 408
Nº 409
Nº 410
Nº 412
Nº 411
Nº 413
ROYAL ARCANUM
M V C

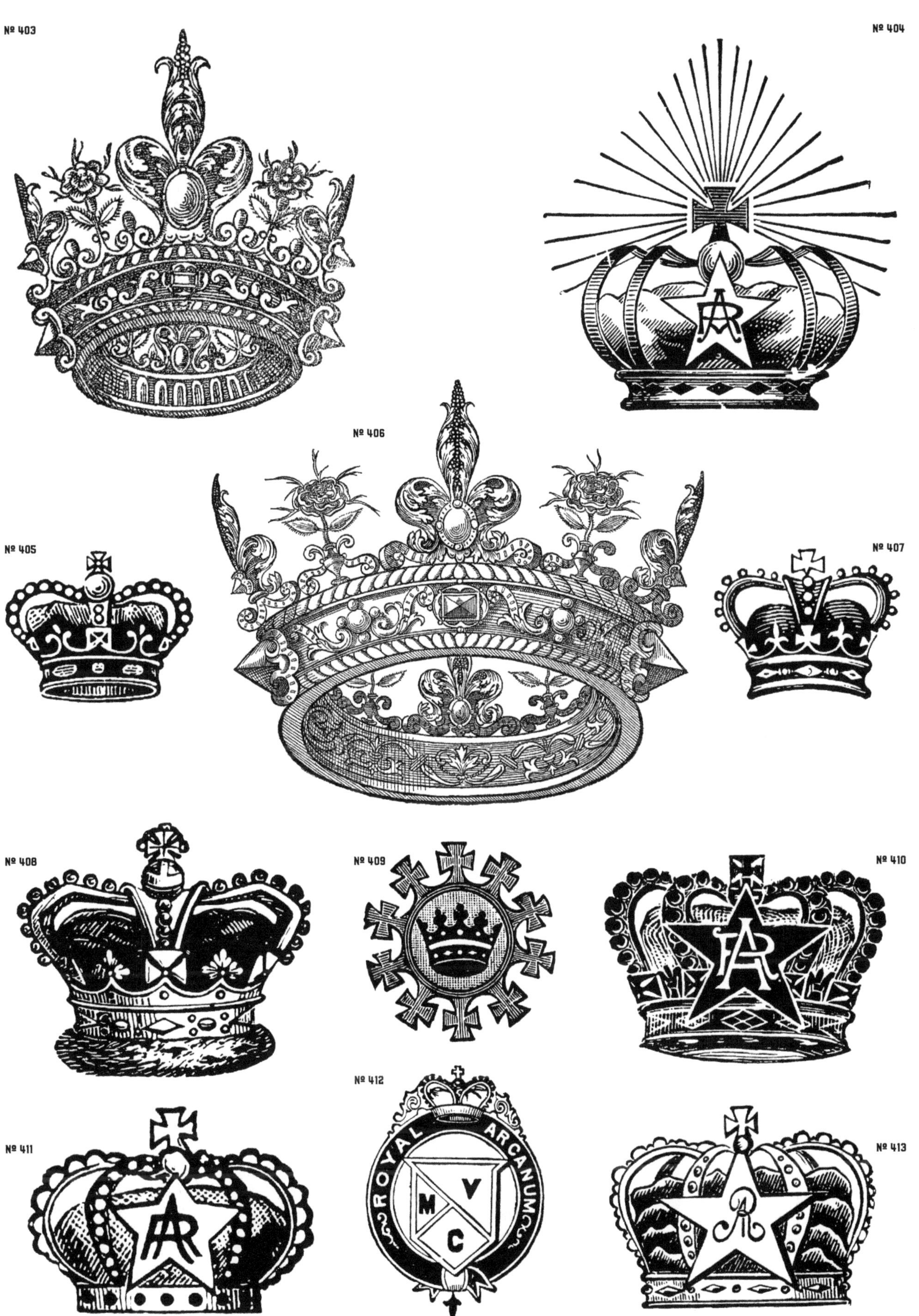

CROWNS

ROSES

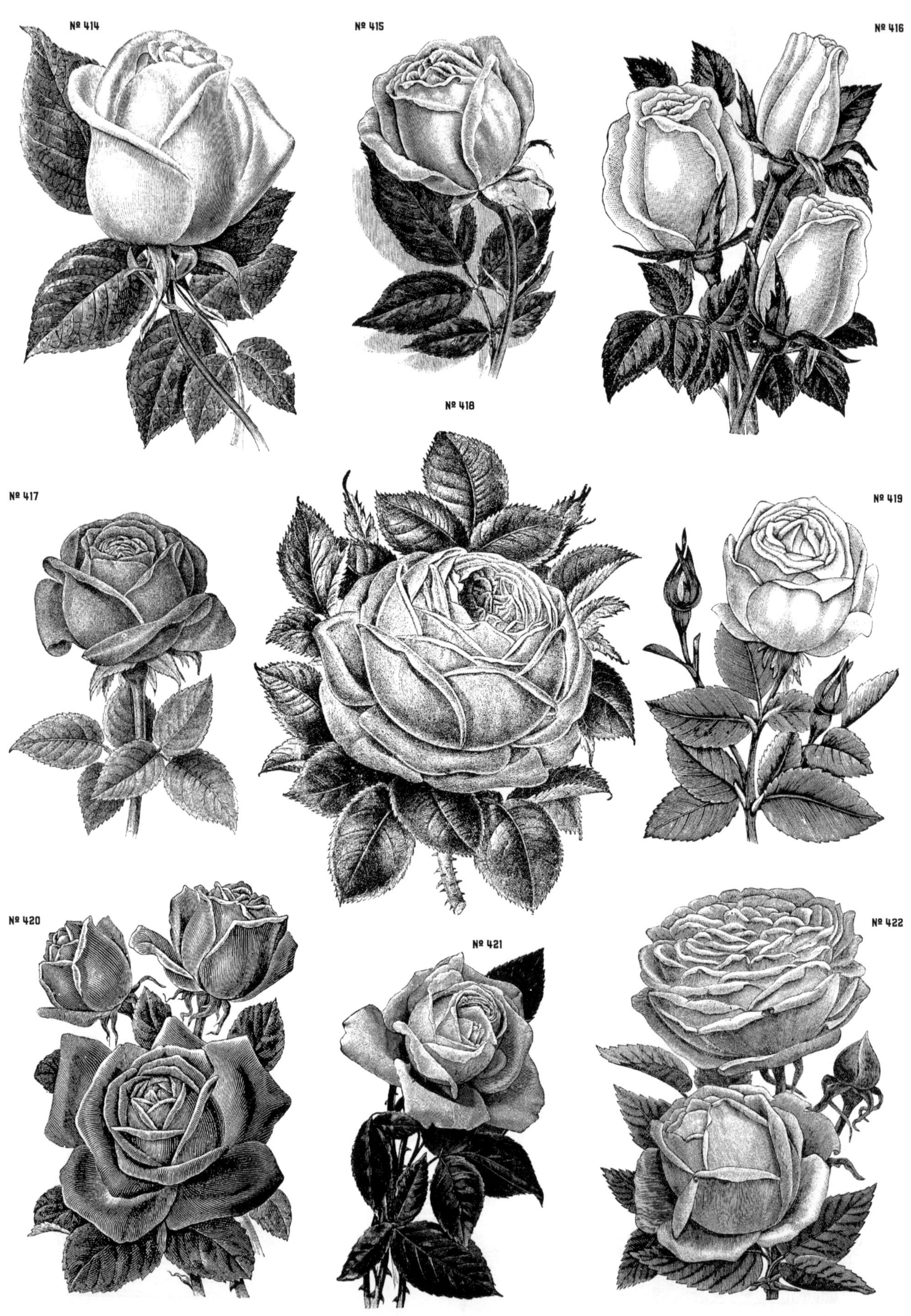

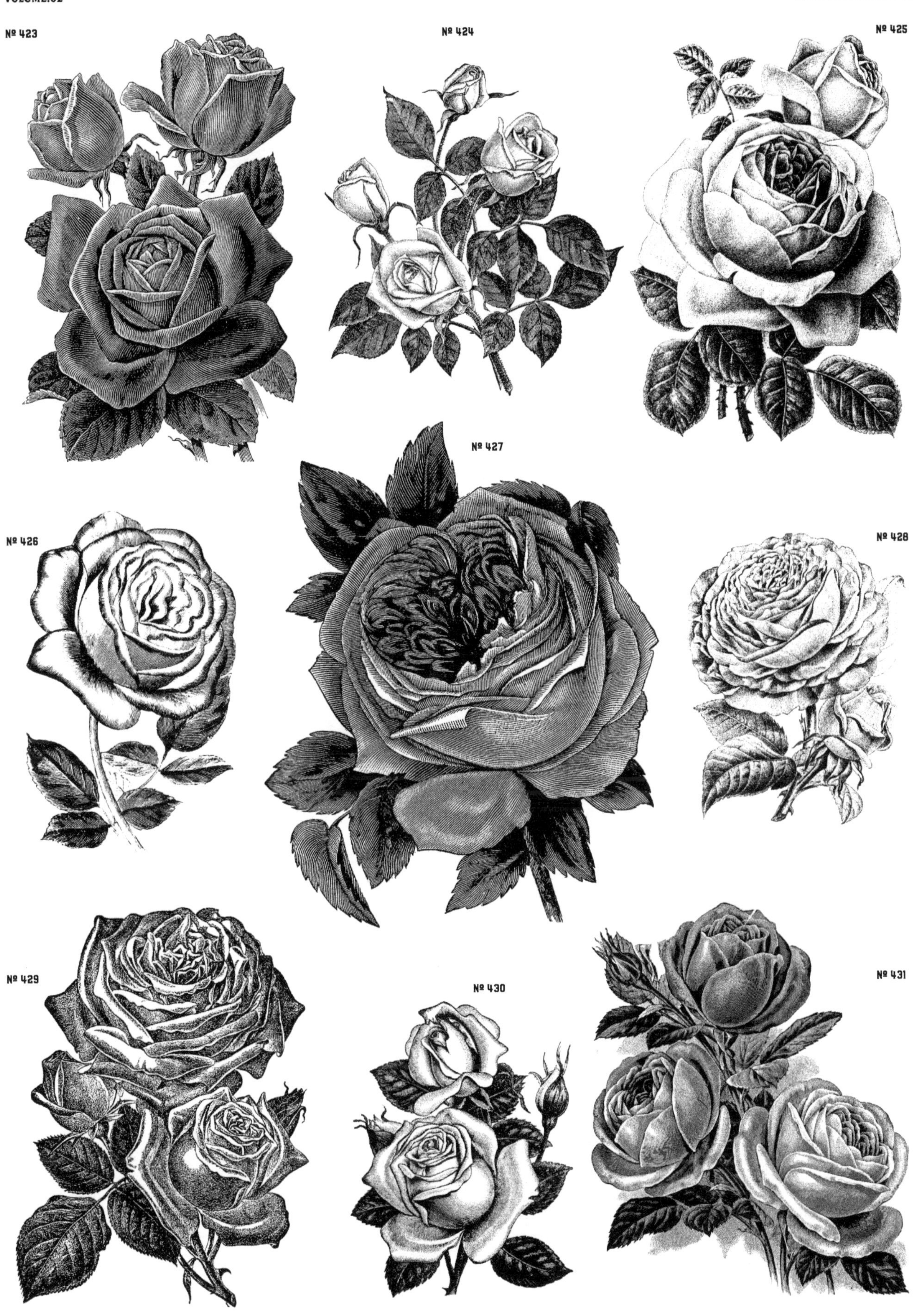

ROSES

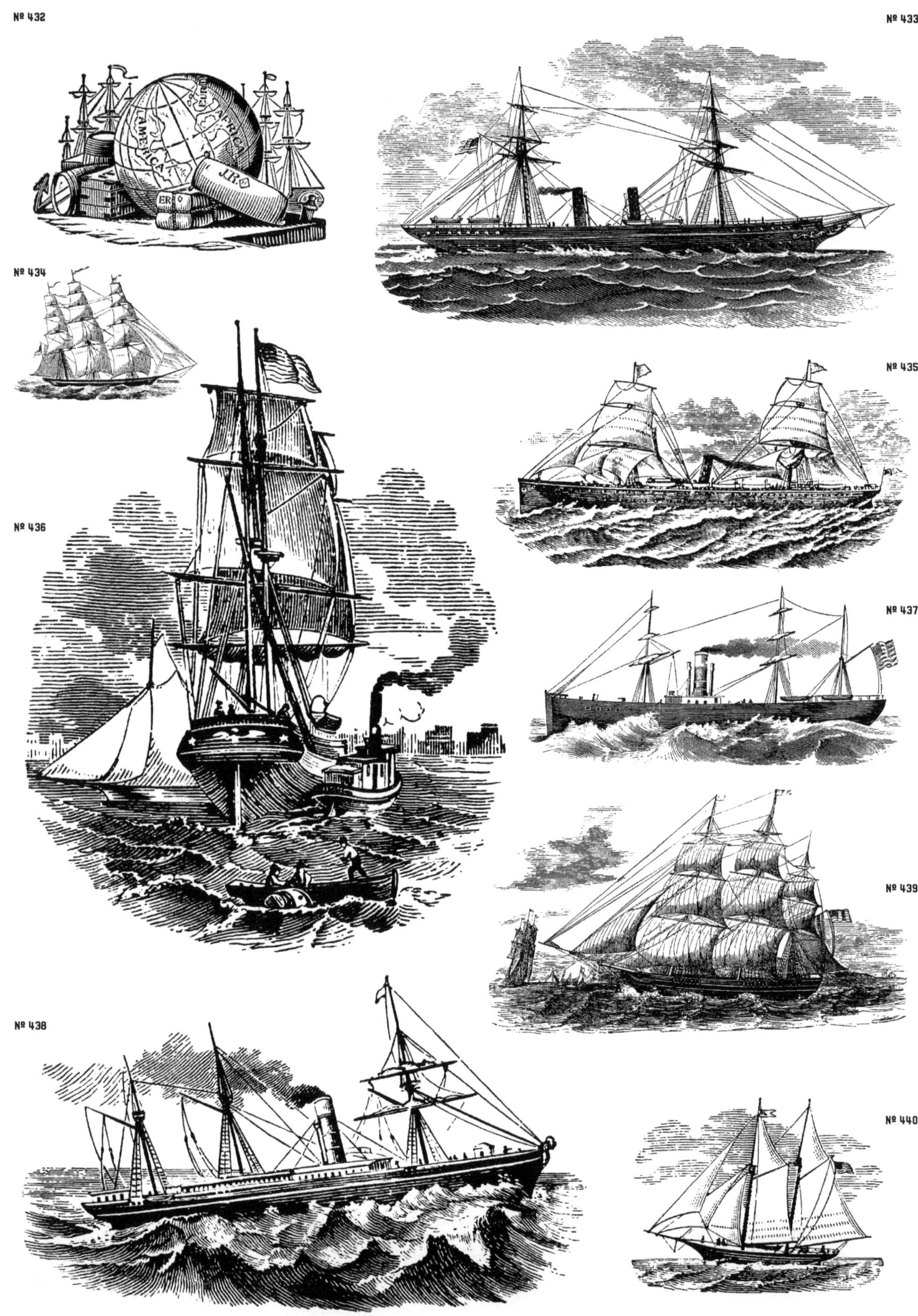

№ 432

№ 433

№ 434

№ 435

№ 436

№ 437

№ 438

№ 439

№ 440

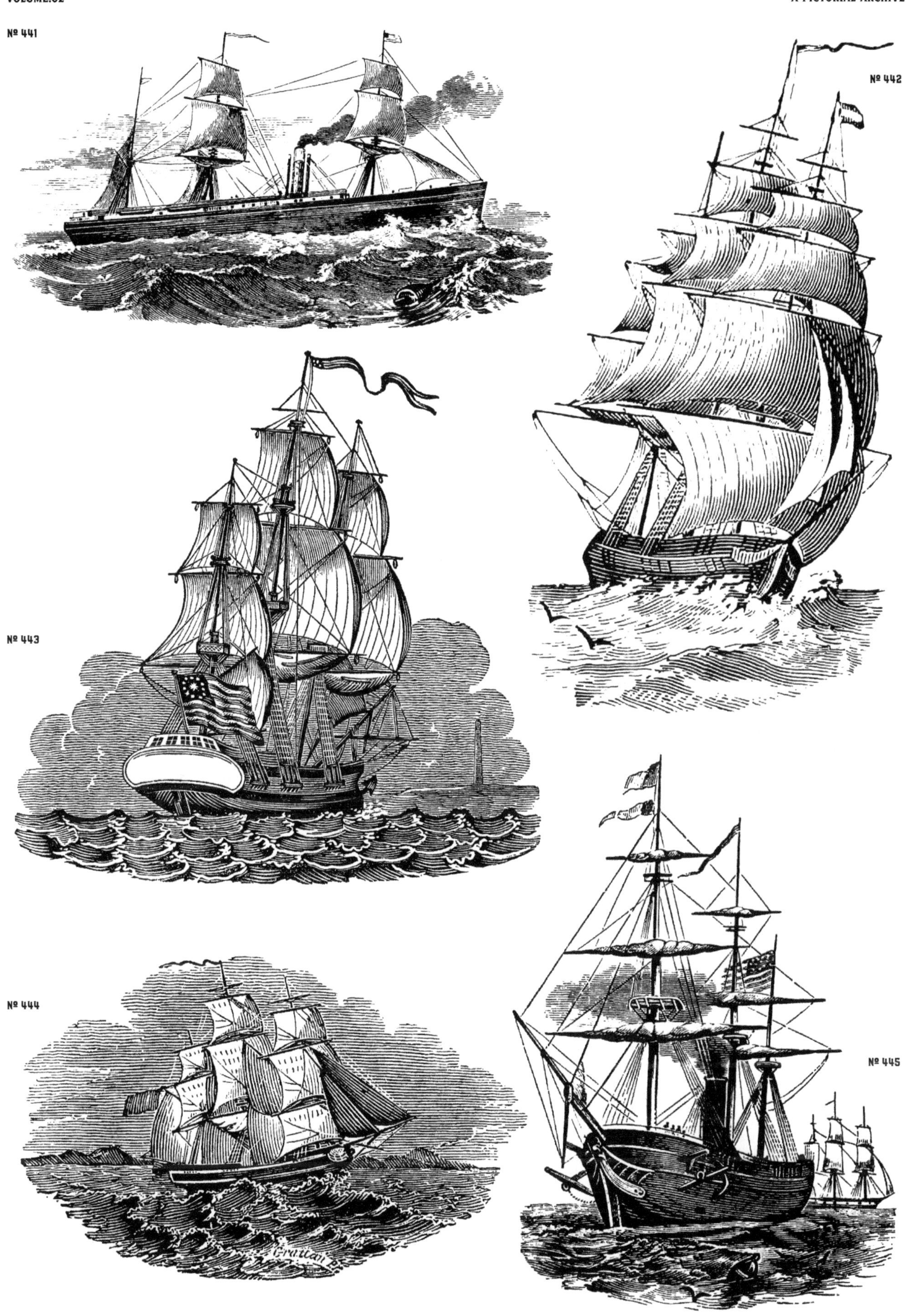

№ 441

№ 442

№ 443

№ 444

№ 445

TALL SHIPS

№ 446

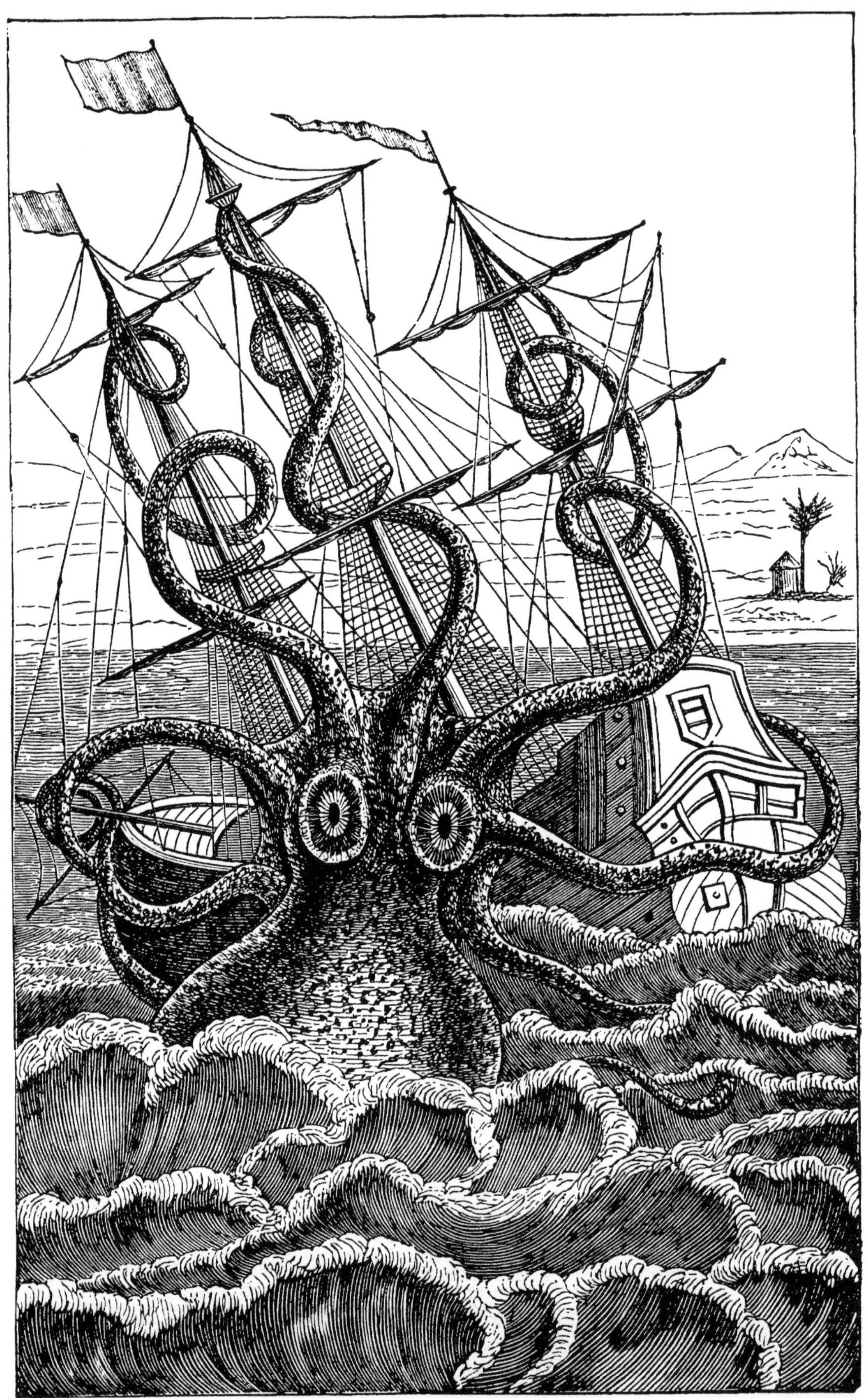

Nº 447

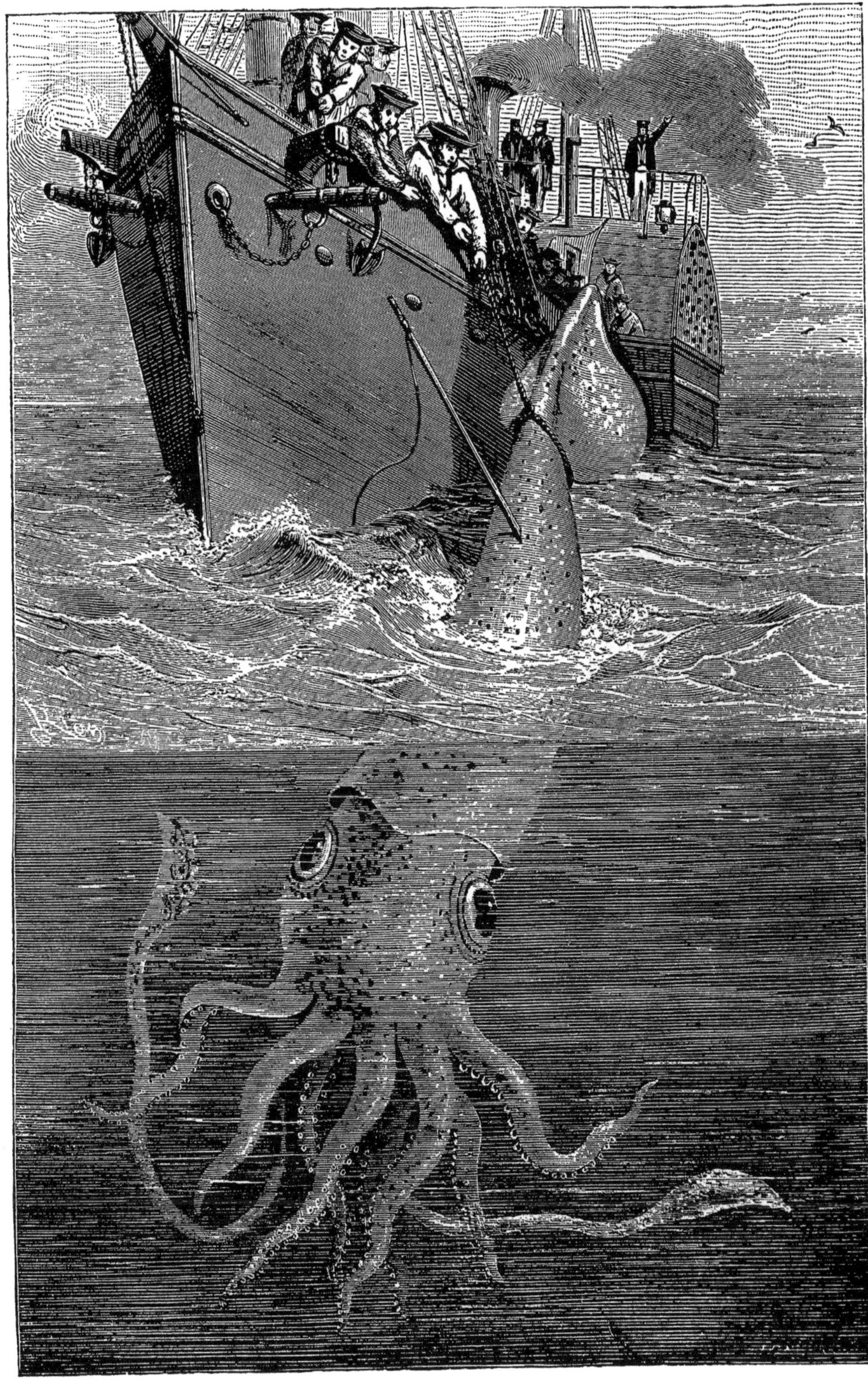

№ 448

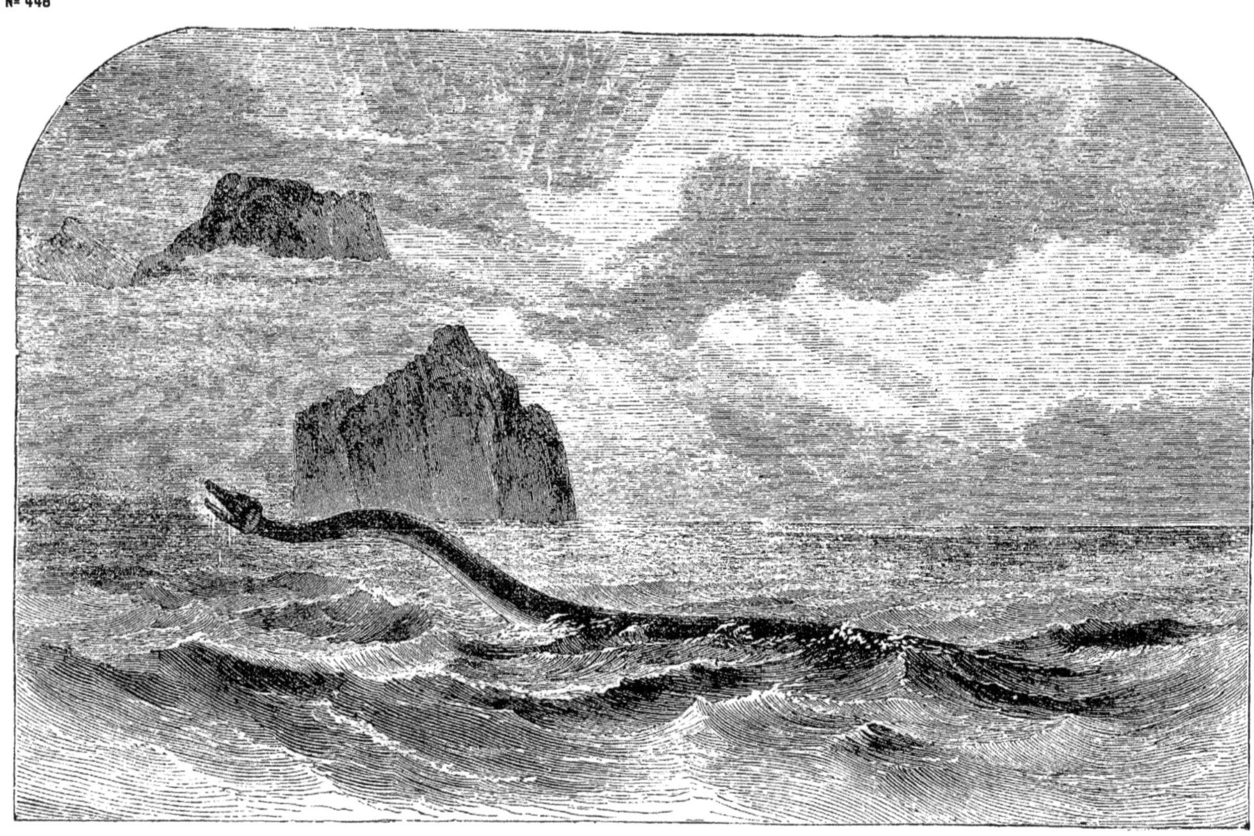

№ 449

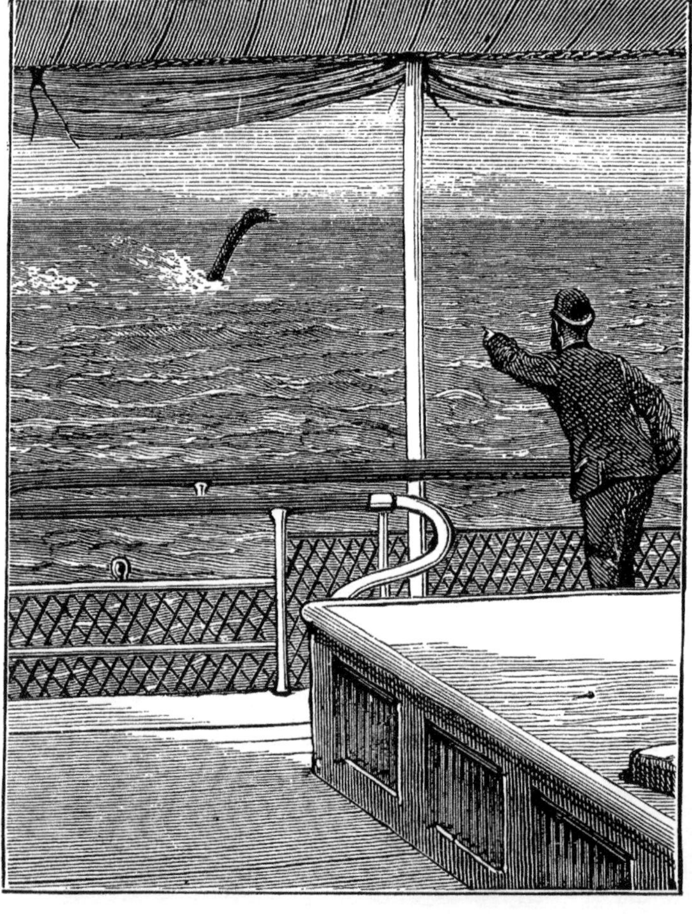

№ 450

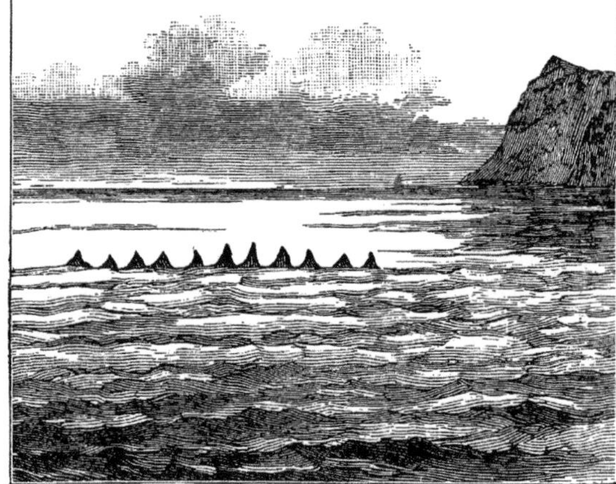

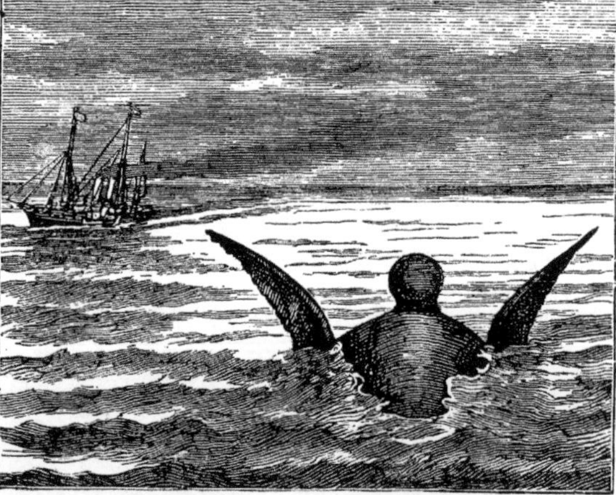

№ 451

№ 452

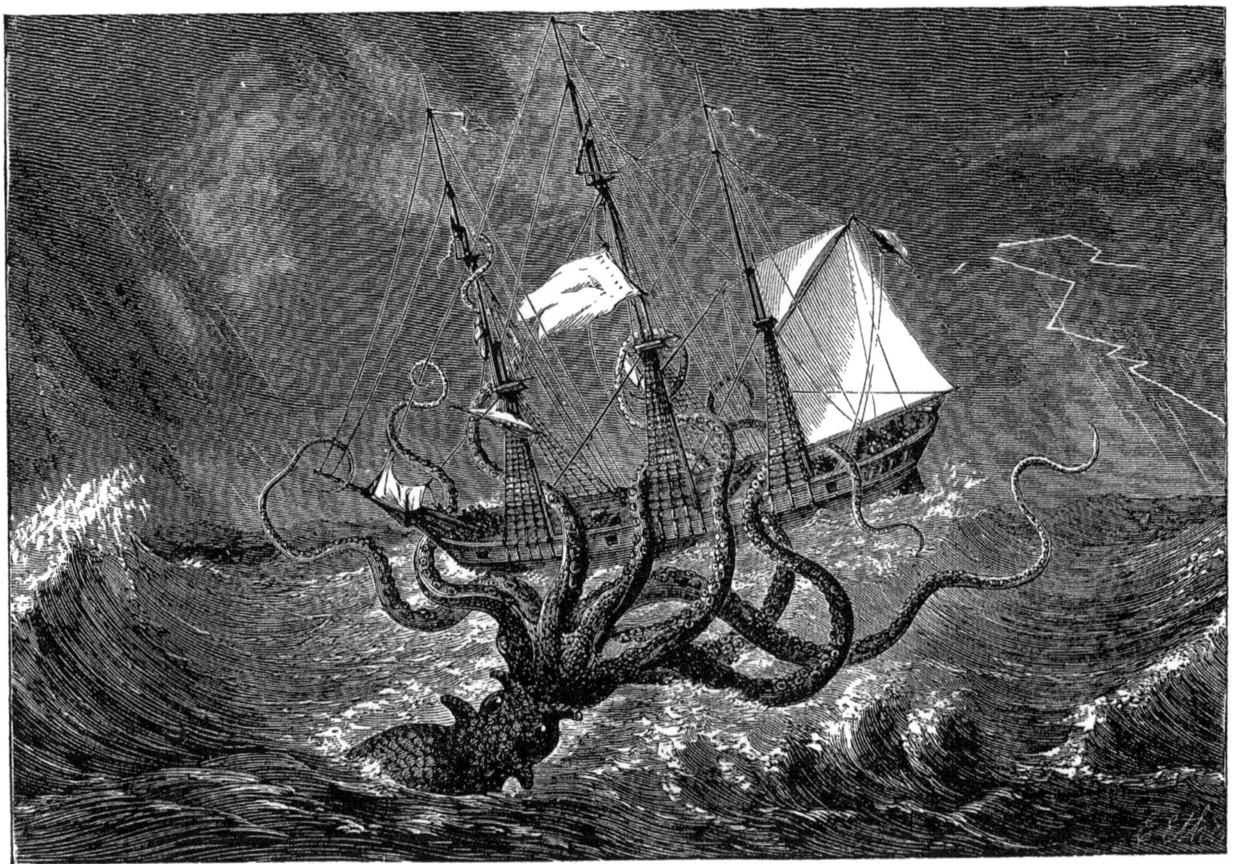

SEA MONSTERS

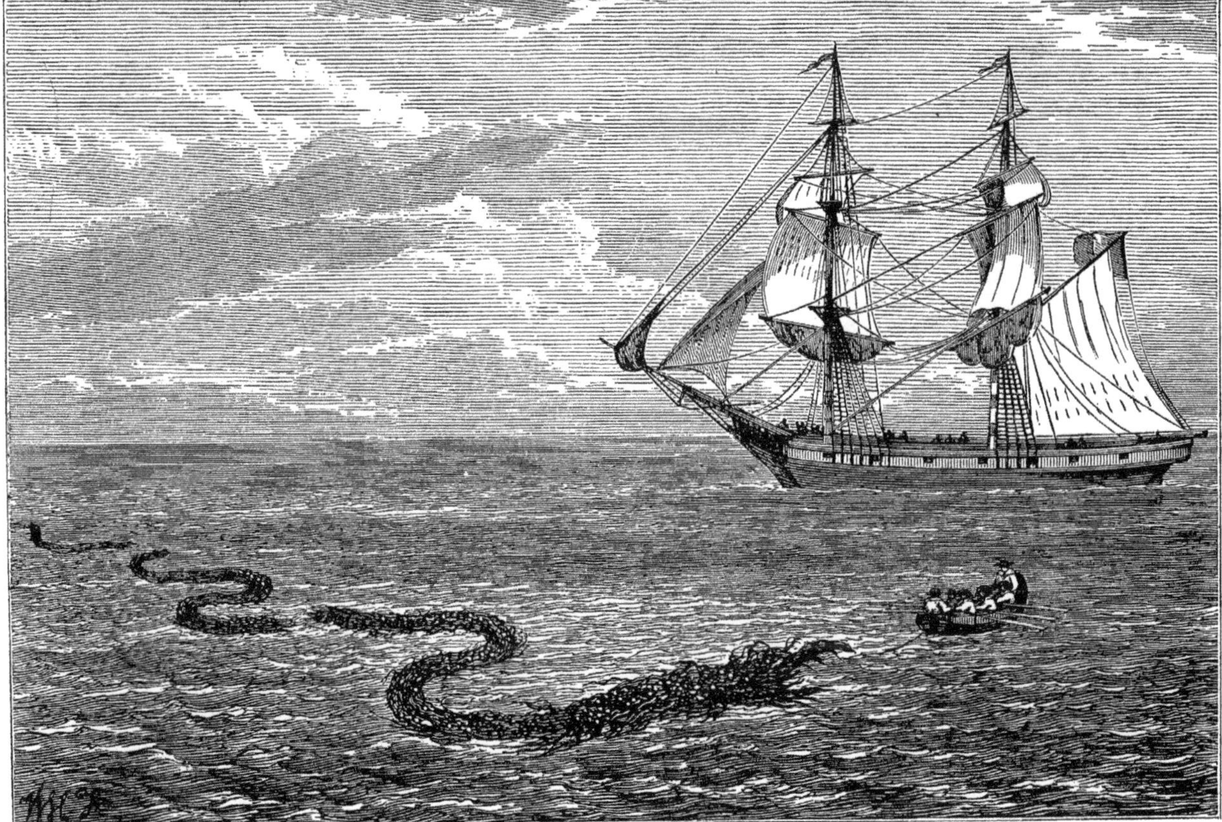

№ 453

№ 454

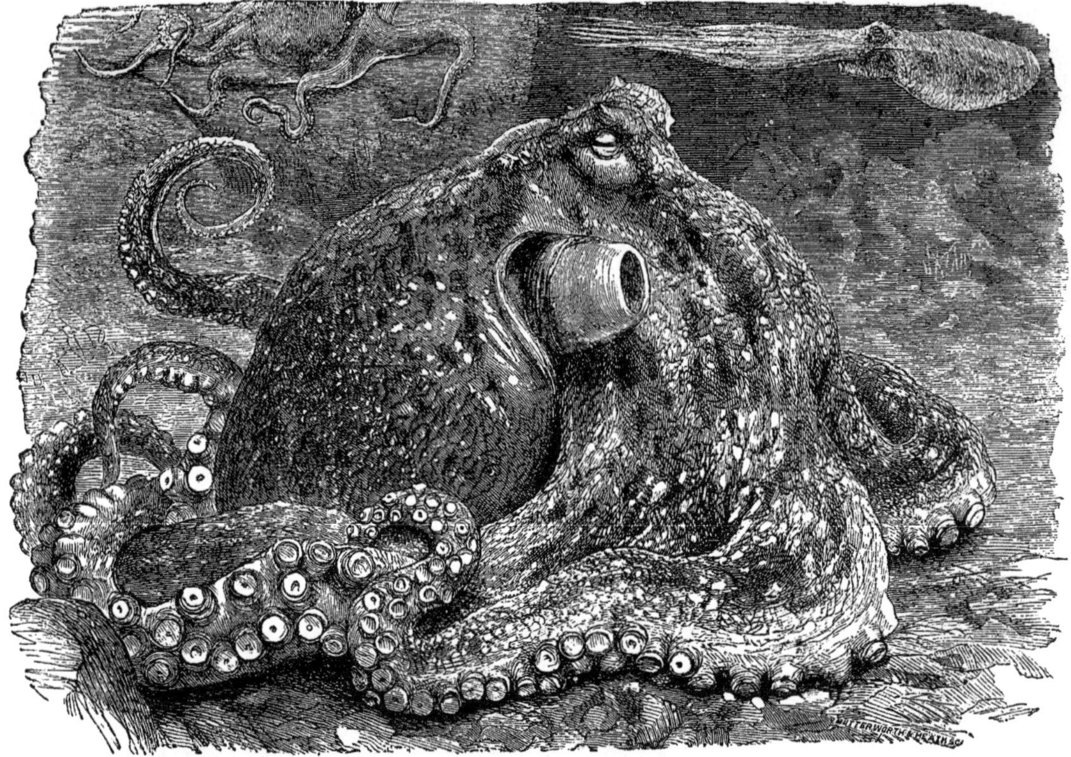

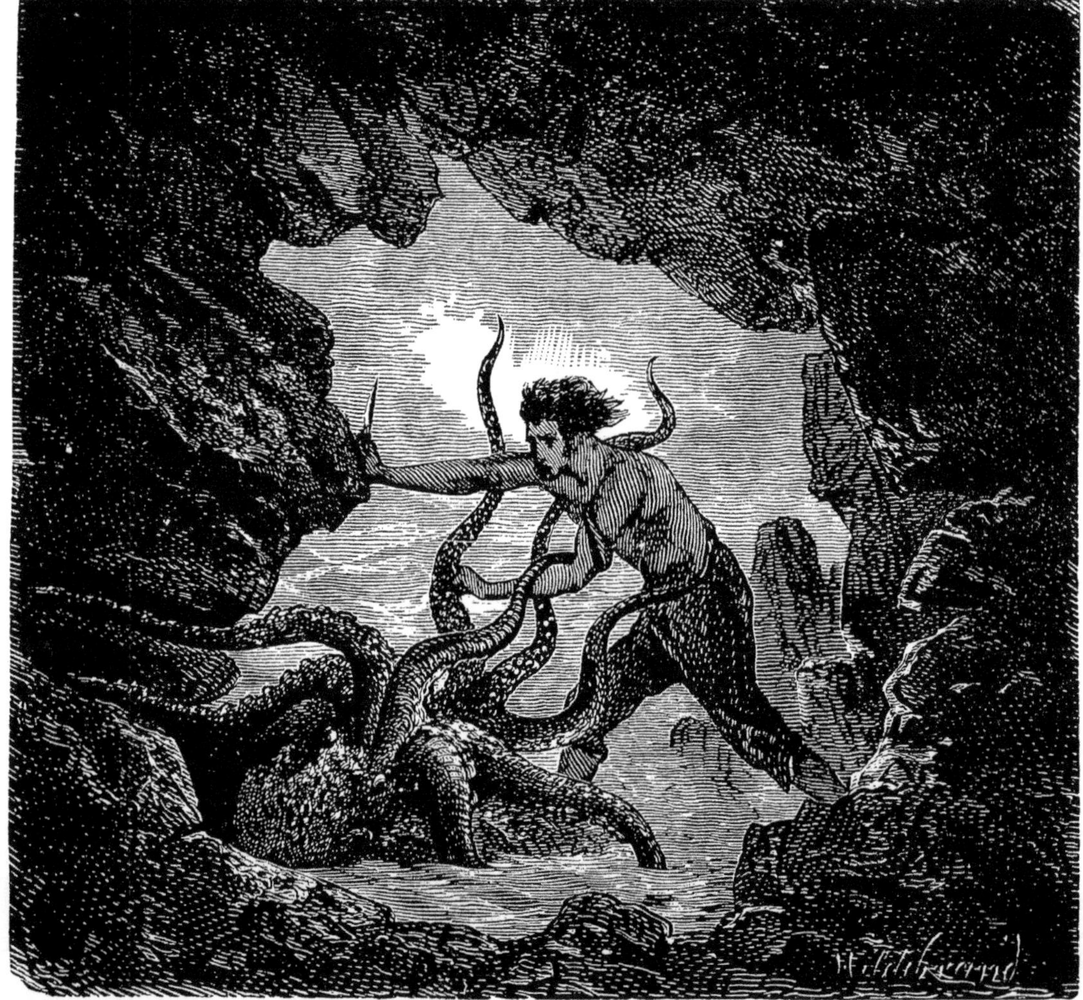

№ 455

№ 456

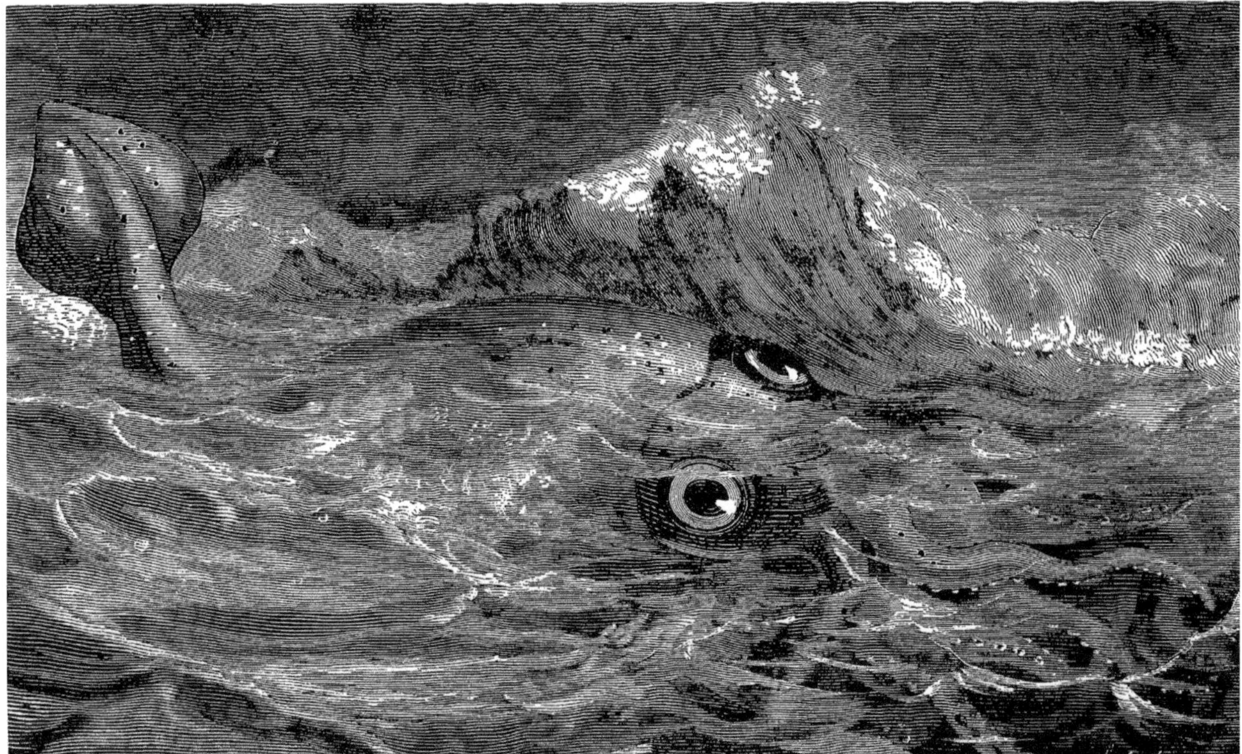

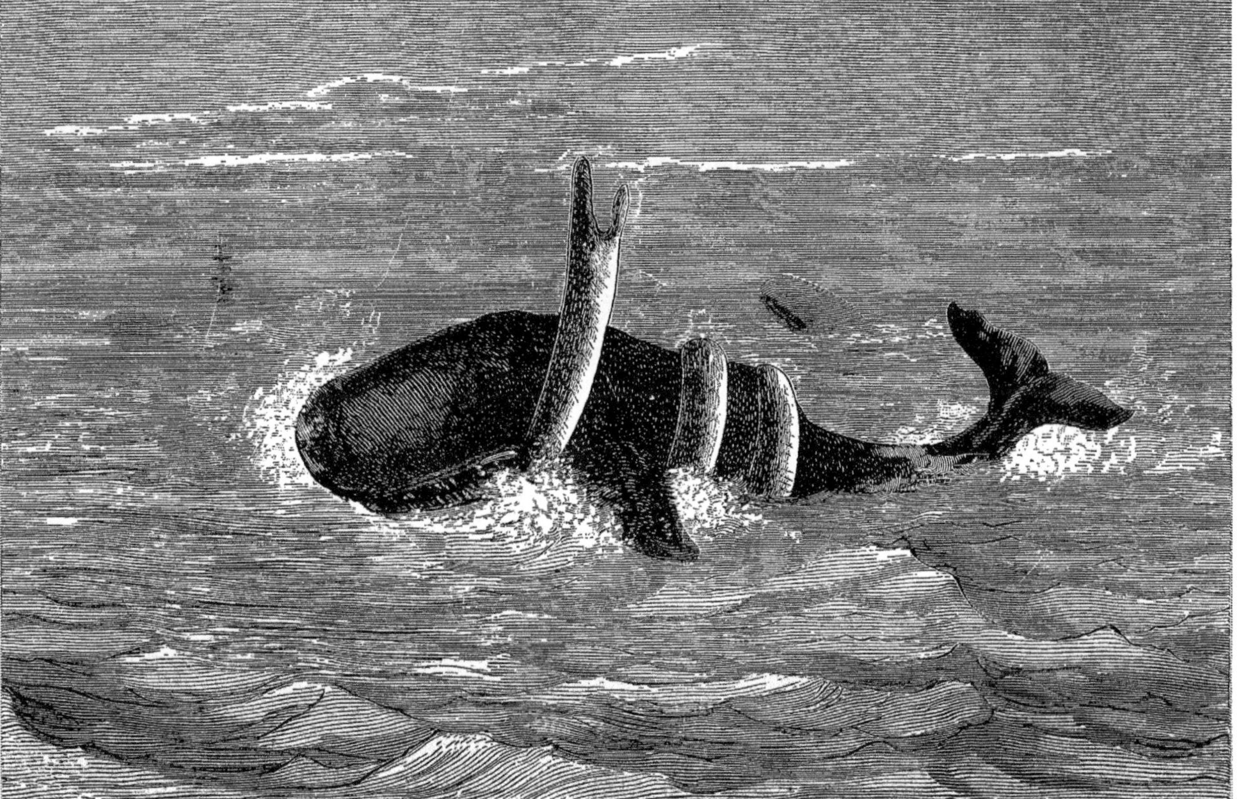

№ 457

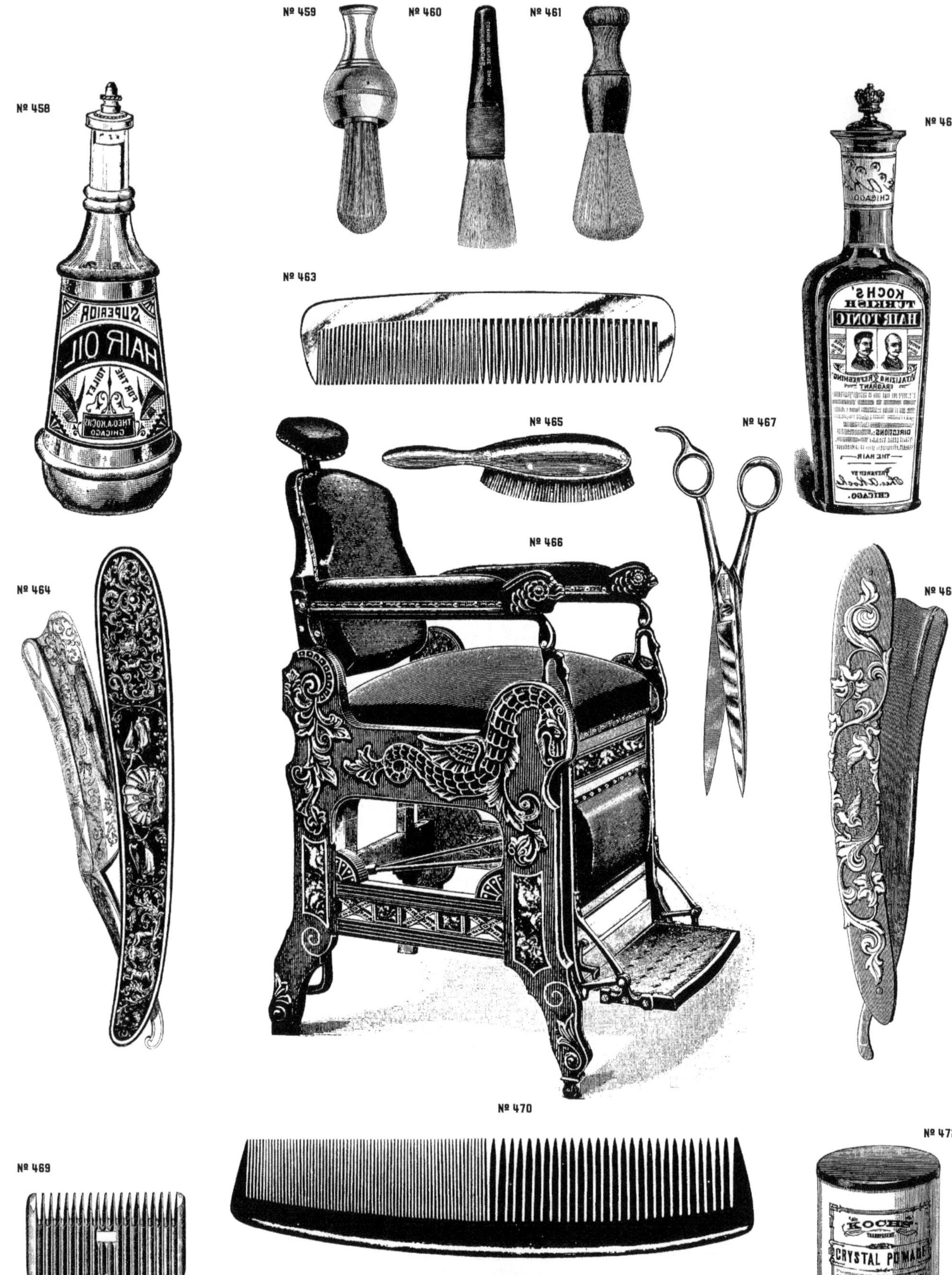
№ 458
№ 459
№ 460
№ 461
№ 462
№ 463
№ 464
№ 465
№ 466
№ 467
№ 468
№ 469
№ 470
№ 471
№ 472
THEO. A. KOCHS
CHICAGO

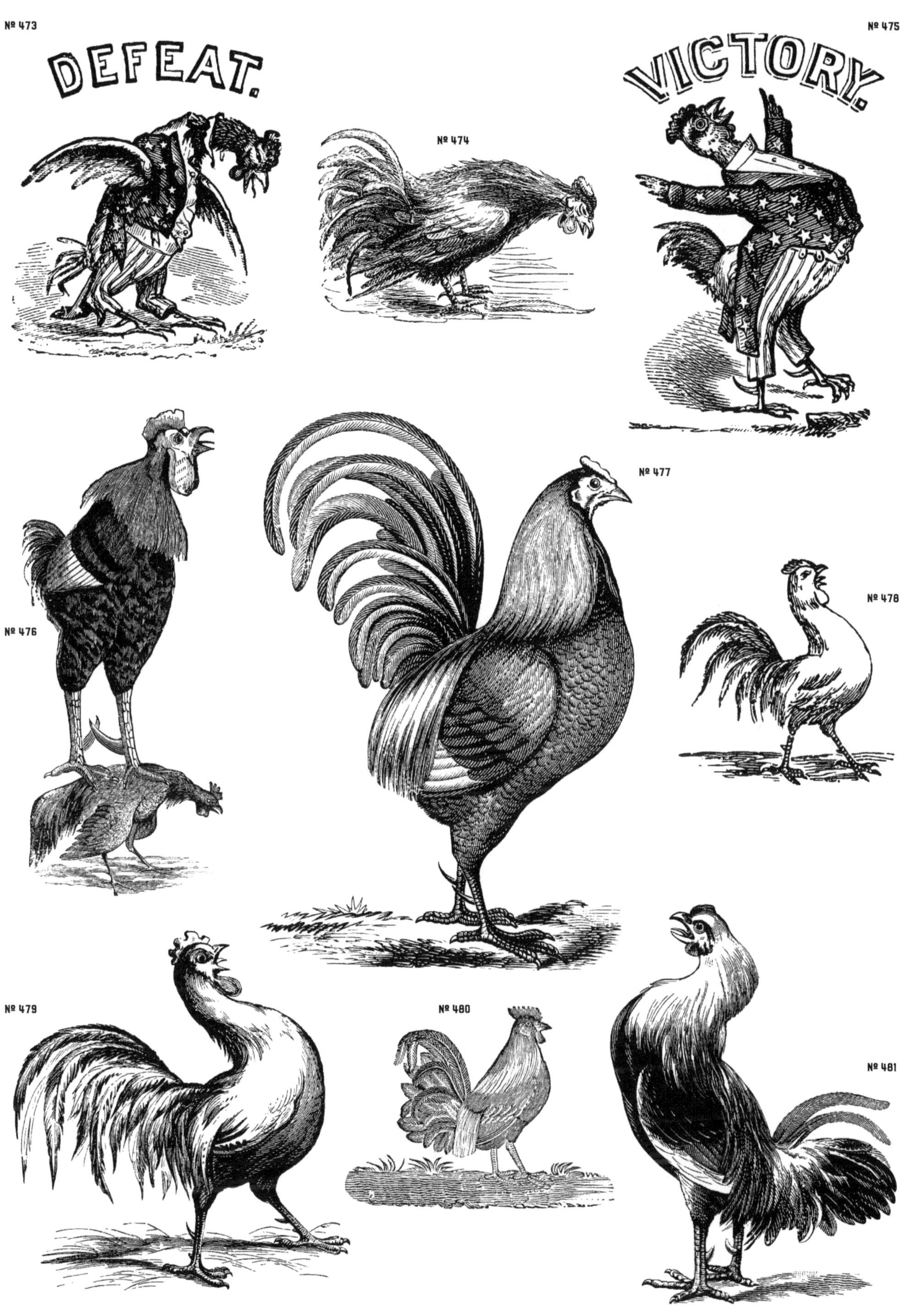

Nº 473

Nº 474

Nº 475

Nº 476

Nº 477

Nº 478

Nº 479

Nº 480

Nº 481

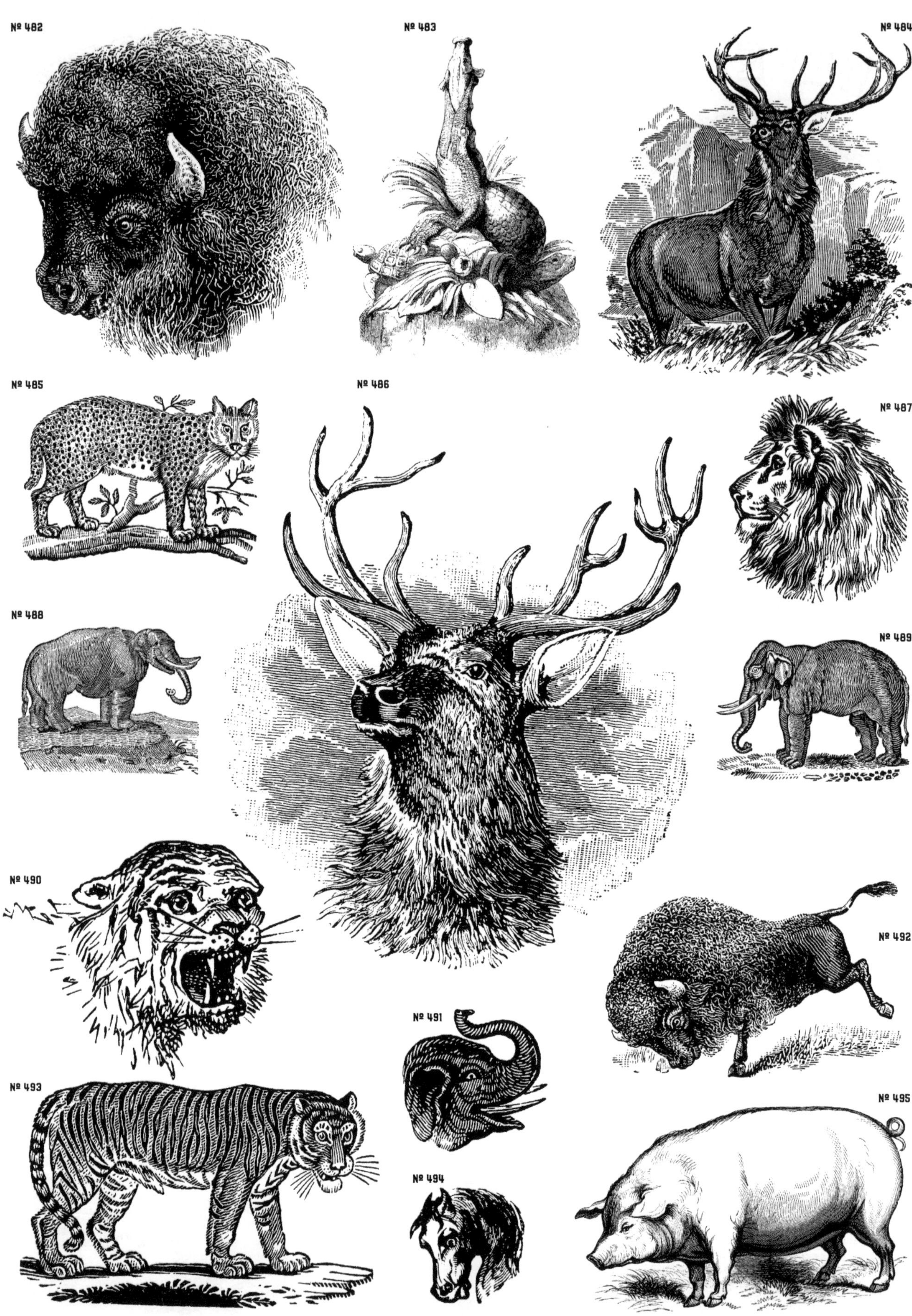

№ 482
№ 483
№ 484
№ 485
№ 486
№ 487
№ 488
№ 489
№ 490
№ 491
№ 492
№ 493
№ 494
№ 495

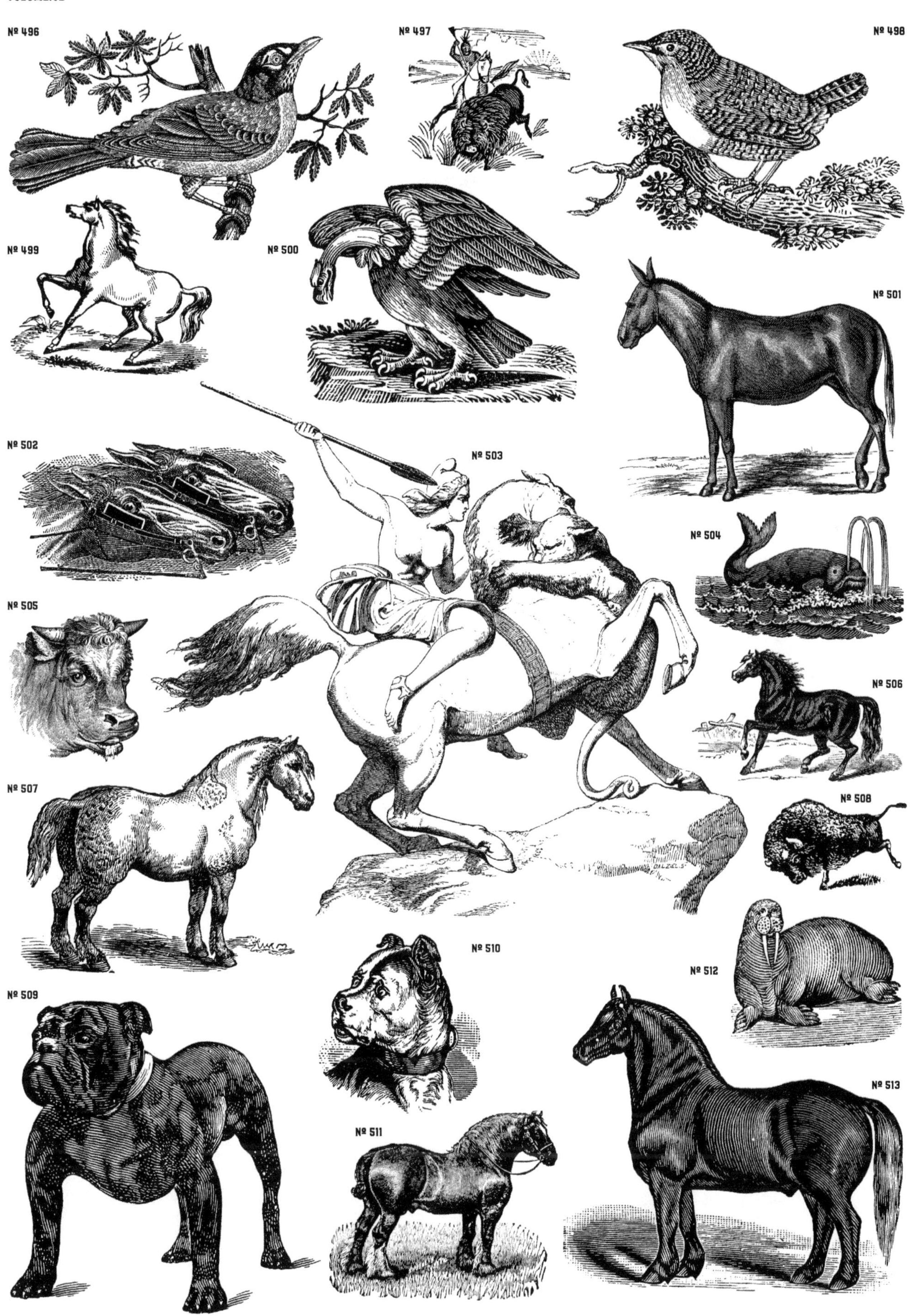
Nº 496
Nº 497
Nº 498
Nº 499
Nº 500
Nº 501
Nº 502
Nº 503
Nº 504
Nº 505
Nº 506
Nº 507
Nº 508
Nº 509
Nº 510
Nº 511
Nº 512
Nº 513

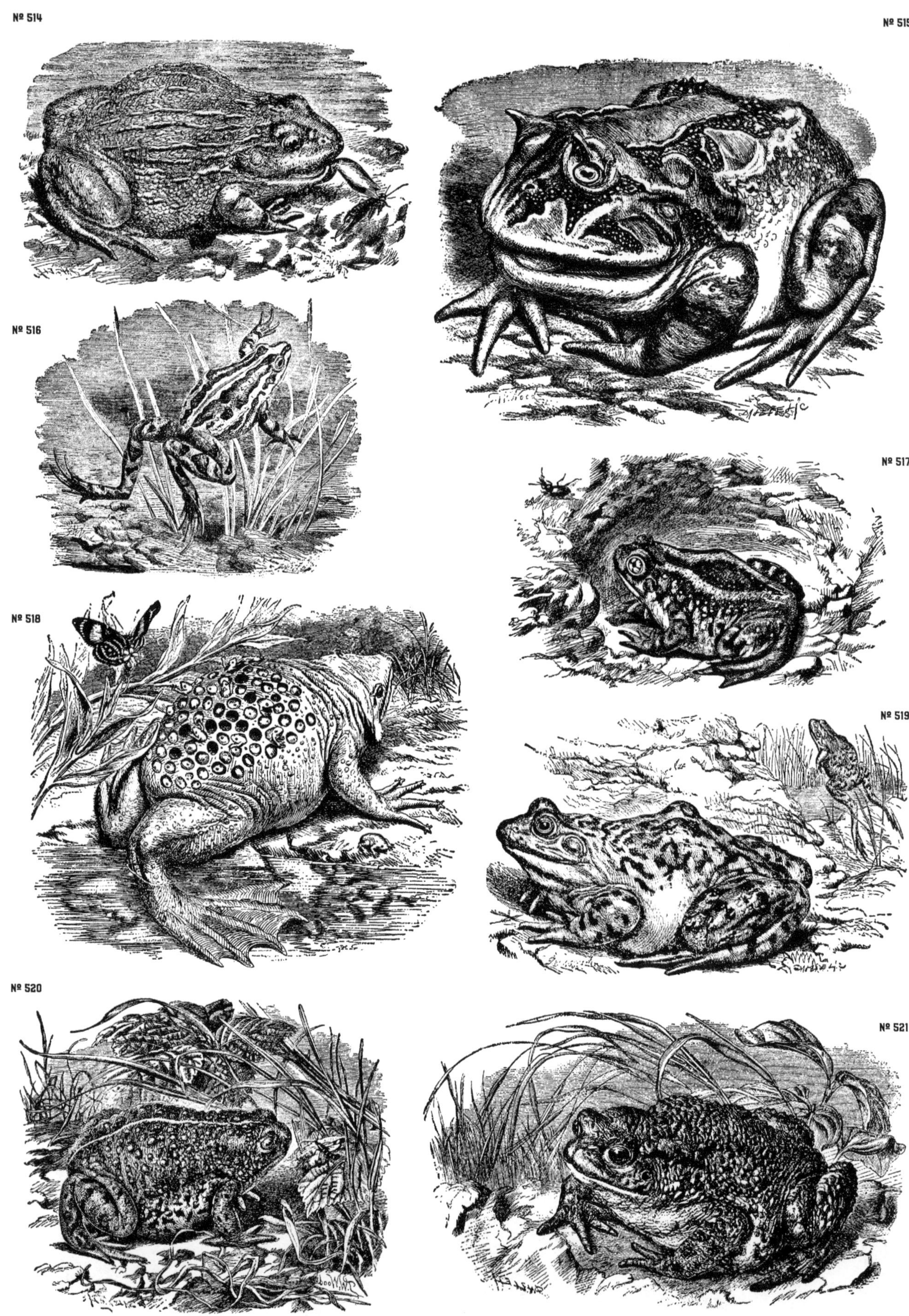
№ 514
№ 515
№ 516
№ 517
№ 518
№ 519
№ 520
№ 521

№ 522

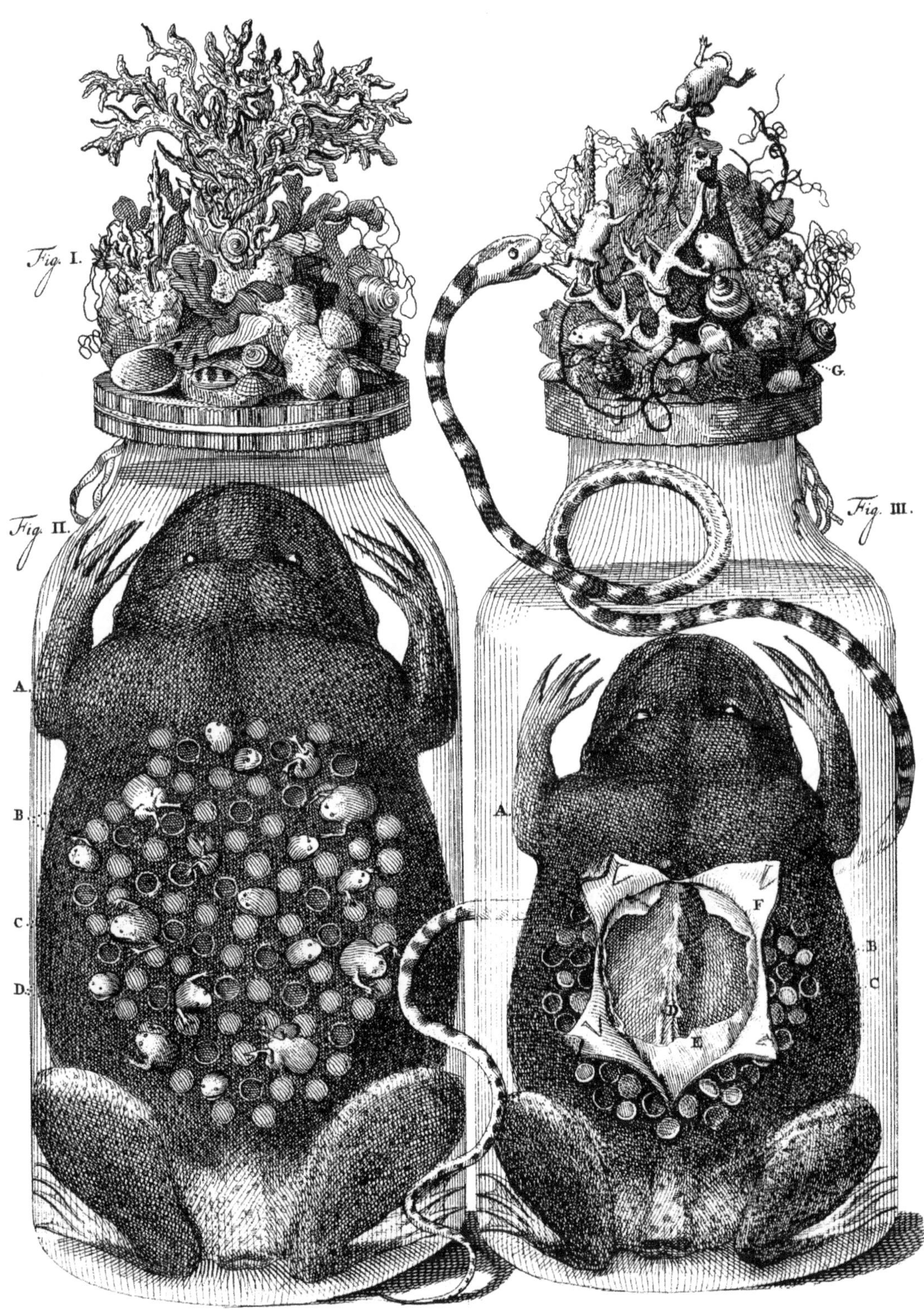

№ 523

№ 524

№ 525

№ 526

№ 527

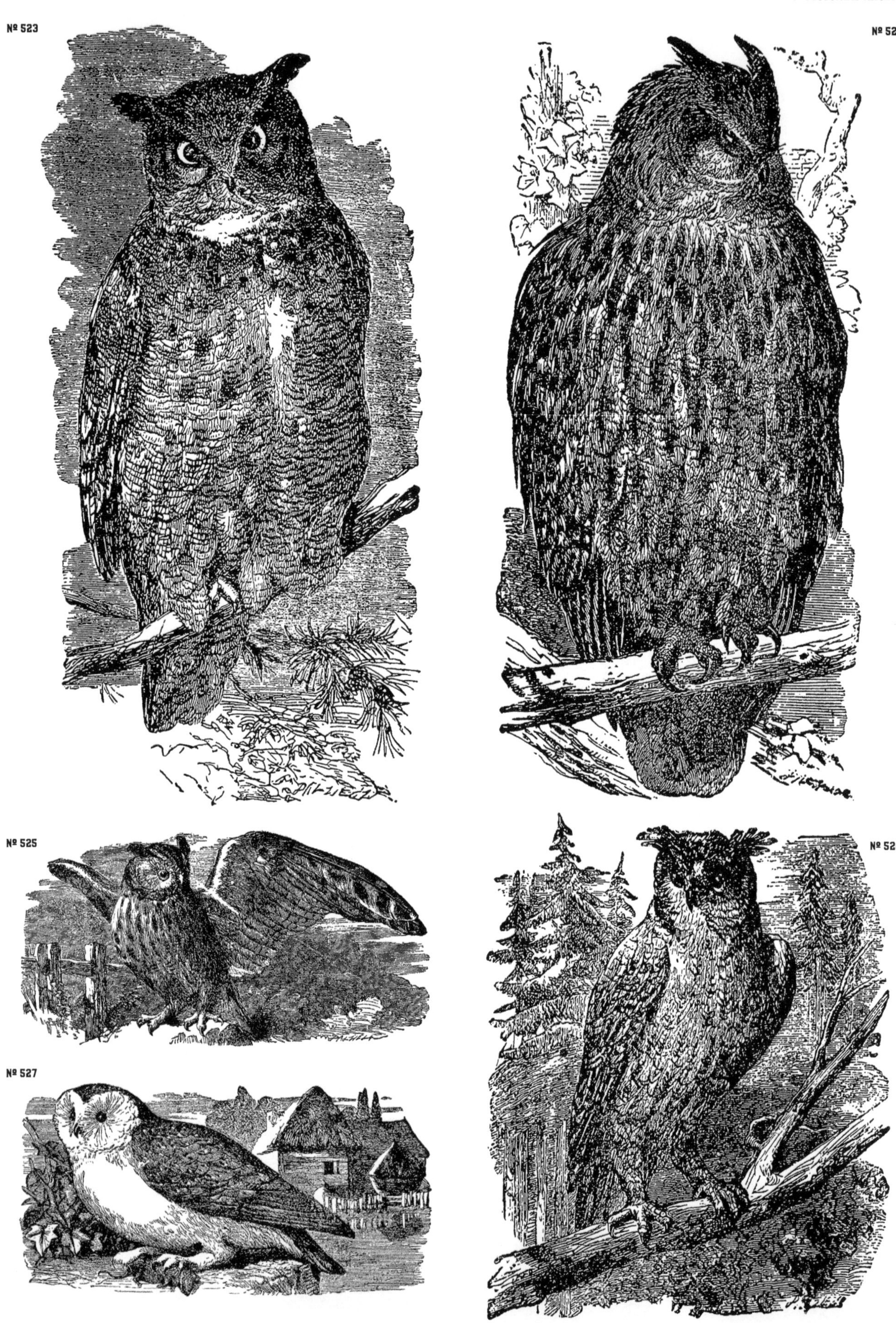

Nº 528

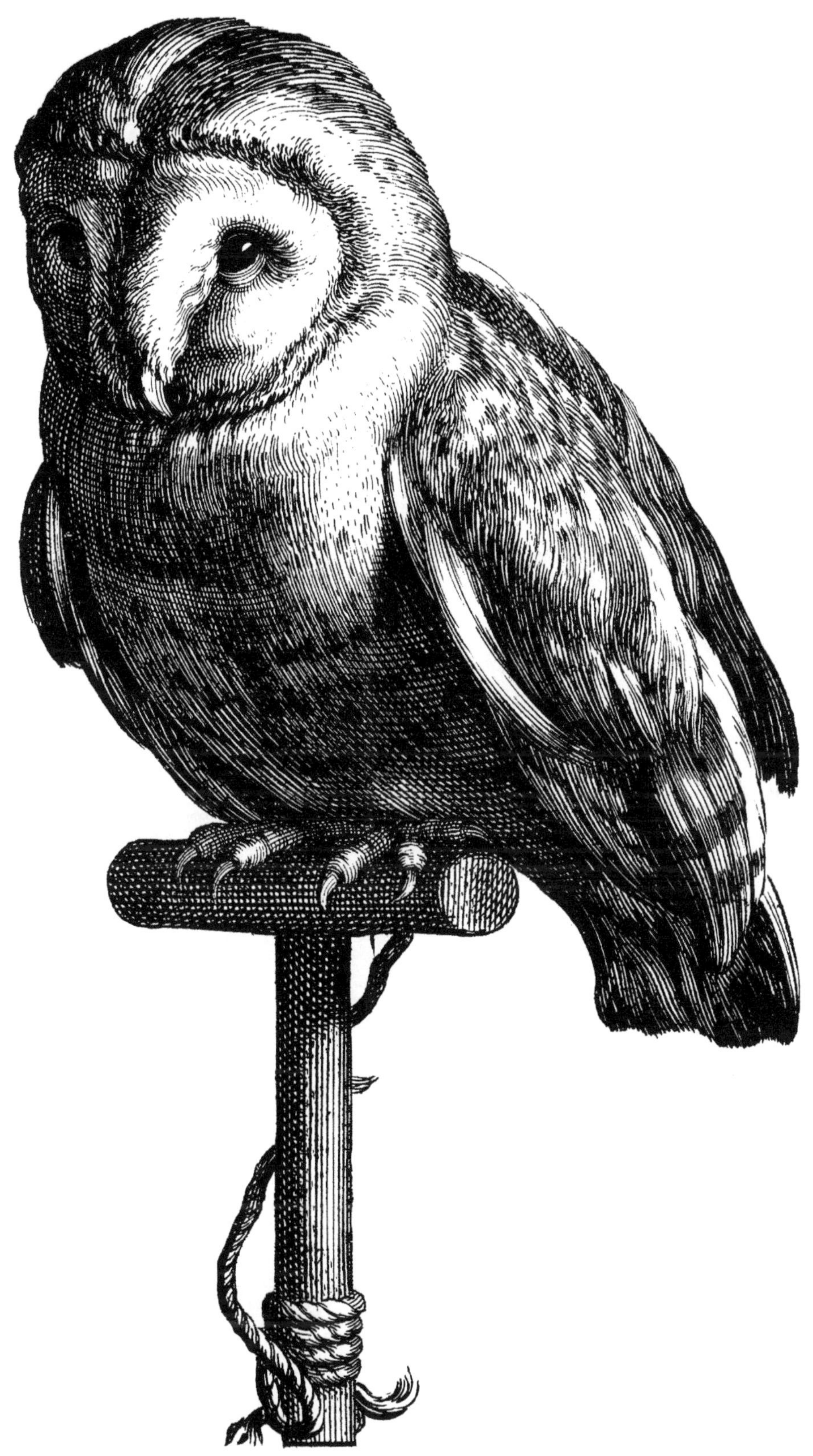

№ 529

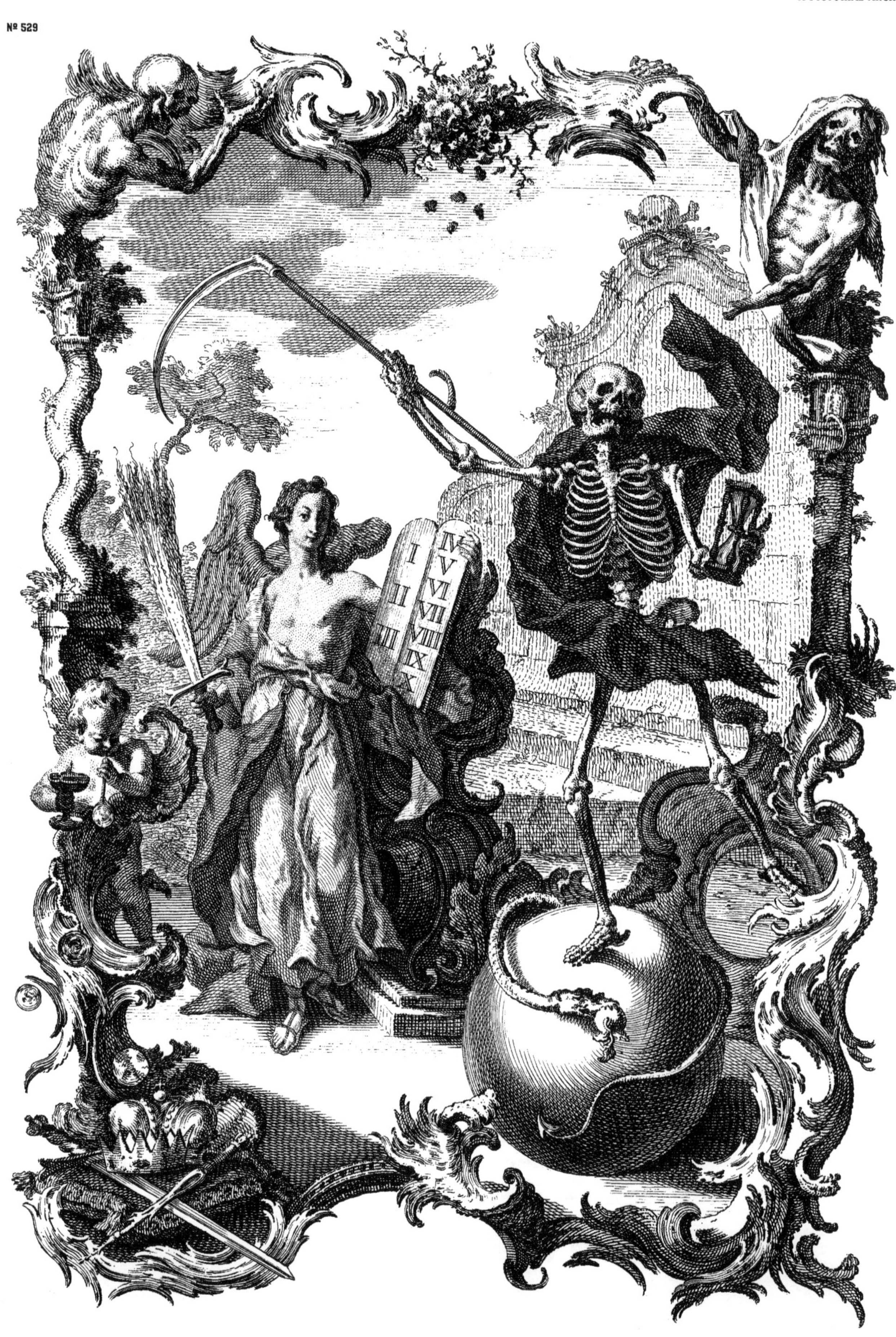

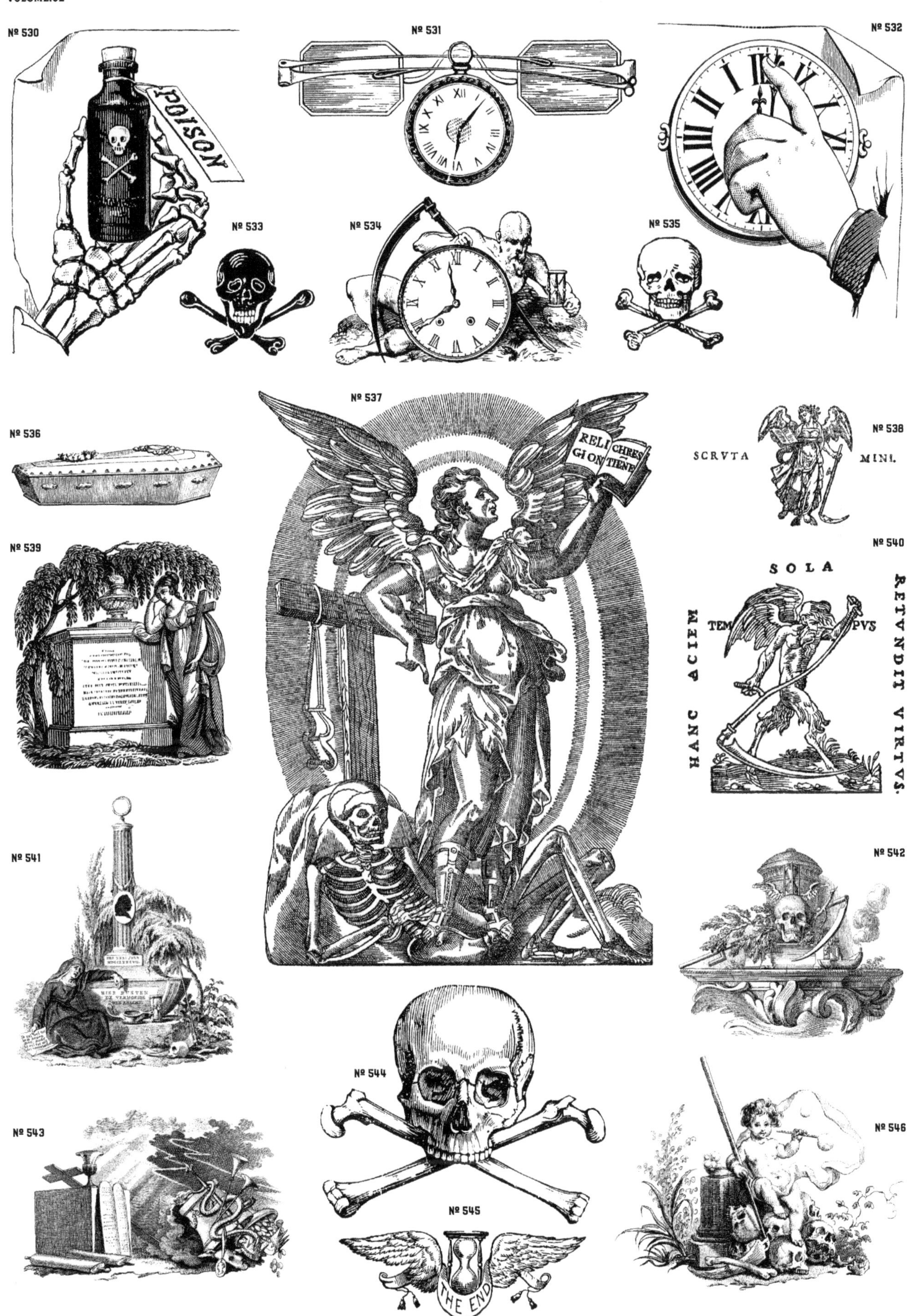
№ 530
POISON
№ 531
№ 532
№ 533
№ 534
№ 535
№ 536
№ 537
RELI GION CHRES TIENE
№ 538
SCRVTA MINI.
№ 539
№ 540
SOLA
TEM PVS
HANC ACIEM
RETVNDIT VIRTVS.
№ 541
№ 542
№ 543
№ 544
№ 545
THE END
№ 546

№ 547

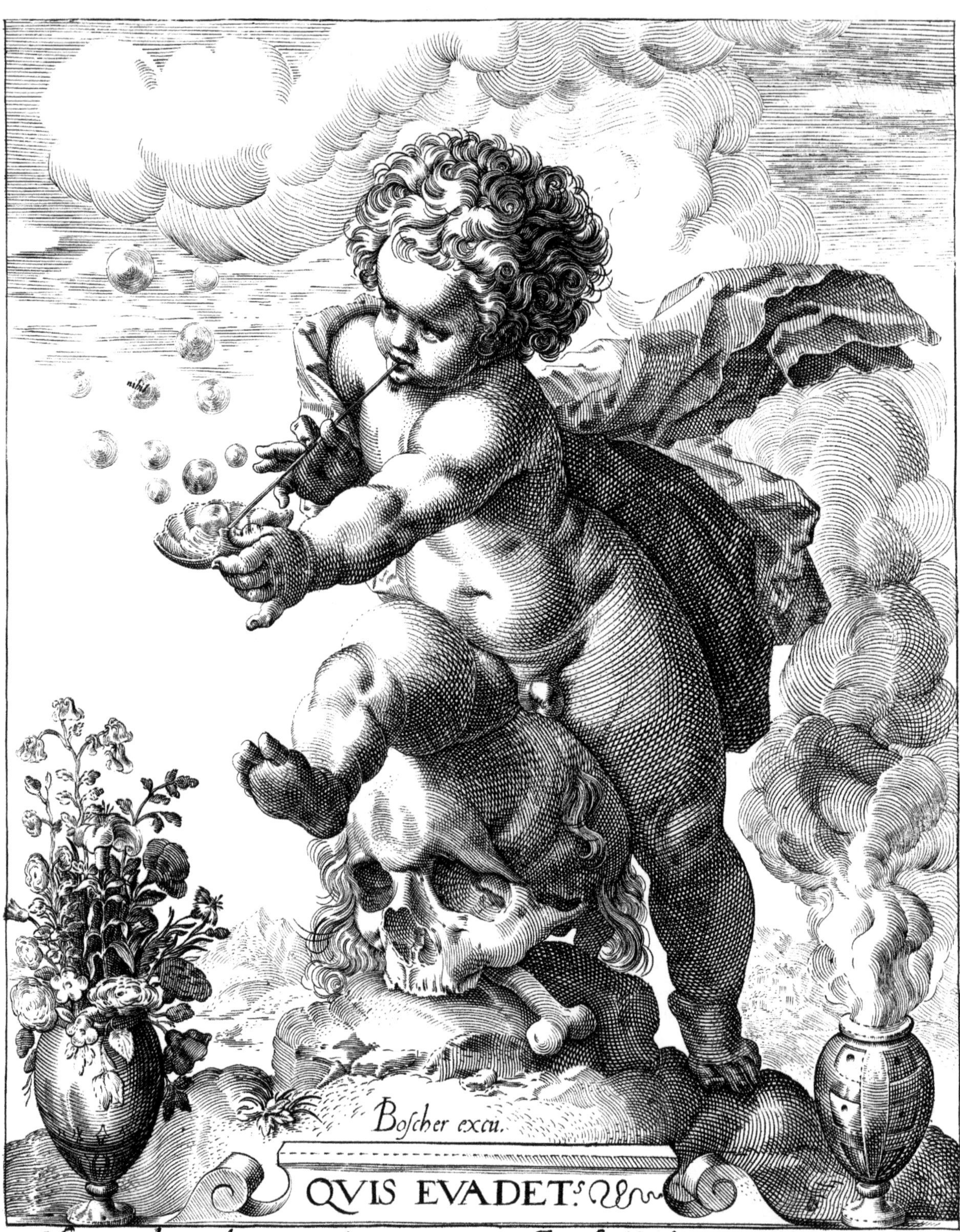

Momento breuis hæc, certeq; obnoxia morti
Vita, quasi fumus, bullula, flosq; perit
Cur ergo teneris (prôh Stulti) fidimus añis?
Cur non sponte mori discimus ante diem?

Excussa blandæ carnis, dum vita superstes,
Compede, post mortem liberiore gradu
Spiritus astra petet iam sedem vbi fixerat ante,
Ciuemq; agnoscet cœlica turba suum

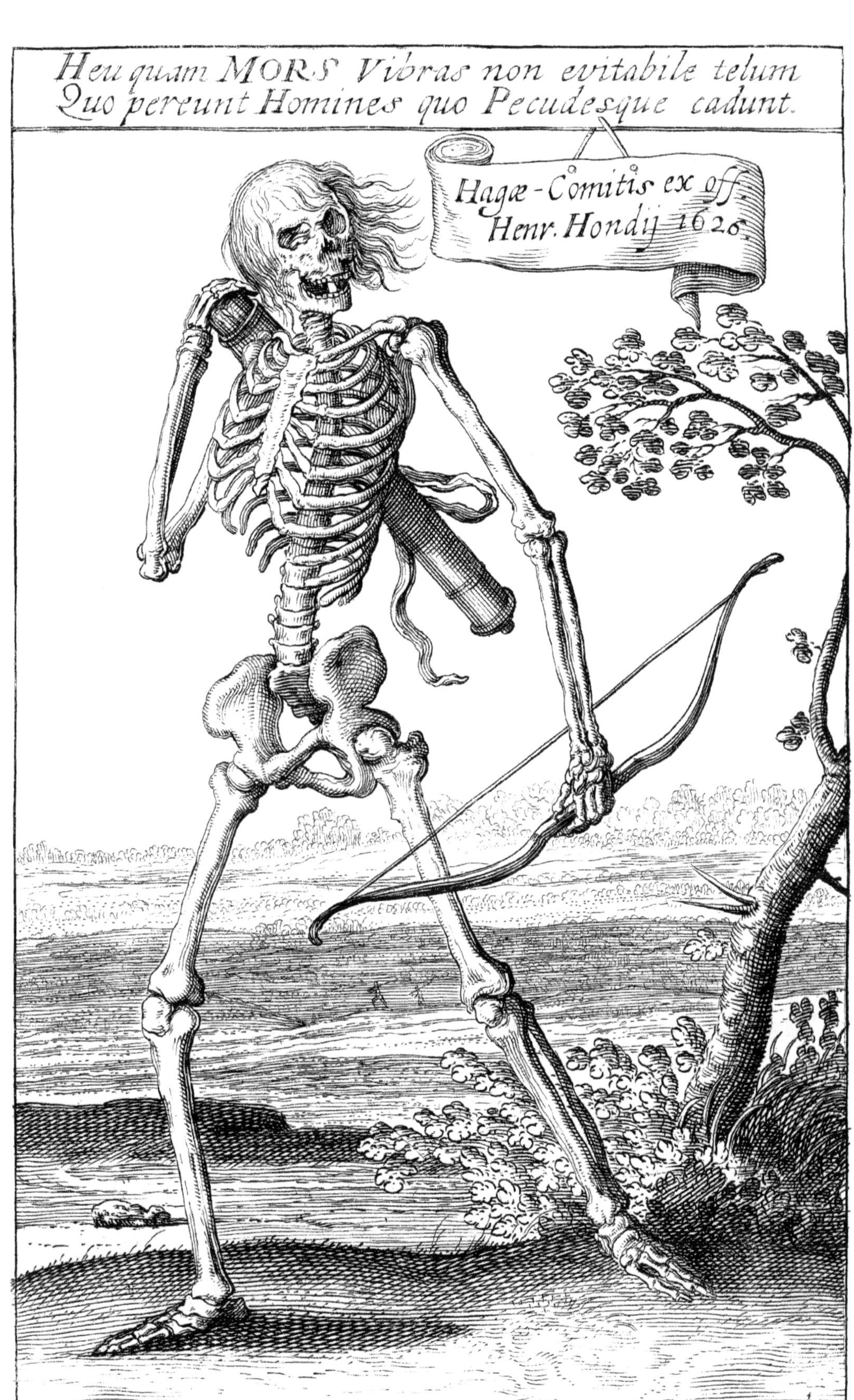
Heu quam MORS Vibras non evitabile telum
Quo pereunt Homines quo Pecudesque cadunt.
Hagæ-Comitis ex off.
Henr. Hondij 1626.

58

№ 551

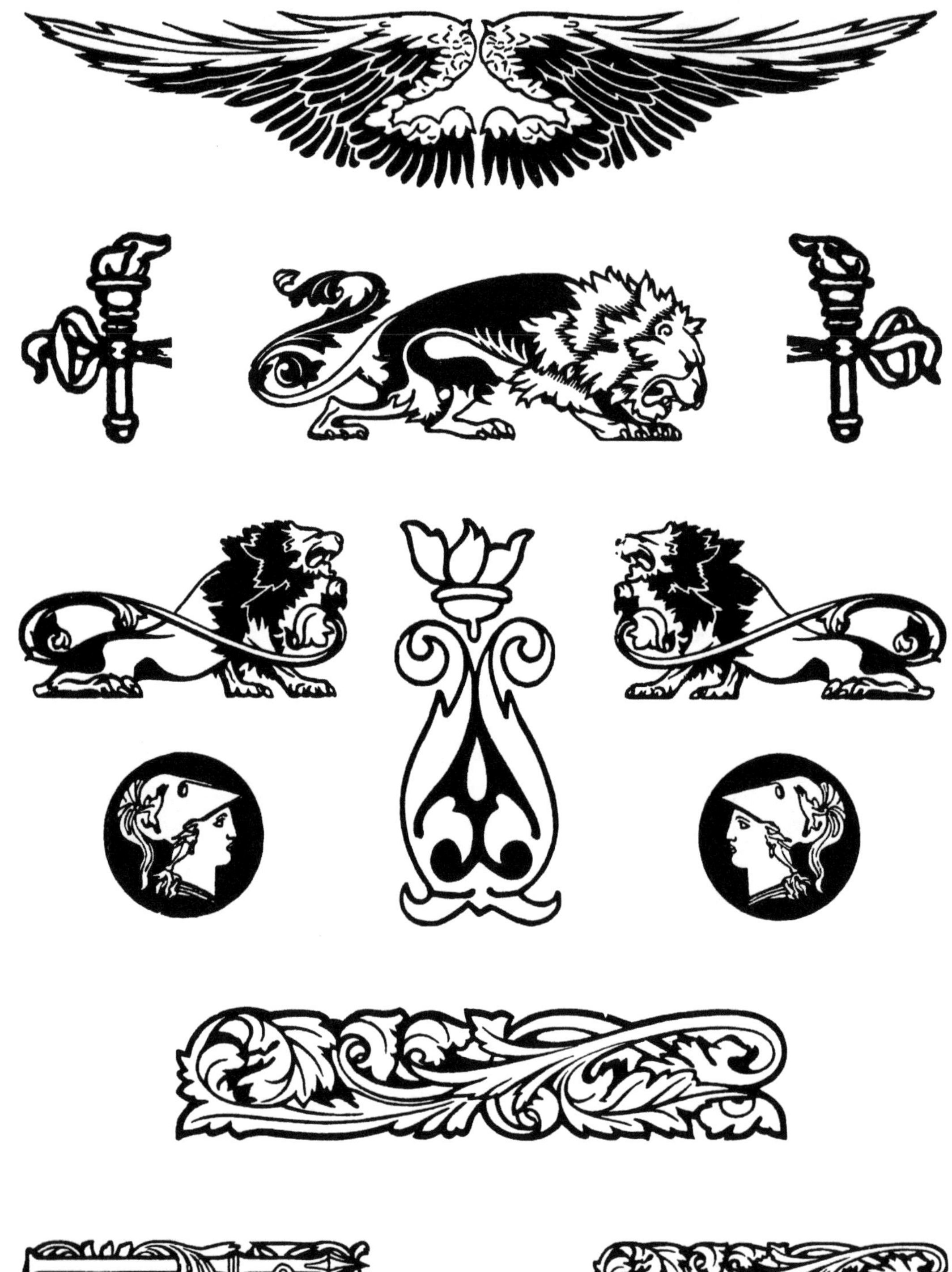

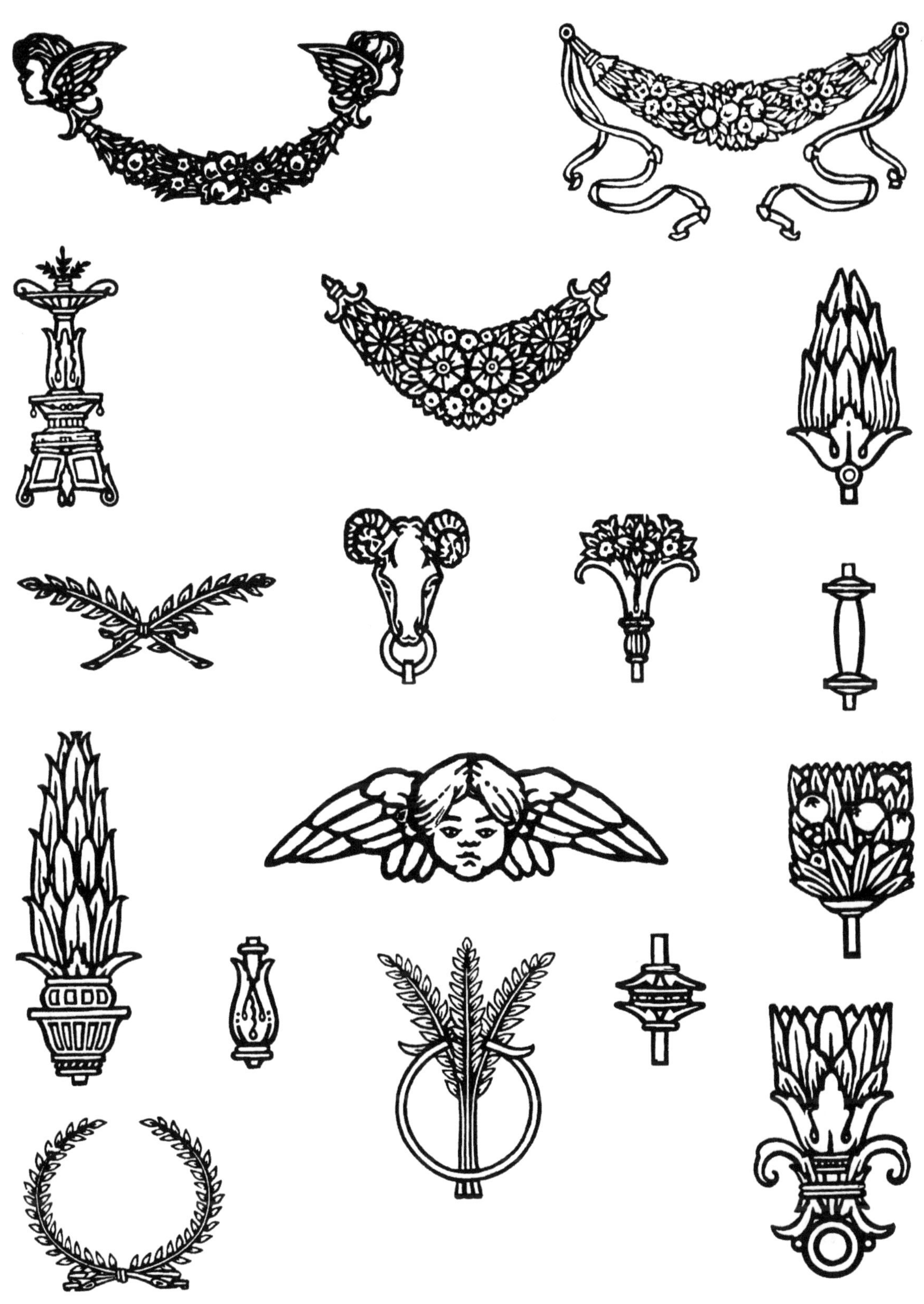

№ 553

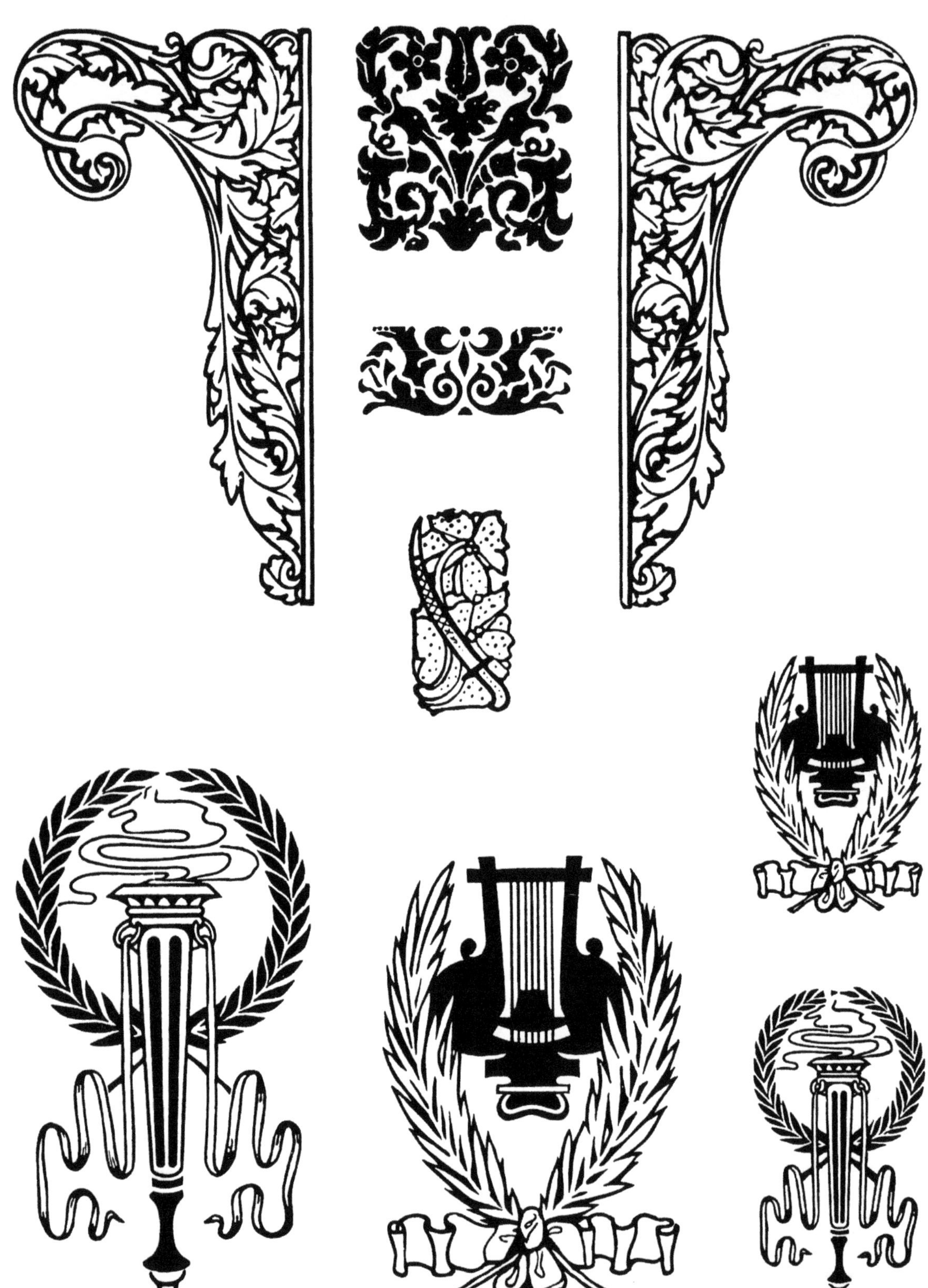

№ 554

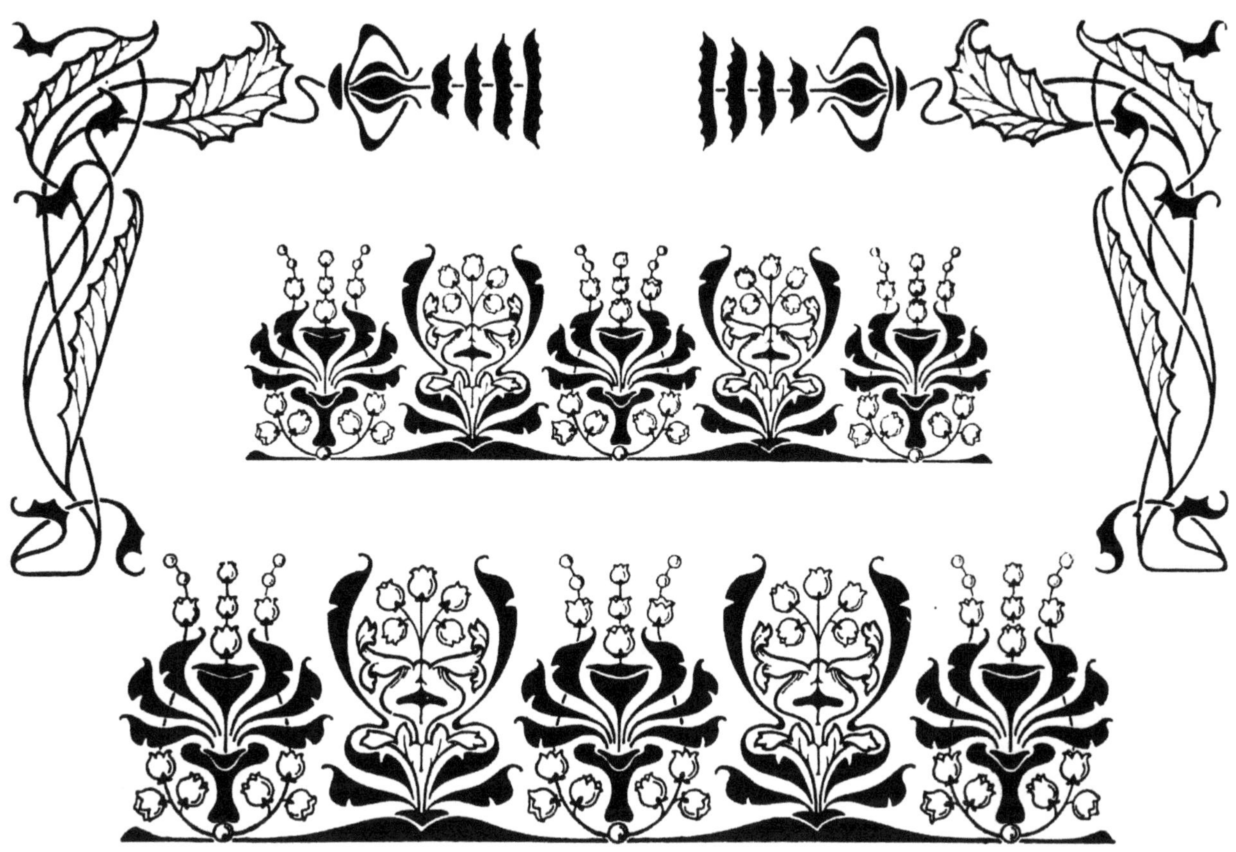

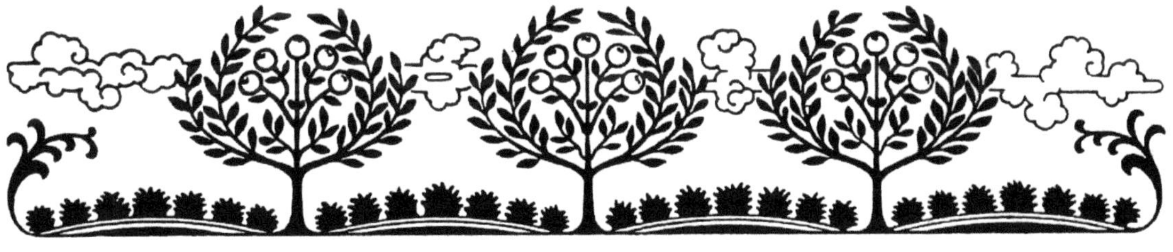

Nº 555

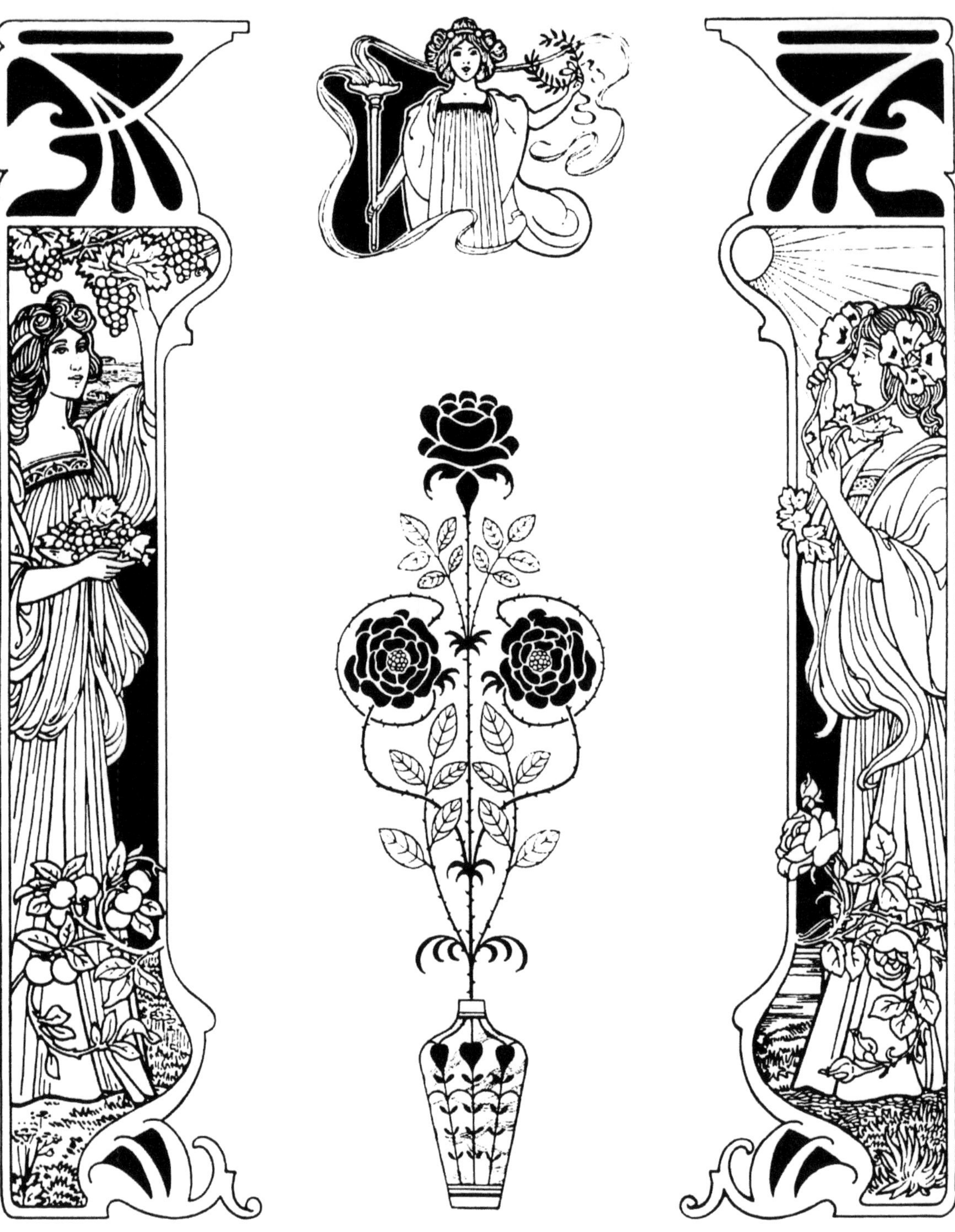

Nº 556

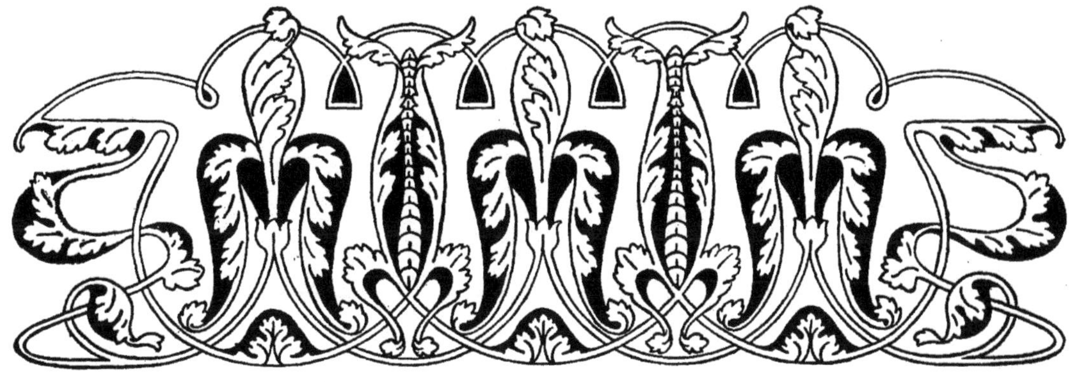

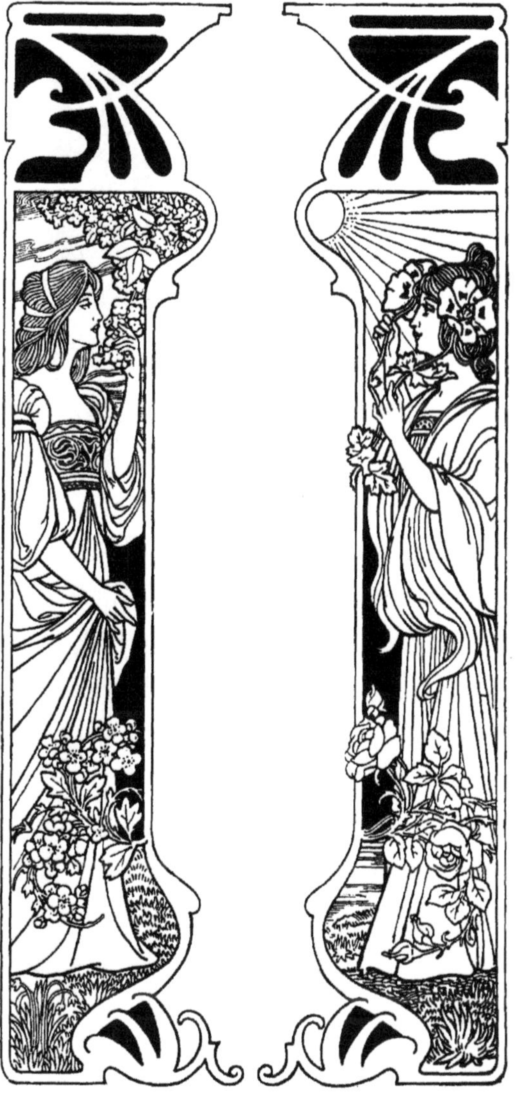

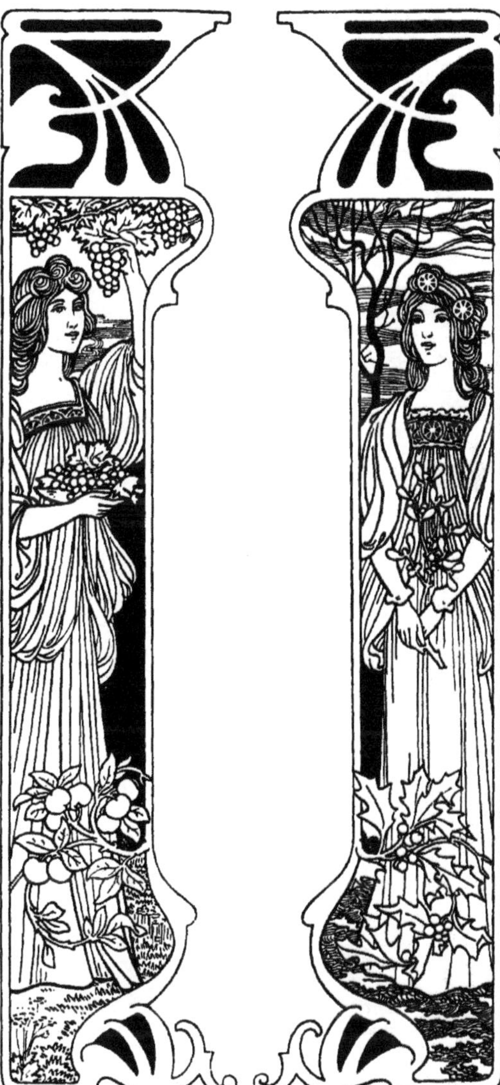

№ 557

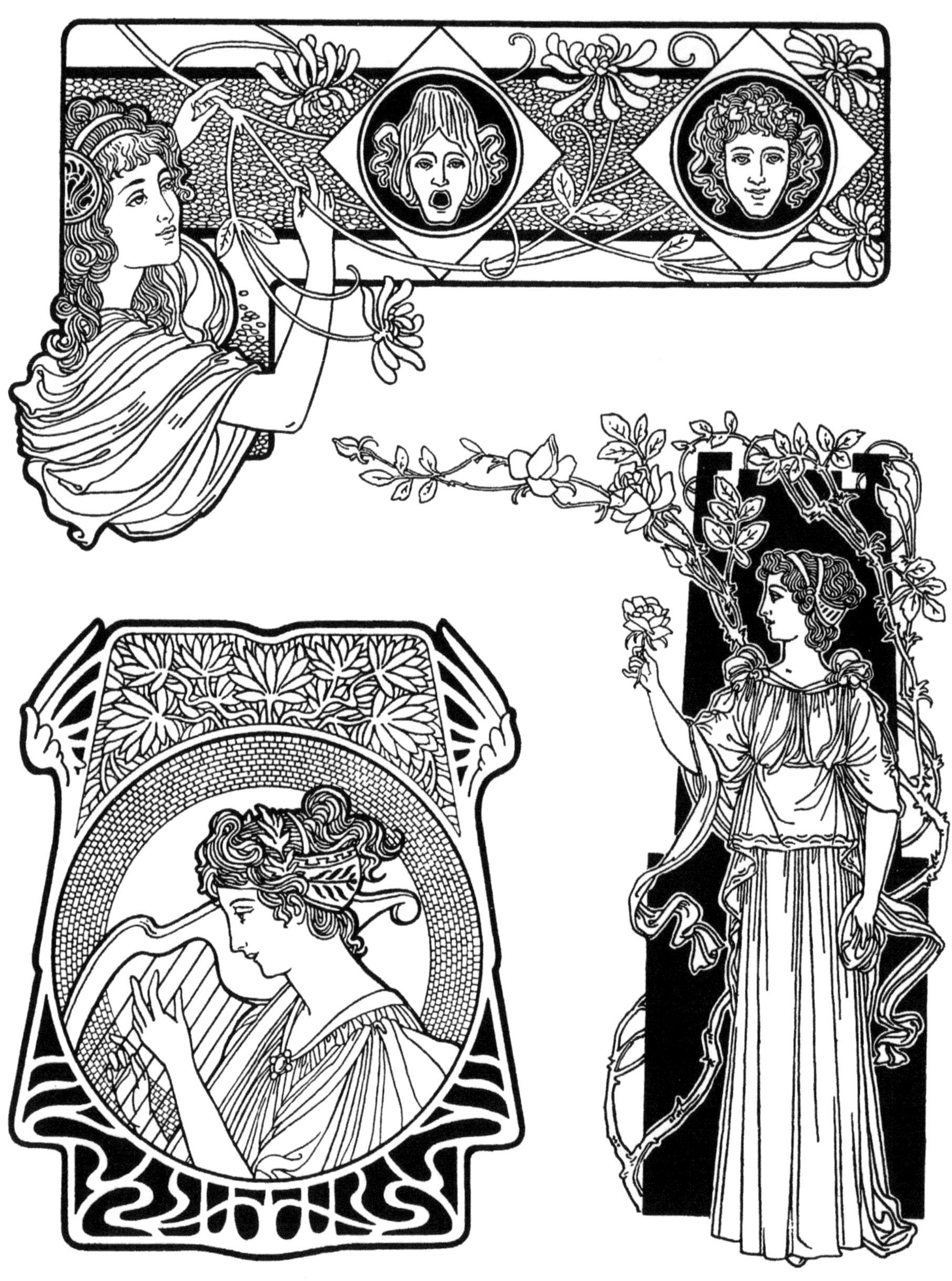

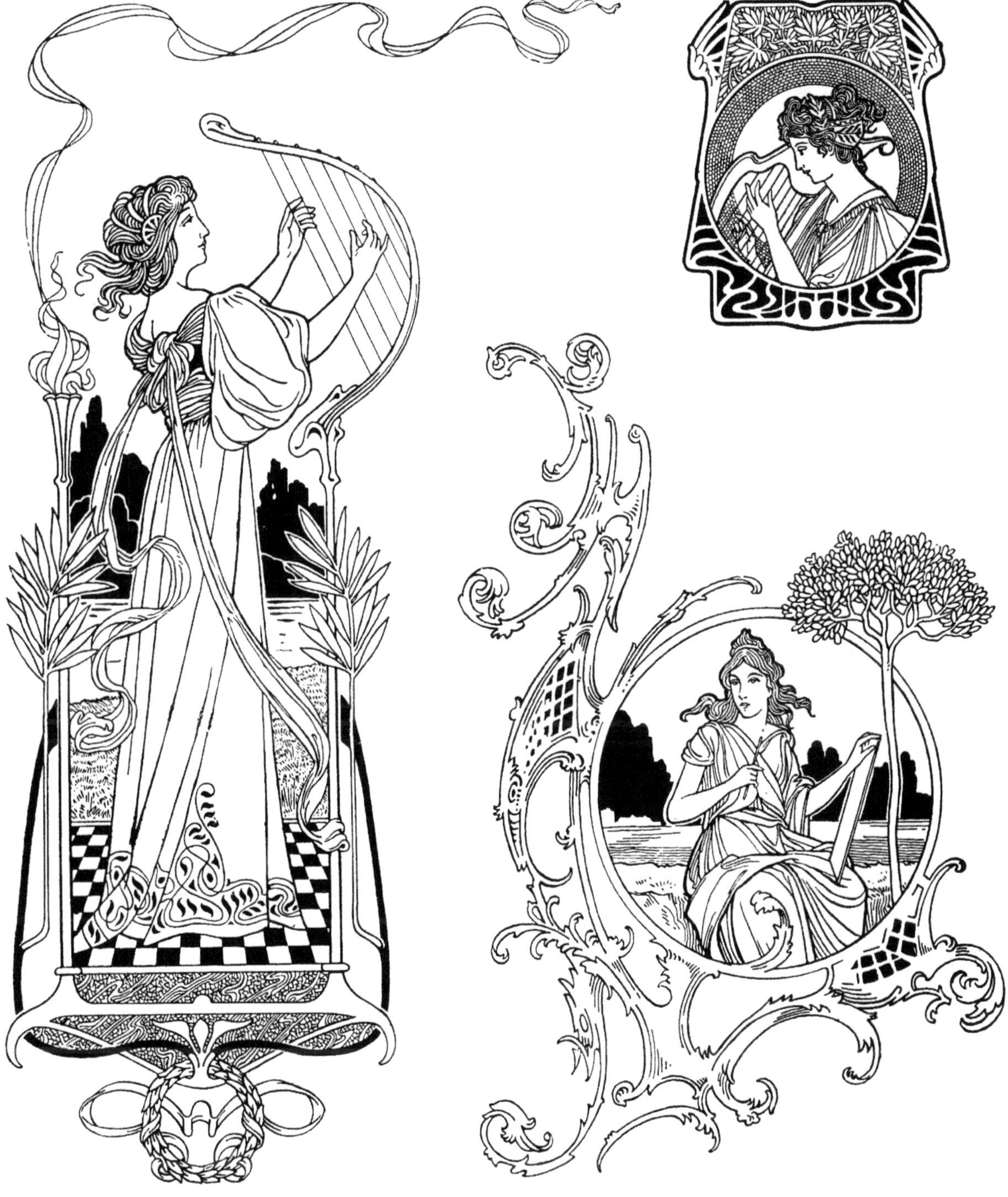

Nº 559

HERALDRY

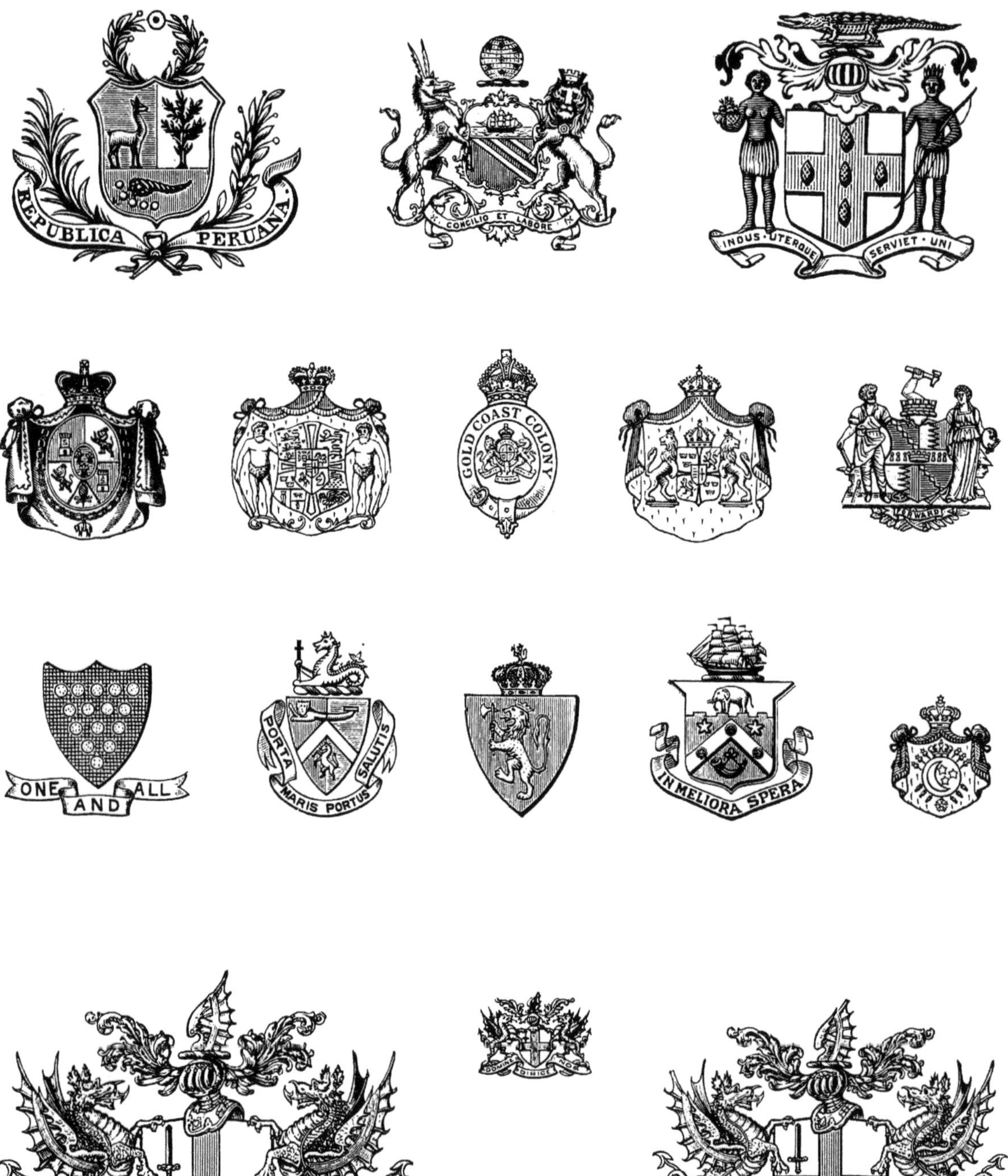

IC DEFERS
IC DEFERS
IC DEFERS
HONI SOIT QUI MAL Y PENSE
DIEU ET MON DROIT
HONI SOIT QUI MAL Y PENSE
DIEU ET MON DROIT
HONI SOIT QUI MAL Y PENSE
DIEU ET MON DROIT
HONI SOIT QUI MAL Y PENSE
DIEU ET MON DROIT

№ 561

ROCAILLE ORNAMENTS

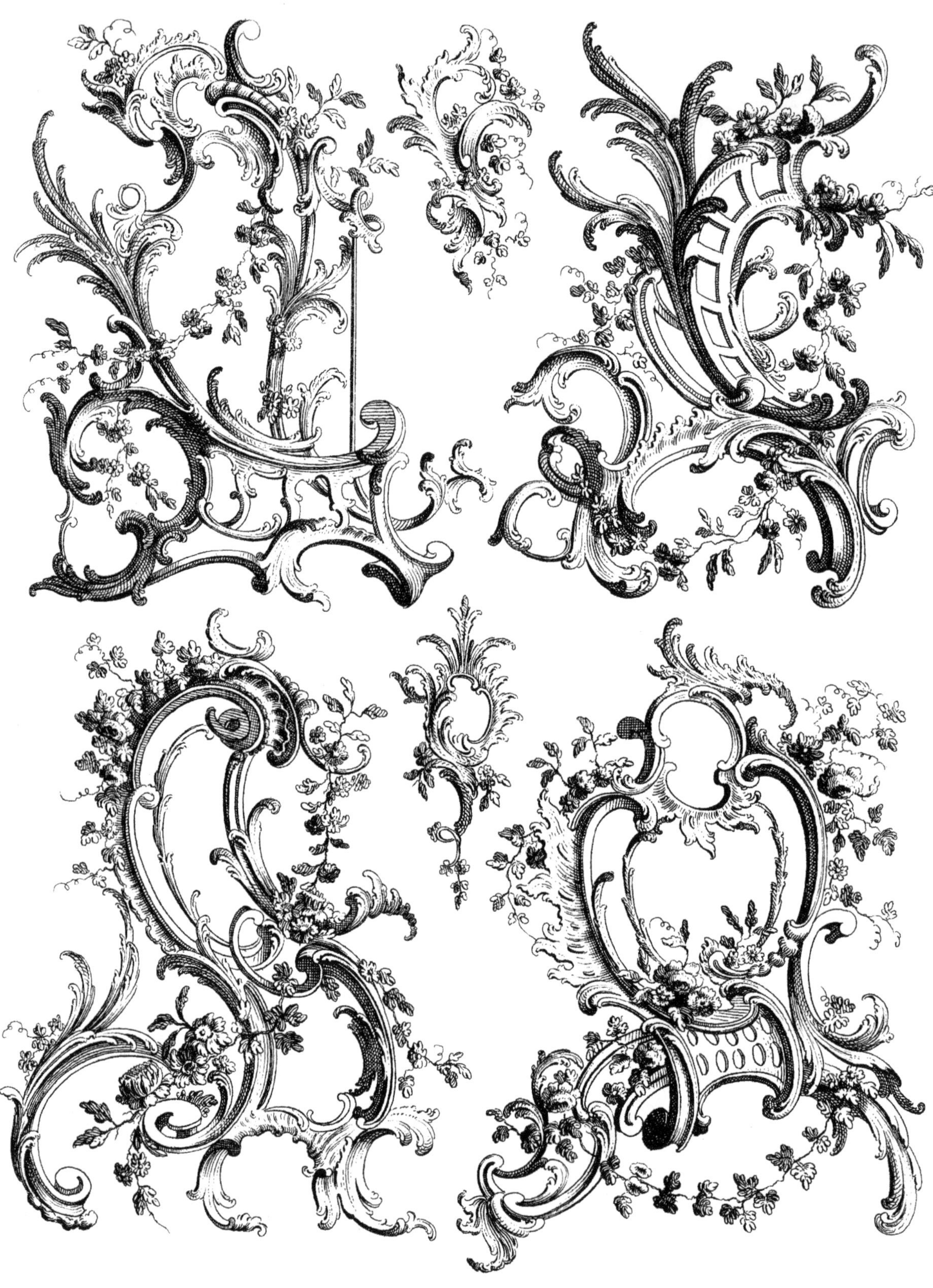

№ 562

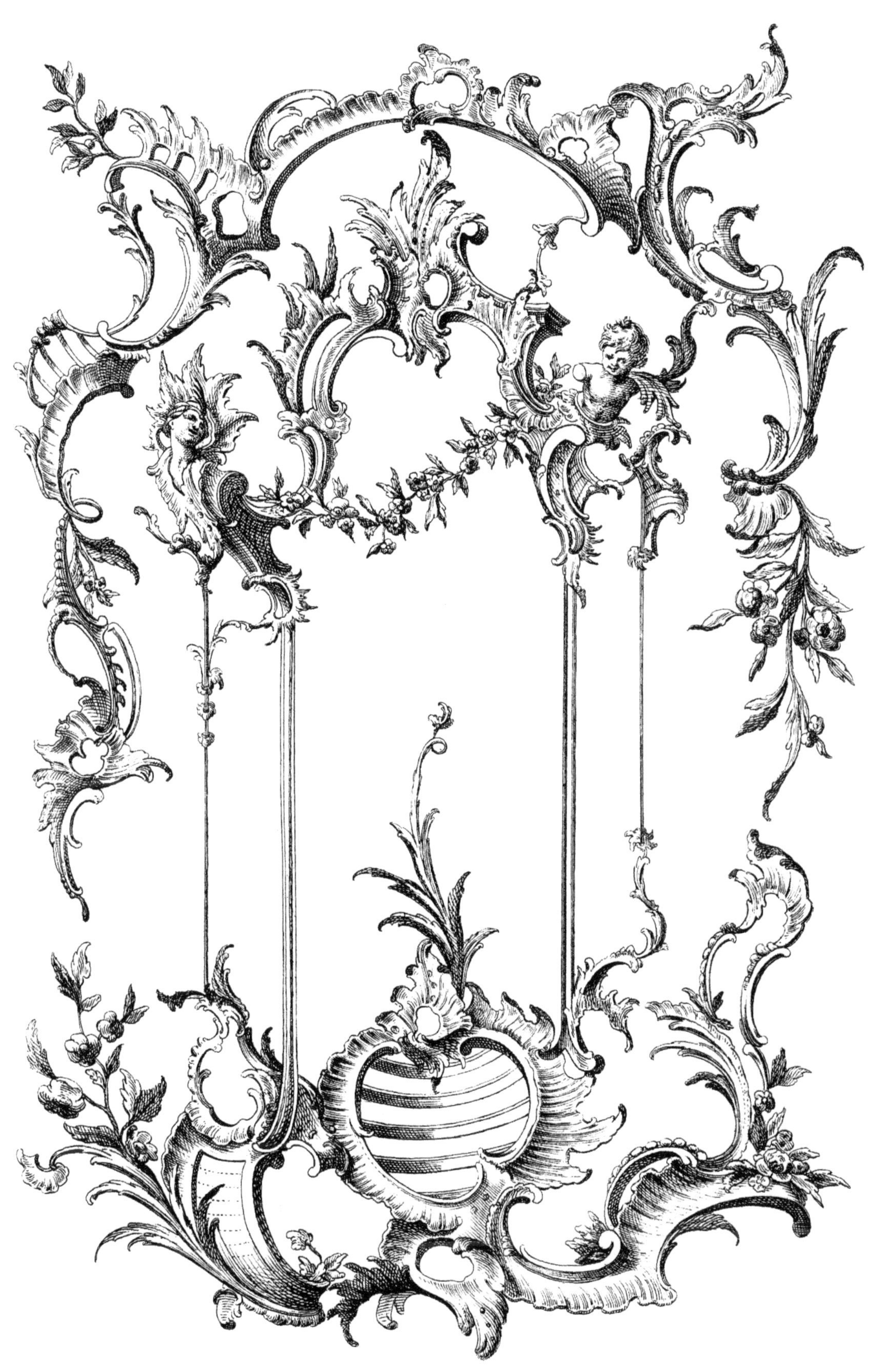

№ 563

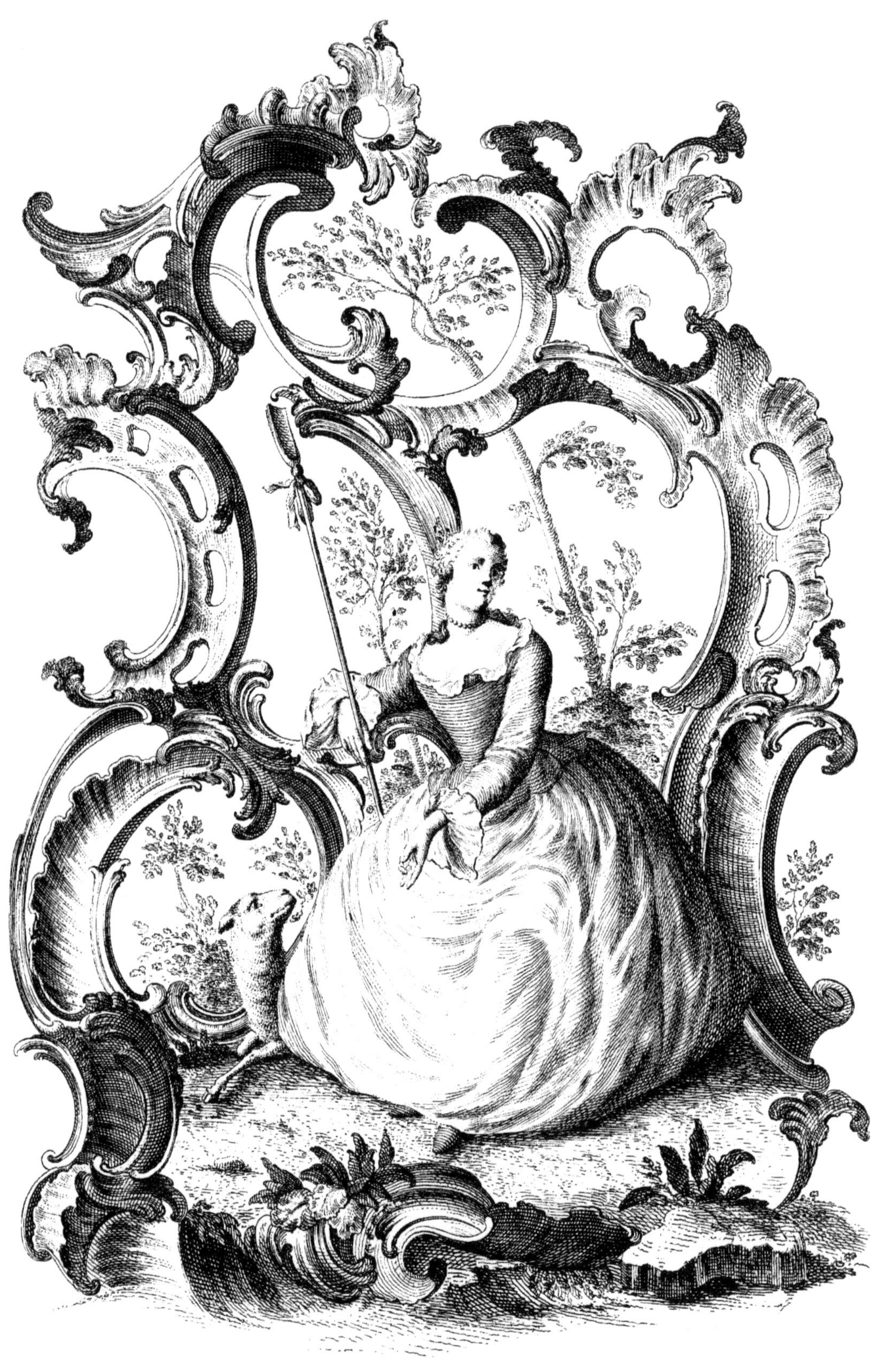

№ 564

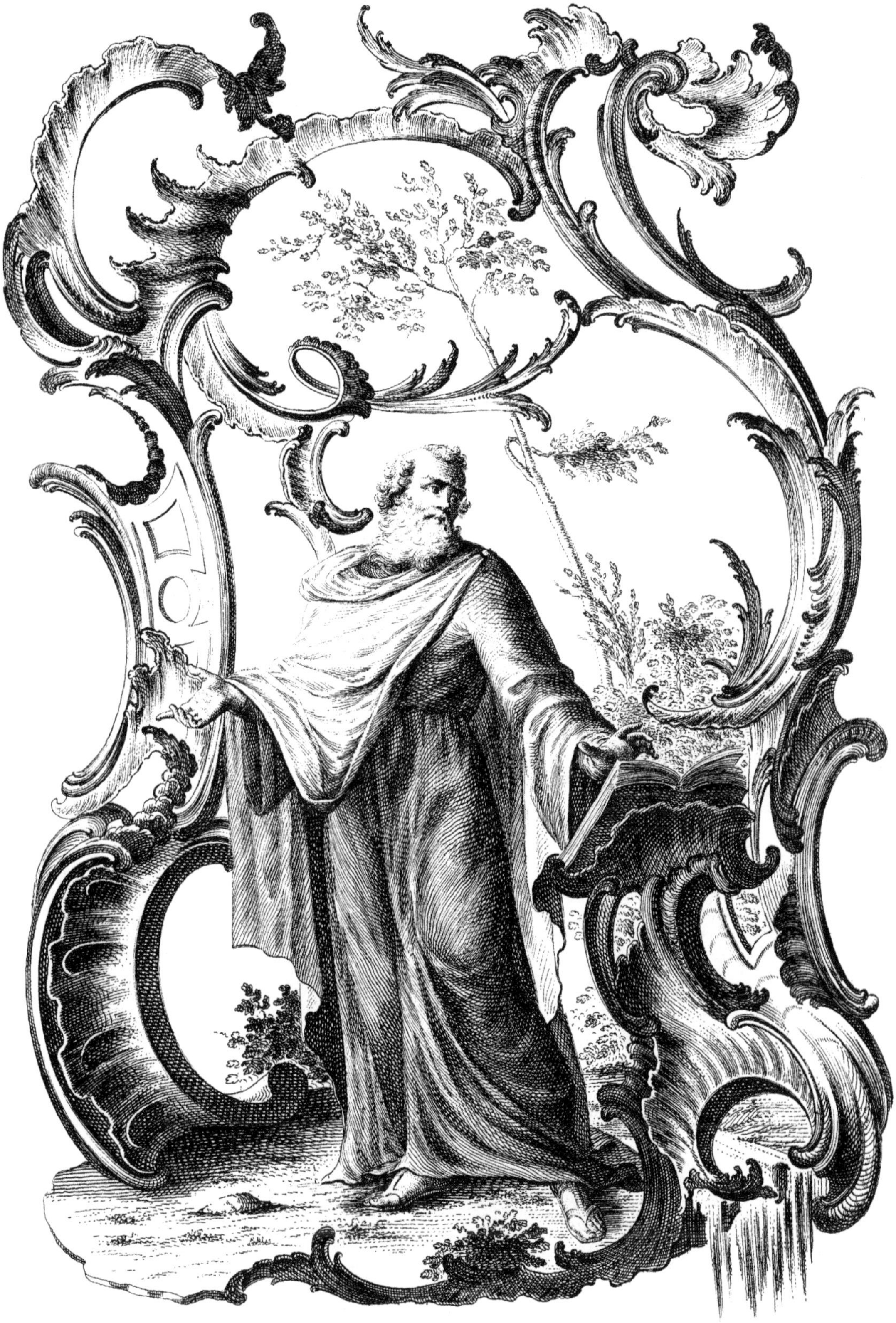

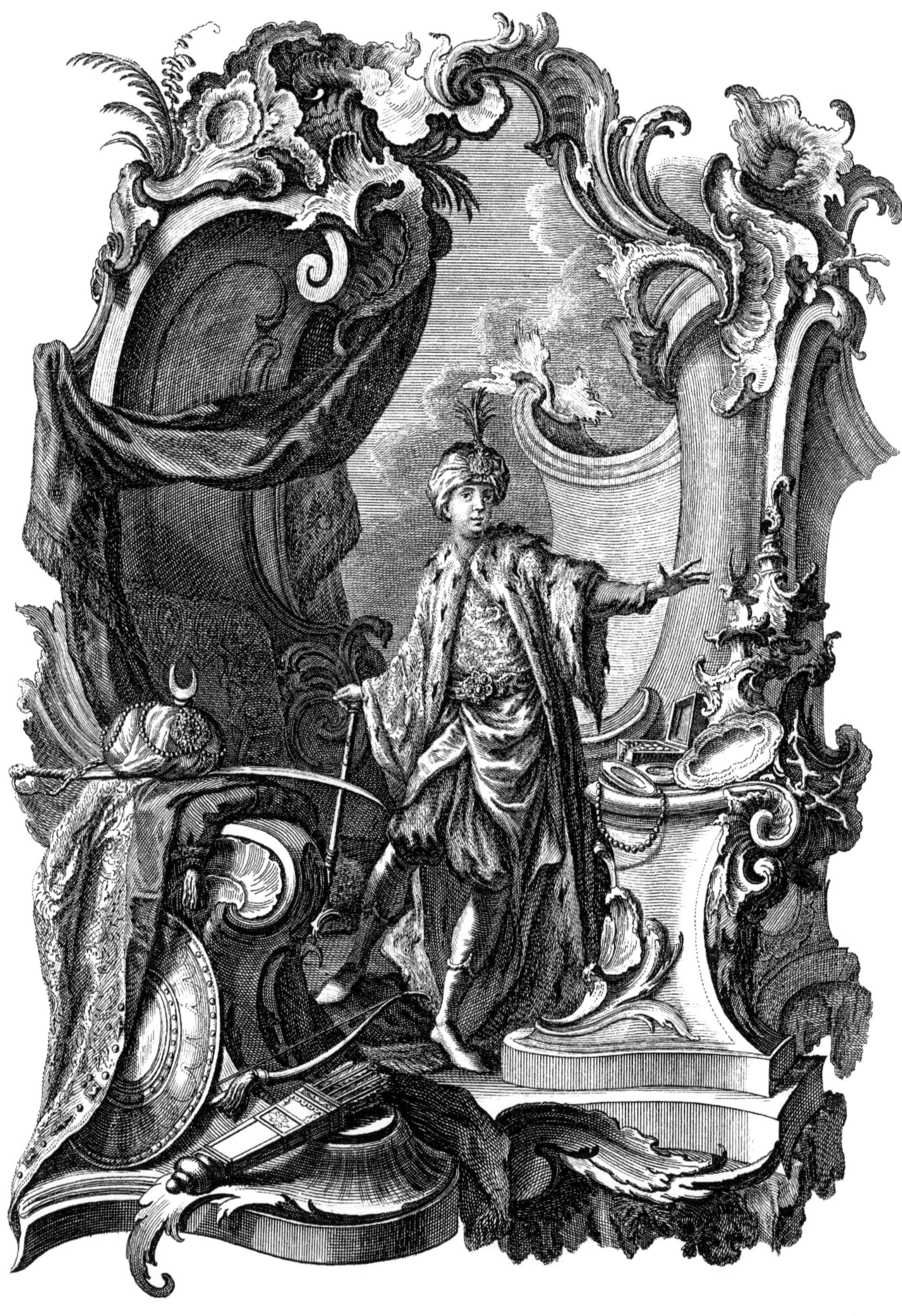

№ 566

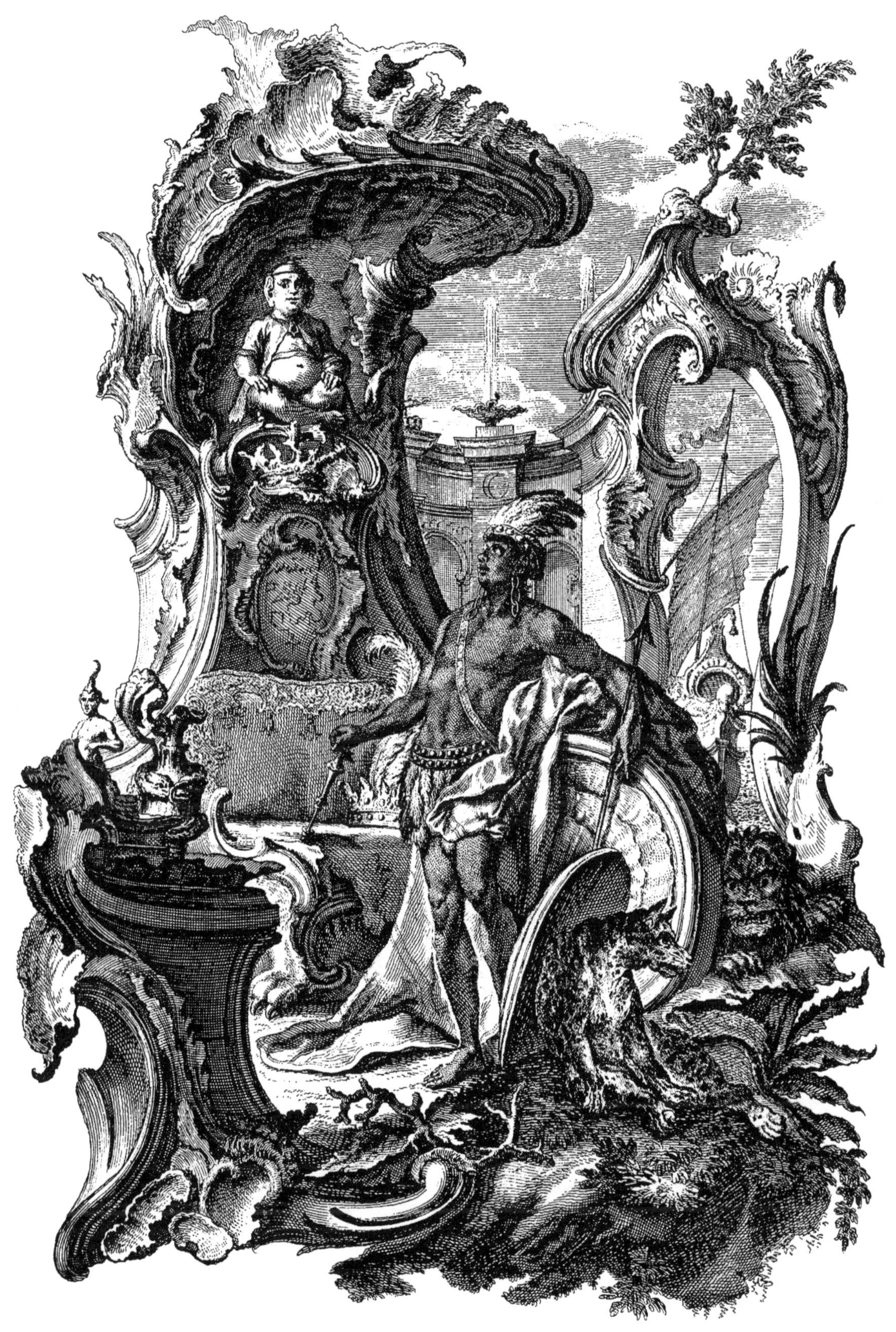

MISCELLANEOUS

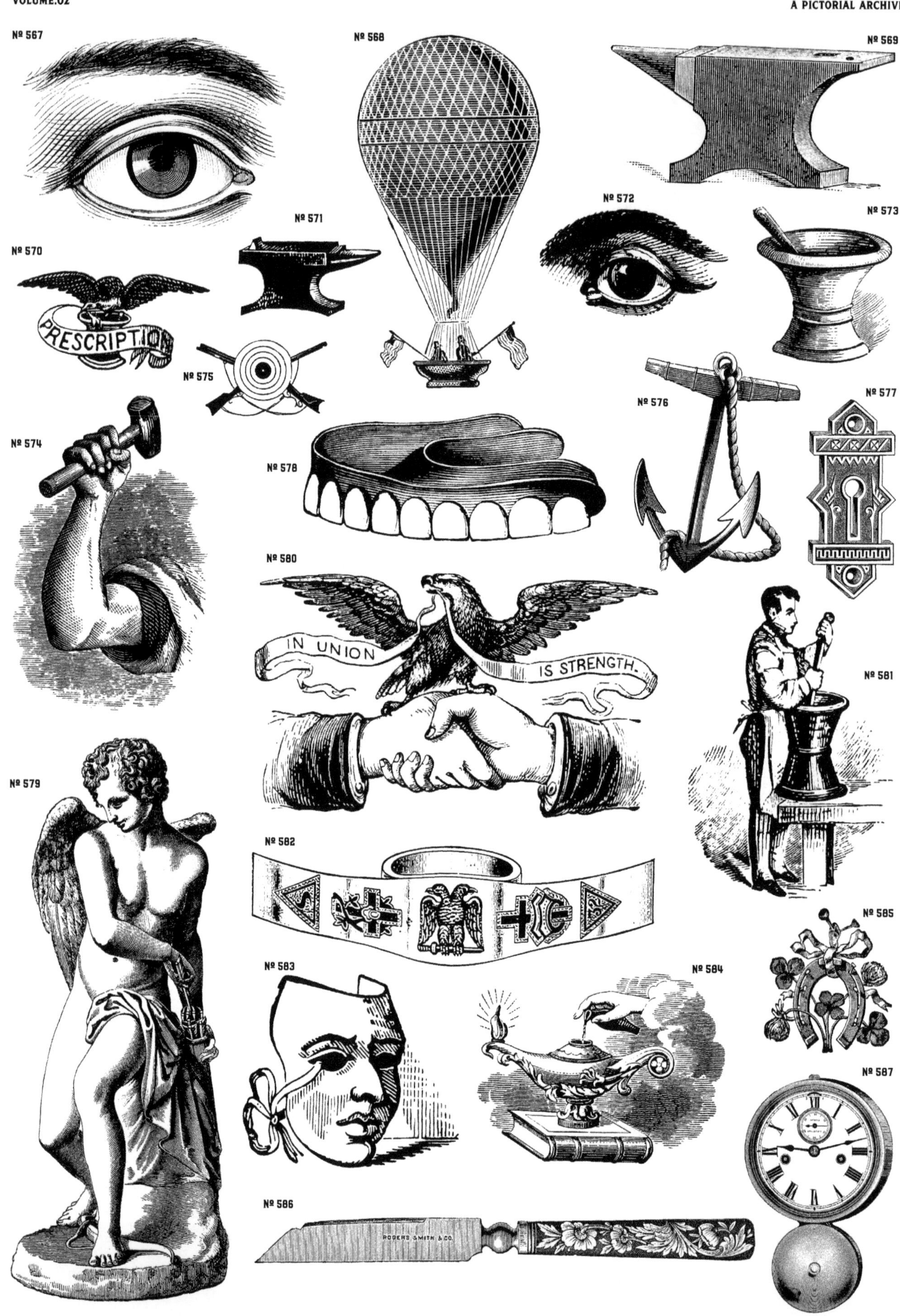

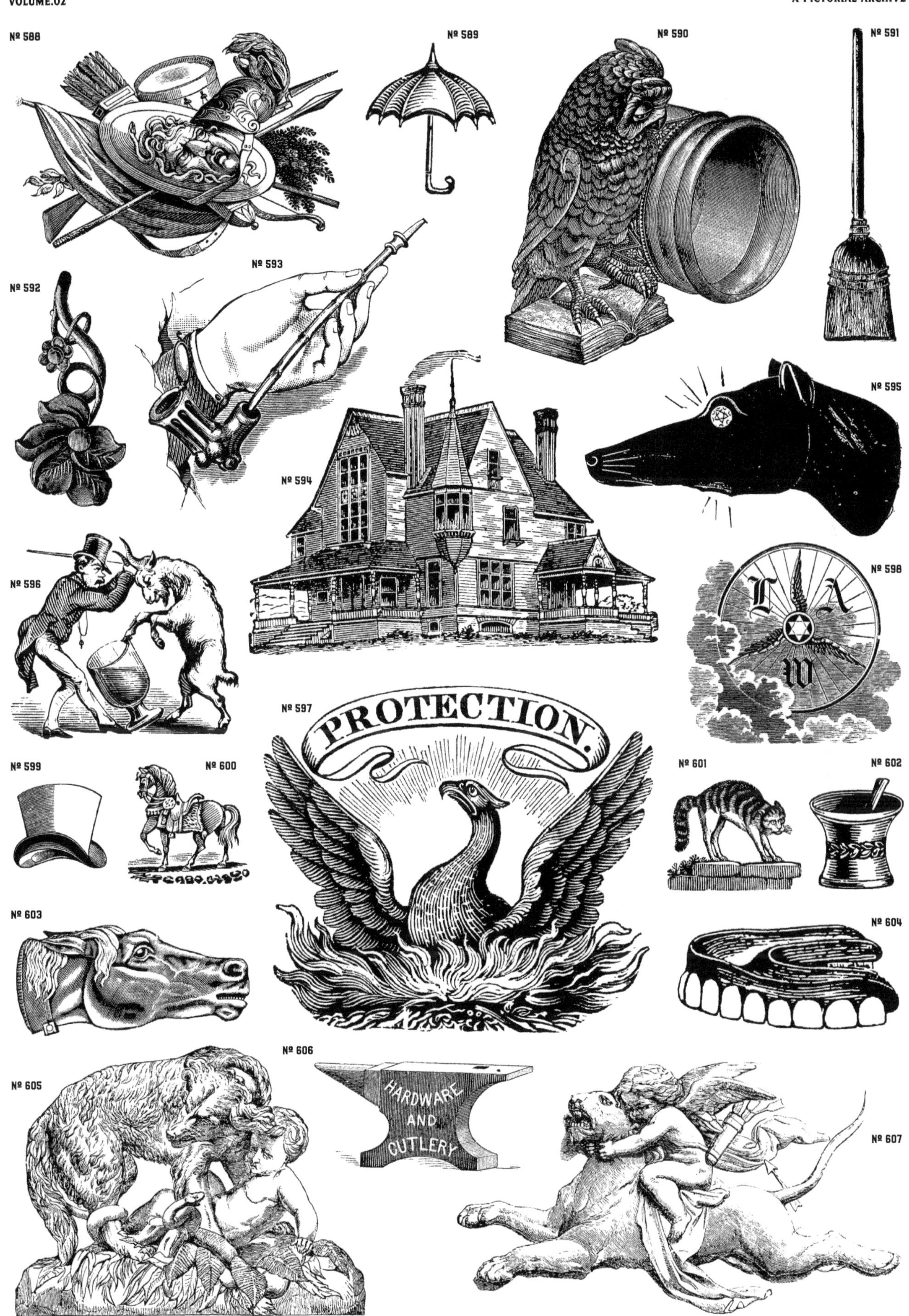

MISCELLANEOUS

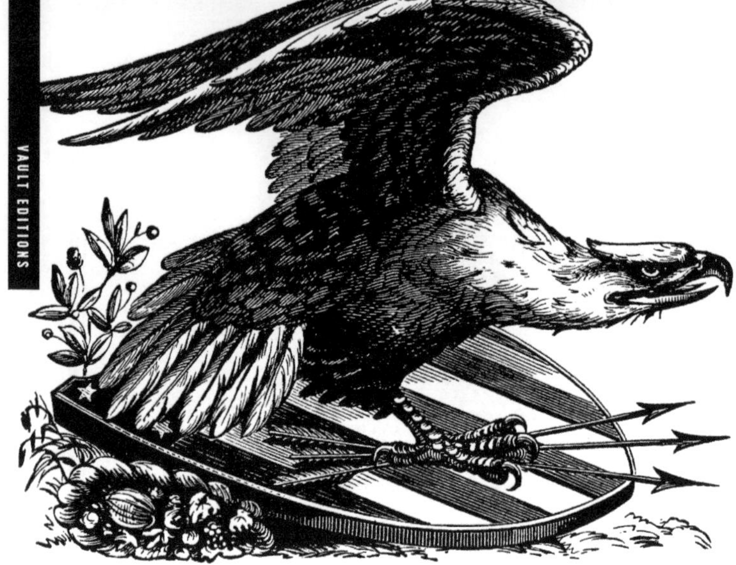

LEARN MORE

At Vault Editions, our mission is to create the world's most diverse and comprehensive collection of image archives available for artists, designers and curious minds. If you have enjoyed this book, you can find more of our titles available at vaulteditions.com.

REVIEW THIS BOOK

As a small, family-owned independent publisher, reviews help spread the word about our work. We would be incredibly grateful if you could leave an honest review of this title wherever you purchased this book.

JOIN OUR COMMUNITY

Are you a creative and curious individual? If so, you will love our community on Instagram. Every day we share bizarre and beautiful artwork ranging from 17th and 18th-century natural history and scientific illustration, to mythical beasts, ornamental designs, anatomical illustration and more. Join our community of 100K+ people today—search @vault_editions on Instagram.

DOWNLOAD YOUR FILES

STEP ONE

Enter the following web address in your web browser on a desktop computer.

www.vaulteditions.com/ticv

STEP TWO

Enter the following unique password to access the download page.

tic38972fsdrx4

STEP THREE

Follow the prompts to access your high-resolution files.

TECHNICAL ASSISTANCE

For all technical assistance, please email: info@vaulteditions.com

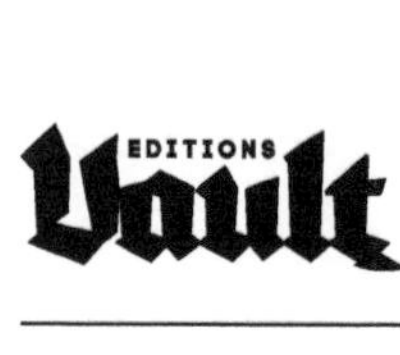

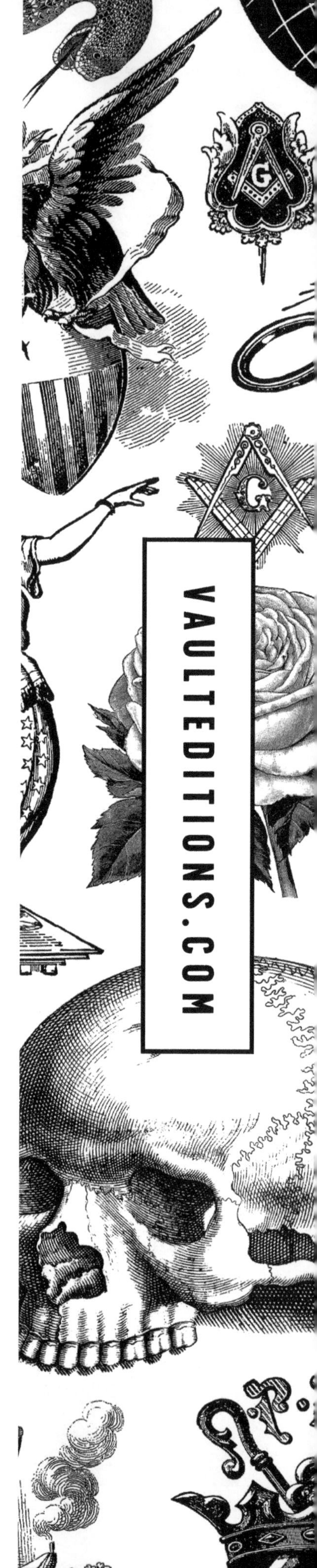

www.ingramcontent.com/pod-product-compliance
Ingram Content Group UK Ltd.
Pitfield, Milton Keynes, MK11 3LW, UK
UKHW051207260726
13967UKWH00011B/3149